ON A WING AND A PRAYER

ON A WING AND A PRAYER

*One Woman's Adventure into
the Heart of the Rainforest*

Sarah Woods

B L O O M S B U R Y

LONDON • NEW DELHI • NEW YORK • SYDNEY

For my precious
daughter Milly

Bloomsbury Publishing Plc

50 Bedford Square
London
WC1B 3DP
UK

1385 Broadway
New York
NY 10018
USA

www.bloomsbury.com

BLOOMSBURY and the Diana logo are trademarks of Bloomsbury Publishing Plc

First published 2015

© text by Sarah Woods, 2015

All photographs in the plate section are © Sarah Woods, with the exception of p1 bottom
© Alfredo Maiquez/Getty Images, p4 bottom © Nina Raingold/Getty Images, p5 top
© Sune Wendelboe/Getty Images, p5 bottom © Alfredo Maiquez/Getty Images and
p7 bottom © Jason Edwards/Getty Images.

British Library Cataloguing-in-Publication Data
A catalogue record for this book is available from the British Library.

Library of Congress Cataloguing-in-Publication data has been applied for.

ISBN (hardback) 978-1-4729-1213-8
ISBN (paperback) 978-1-4729-1214-5
ISBN (ebook) 978-1-4729-1215-2

2 4 6 8 10 9 7 5 3 1

Typeset by Deanta Global Publishing Services, Chennai, India

Printed and bound in Great Britain by CPI Group (UK) Ltd, Croydon CR0 4YY

To find out more about our authors and books visit www.bloomsbury.com
Here you will find extracts, author interviews, details of forthcoming events
and the option to sign up for our newsletters.

Contents

Prologue

I'm in a taxi crossing Panama City, earphones filling my head with the mellow sounds of the Steve Miller Band. When I left London, my friends gave me a track list tailored to Panama, a cleverly conceived collection of downloads themed around hats, cigars, jungle and birds. At this moment the track just happens to be 'Fly like an Eagle'.

The nation is preparing to party, now that news bulletins have confirmed what many Panamanians had only dared hope: that the Americans will no longer own, control and dominate a part of their country roughly the size of Barbados. The Canal Zone is being handed back to Panama. Within days, annual tolls of around one billion US dollars will go straight into the country's purse, once America's final rent cheque of a quarter-million US dollars has cleared. More than two million Panamanians are literally jumping for joy. Streets are festooned with blue, red and white streamers, flags and bunting. Political murals depict grotesque, fat American bigwigs sailing home in leaky rowboats. Slogans scrawled on walls throughout barrios in the city read: 'Finally we have achieved sovereignty' – a poignant reminder that Panama will soon have control over its entire land for the first time since independence in 1903.

Steve Miller and his flying eagle are still swirling around my head as the taxi screeches its way round a busy cross-town junction, navigating a 180-degree curve at considerable speed. Splat! A large poster, presumably liberated from a wall by a Pacific breeze, lands face down across the windscreen. It renders the driver blind in fast-moving traffic, and he screams as panic sets in. He flicks the wipers on, slapping the inside of the windscreen in desperation. With stoic *que sera sera*, I fix my gaze as blaring horns all around us warn of our imminent doom.

The poster stares back at me with a pair of penetrating steely eyes, a prehistoric-looking winged creature, unlike anything I have seen before. It is certainly an eagle of some sort. But one with dark, menacing features. A blade-sharp beak as black as soot,

and a neck as thick as a tree trunk. Eyes wide, super alert. Talons
at the ready. It looks as if it is about to strike. Christ, it's one
sinister bird.

And then it is gone, torn from the windscreen by the taxi
driver, who has cajoled his pudgy hand just far enough through a
gap in the driver-side window. I watch as the paper sheet barrels
and cartwheels across a lane of cars before attaching itself to a
custard-coloured school bus. The driver speaks to me through his
rear-view mirror, swearing colloquially at the drama as sweat
leaks through his wash-faded red T-shirt.

'What's the bird?' I enquire when eventually he pauses for
breath. 'Harpy eagle, it's a harpy eagle,' he confirms. 'Panama's
national bird. There's one at the zoo, maybe. Enormous. Flies as
fast as a motorbike. Like a dinosaur with feathers. Kills anything, it
ain't afraid of nothing. No. Nothing. Scary shit.'

Jungles in the City

Panama
1999–2005

It is barely 4.30am, and the sky is still a marbled inky black, but globes of sweat are already strung across my brow. I never struggle to make an early flight, but after a troubled night wriggling in damp, hot sheets I feel poorly prepared for the day ahead. The air is so cloying, I feel choked by its weightiness. Everything, bar the insects and my itchy feet, is silent and still. I have never felt so close to the equatorial belt as I do at this moment: everything I touch feels hot, humid and wet. Even my scalp is clammy. Panama City's daily temperature hovers around thirty degrees Celsius for 365 days a year. Only rainfall denotes a change in season. Year-round, overnight, the cloud knits together to trap the heat. So, even then, it rarely drops below twenty-two degrees: the winter setting for my electric blanket on my bed in the UK. I breathe in – a trio of steady, deep breaths – then expel the air in a slow, controlled exhalation. Fearful thoughts flicker behind my eyes. My limbs seem weighty. I feel restless. It is time to move on.

Panama. The very name dances on my tongue. Pan-a-ma. I can remember first tracing the contours of this country with my finger on the map, running east to west, and marvelling at how tiny it is. This S-shaped land bridge between South and Central

America, famously sliced in half in the name of sea trade, is so slight it is barely there. At just over 75,000 square kilometres, it is smaller than South Carolina and less than half the size of Italy. Yet Panama's stature is so much bigger than its size. Squeezed against Costa Rica to the west and the wildest of Colombia's jungle frontiers to the east, Panama offers incredible biodiversity. Around 1,000 species of bird, more than 200 mammals, almost 250 reptiles and over 160 amphibians have a home in its tropical mix of rainforests, scrubland, grassland savannas, swaying crops and mangrove swamps, which are neatly intersected by the ridge of the Cordillera Central running like a backbone along the centre of the country.

When I first arrived in Panama City, in 1999, I had an insatiable appetite for its irrepressible salsa music, the collective human psyche of its peoples, its delicious regional foods and its landscape and architecture. I wanted to take photographs of a variety of different faces, from the black-skinned Afro-Panamanians on the Caribbean coast, descended from banana workers and canal labourers, to the pale-faced residents of Parita, with their angular Spanish features and bull-fighting customs, and the diminutive, creased-skinned Kuna people, whose bright, beaded anklets and colourful robes are as twinkly as their deep-set eyes. I wanted to pace around the places in which they lived and observe ordinary, daily life in the colourful backstreets of Panama City's historic old centre, Casco Viejo. To watch queues of workers boarding the fume-spewing, gaily painted buses that swarm westbound along the streets of Avenida Central and the net-mending fishermen at the Mercado de Mariscos (seafood market). To witness the gigantic swarms of flies descending over the city beaches at twilight, like dark grey plumes of smoke or the swirls of starling murmurations that billow over Brighton's west pier.

These weren't the reasons for my visit, of course. I'd arrived to report on the Canal handover and something struck a chord deep down inside me. Euphoric hope. Optimism. Belief. Joy. With my heart lifted and cheeks flushed, I watched Panamanians rejoicing. The journalist in me wondered if the mood would last.

By 1999 I'd been travelling pretty much non-stop for three years: Australia, New Zealand, Asia and the US, where my favourite city was Miami. I stayed in the heart of the Hispanic district, where hundreds of thousands of Spanish-speaking migrants and their families shopped for plantain, bought hand-rolled cigars and sipped twenty-five cent coffee at *cafecitos* that evoked the charm of old-time Cuba. I'd eat Panama-style shrimp tortillas and authentic Nicaraguan dishes in bars full of Latin American émigrés playing dominoes. Wherever I went, salsa and merengue music blared out of boom boxes and car stereos: an audio backdrop that pulsed right through me, day and night. First, I tapped my feet. Then I found myself moving, instinctively, to the rumba, mambo, salsa, samba and cha-cha. I joined a class to ease my stiff, awkward British hips into the seductive sway of the Latino quick-quick-slow timing. Click of a heel, extended arms, arched back, a pout of the lips, straightened leg and a hand on tilted hip. It felt really good to move so freely.

And so it was that through the pure pleasure of salsa music, Cuban sandwiches, ceviche and bowls of gallo pinto I fell in love with South and Central America. As a flight hub for a hundred or so Latin American cities, and with seventy per cent of its population Hispanic, bright and ballsy Miami had allowed me to dip my toe into a vibrant mishmash of different cultures. Anointed, it wasn't long before I was ready to run, jump and fully submerge myself in all that Latin America had to offer. I boarded a plane with a skip in my step, a ticket to Panama in my pocket and a song by Rubén Blades – the Cliff Richard of Panama – on the tip of my tongue.

I knew of the country's remarkable natural scenery and mind-boggling list of endemic wildlife, but I had wrongly assumed that they were out of the reach of the 'ordinary' tourist. That was, until I moved to Cerro Ancon. After my initial visit in the aftermath of the handover, I had flown back and forth from either Miami or the UK, couch-surfing with friends of friends or staying in soulless chain hotels. Then I decided – on the basis of cost, flexibility and local immersion – to rent a room in an apartment on the glorious, jungle-clad hill in the middle of the city.

Wedged between the city's modern infrastructure, crumbling slums and maniacal traffic, Cerro Ancon offers a rainforest escape blessed with wildlife. A madly flapping Panamanian flag denotes its summit – the highest natural point in the capital, at

199 metres – which lies just a half-hour walk from the city. The
trail through this nature-rich enclave is guarded by giant spiders
in glistening webs the size of double duvets, which engulf entire
trees. This was my 'backyard' in Panama City, and I took every
opportunity to delve into its towering palms, thick ferns and
tropical fruit trees, and to marvel at spellbinding views. The
panorama from the top is utterly magical, sweeping over the
rooftops of sleek office towers, snaking trails of traffic, transit
terminals and the charming old buildings of Casco Viejo towards
the illuminated arc of the Bridge of the Americas that marks the
Pacific entrance to the Panama Canal.

Cerro Ancon (meaning Ancon Hill) was part of the Panama
Canal Zone until 1977, when it was returned to Panamanian
control under the Canal Treaty of the same year. For centuries the
Ancon district had been synonymous with cargo and transit.
When the Spanish arrived in 1501, they formed a mule-train path
between the Atlantic and Pacific oceans, an early forerunner of
the Panama Canal. This mariners' cut-through became a crucial
strategic lookout for sea pirates intent on stealing the Spaniards'
gold. Four hundred years later, the area was developed into a
township for employees of the Panama Canal Company. Neat,
boxy houses with pocket-sized lawns in linear formations
characterised the residential neighbourhood. The first ship
officially to transit the canal, the SS *Ancon*, was named after the
district, which today is renowned for noteworthy administrative
buildings, including Panama's Supreme Court and several offices
of the Smithsonian Tropical Research Institute. The Panamanian
Government plopped the huge Panamanian flag on top of the hill
within hours of regaining custody, transforming it into a national
landmark and conserving it for posterity.

Because it was partitioned for much of the twentieth century,
Cerro Ancon escaped the bulldozers of city developers and so
remains a jungle oasis inside the city's inner core. I share my early
morning walks with numerous species of bird, including toucans,
as well as various lizards and mammals, such as sloths, agouti,
white-nosed coati, Geoffroy's tamarins, nine-banded armadillo
and deer. The rough trails through rustling, squawking bushes
never fail to intrigue me, altering each day with every turning leaf

and shooting vine. I rarely see another human soul, other than when I bump into the guy whose job it is to swap the flag over. Apparently it is replaced each month due to the ferocity of the high winds that batter the flag from the Pacific Ocean at speeds of up to 140 kilometres per hour. As it is way too heavy for him to raise the flag by hand, he uses an electric winch. He is visibly proud when he tells me that, at fifteen square metres, the flag is roughly the same size as a basketball court.

For a while, as an experiment, I change the tempo, swapping my well-worn muddy walking boots for a second-hand mountain bike. It is exhilarating to cycle up from the foothills before the slow-burning pain in my calves begins fully to register. It also feels good to rise up out of my seat and stretch up my head as far as I can towards the cool of the clouds. Contentedly patting the pedals on the final, flatter stretch feels amazing after a single-track gully has jolted and jarred every bone in my body. After gulping down a bottle of water, I swallow up the damp mist and drink in the all-consuming quiet. There is, undoubtedly, a certain adrenalin thrill in reaching the top before debilitating fatigue kicks in. Within a few brief weeks, however, I develop a pathological hatred for my saddle. Once so relatively comfy, it is now an instrument of torture. Exertion in the early-morning sunshine is beginning to cause some rather peculiar hallucinations. And the rough terrain that, on foot, felt merely bumpy is making me dream of a few smooth metres of concrete. During epic vertical descents, the velocity of my heavy, fifteen-gear bike means that, in truth, there is little chance to spot any wildlife at all. I shriek, rattle, bang and clang, ensuring that every creature within earshot gets early warning of my arrival. The wilderness I once explored at walking pace now whizzes by at such a rate that I screw my gravity-shy eyes tight shut.

After a particularly hair-raising downhill mishap, I vault a fallen tree at around twenty-five miles per hour. A warm-hearted woman from the nearby offices of the conservation organisation ANCON (Asociación Nacional para la Conservación de la Naturaleza) sees me lying on the ground, limp and winded, and rushes out with a water-soaked copy of the national newspaper *La Prensa*: a makeshift wet towel that baffles me until she presses it firmly to my head. Bits of me are purple, red and blue, bruised, raw and saddle sore. I dig out my walking boots later that day and stow the bike in a cupboard.

Later that night, on my balcony, I realise that Panama's capital is a rarity among cities. For this fume-filled metropolis is in the countryside. And there is countryside in the city. Not on the edge, or at the end of a day-trip excursion. But right in the centre of the urban sprawl. As if to order, a sloth plops down onto the terrace from a large overhanging bough: unscheduled, dishevelled and a little dazed. With his rag tail, he looks like a cheap puppet, hand-made from a pile of scruffy old mopheads. Together, in proximity and spirit, we share the breath-gulping panoramic view across the moon-dappled waters of the Port of Balboa. It dawns on me that I have shared a space with wildlife almost every day of my life, but that I haven't always seen it or had my eyes open. Cerro Ancon has shown me, in exaggerated terms perhaps, that the wonder of nature and its amazing birds and bizarre creatures are never far away – even in a gridlocked urban sprawl.

Overlooking the bay, where a trio of ships is waiting to transit the world's most famous waterway, I have my own watershed moment. I feel fulfilled; blissful. Panama, its curious creatures and exciting landscapes, have enriched my world. 'I'm at home,' I whisper to nobody but myself. For me, travel has become so much more than, well, travel. I'm on a journey. And I'm ready to make bigger plans. I grab a pad and scribble out a flow chart that looks like a muddle of wires. Squiggles lead to circles in which I make inky suggestions. Each is an idea for a big, bold adventure. Arrows point to oblongs containing estimated times and durations. Rotating the pad, I add notes on weather, travel issues and risks. Other squiggles lead to purposes and outcomes. I've underlined these. Dolphins on the Caribbean coast; bats, tree frogs and toucans in the Bocas del Toro archipelago; hummingbirds in the rainforest; monkeys, sloths and birds of prey in Soberanía National Park. To top it off, I add a big box in which I scrawl one final goal. A harpy eagle in the wild.

Much as I love to travel solo, a real downside of lone adventuring is having nobody to confer with when an unknown giant furry, flappy or crawly thing takes me by surprise. I've lost count of the times I've hissed: 'Shit! What the hell was that?' to myself. I long to be able to differentiate, with some degree of accuracy, between the jungle's cries and squawks. My neighbour, Tammy Liu, who comes from Hong Kong and once owned a florist's shop in Southampton, now runs a small, independent tour company and B&B in Cerro Ancon. She suggests I meet with an expert from ANCON, and sets up a meeting with Mario Bernal, a seasoned guide with an incredible breadth of knowledge and a keen zest for life. He listens to what I have to tell him with interest, smiling at my tales of early-morning hilltop slogs and bird-rich free-wheeling. Mario, who hails from the town of El Valle in Panama's central Coclé Province, is warm and easy-going. Aged about fifty, he has the gentle contentment of someone who has been lucky enough to earn a living doing what he loves. His spare time is ploughed into local conservation; his spare energy devoted to friends and family. Mario Bernal never felt dressed without a pair of binoculars looped around his neck, or pressed to his eyes. 'So, Sarita,' he ventures. 'You found your thrill-ill, on An-con Hill . . .' He bursts into a tuneful, bluesy twang, and I warm to him instantly as he unfurls a huge map and sets about conjuring up exotic itineraries and quests. With a thin-tipped red pen, Mario translates my illegible doodles into a sensible draft programme. Logical stages link point-to-point on the map.

'Anything specific you definitely want to see? It's always good to have a goal,' Mario urges. Without hesitation, without pausing for breath, I blurt it out, louder than I intend to. 'A harpy eagle. Yes. I want – really want – to see a harpy eagle.' Mario stabs the eastern portion of the map, hard, with his pen. 'Then it's the Darién, no question,' he states, matter of fact. I gulp, but Mario is already rolling up the map. Once the idea is rooted, it's way too late to backtrack. The bottle is empty and the genie is out.

My fascination with the harpy eagle has amplified during the years since that unforgettable taxi ride through Panama City's jubilant streets. Then it hadn't yet been crowned Panama's official national bird – that honour was bestowed upon it in 2002. At more than one metre tall and able to kill a monkey with a single swipe of its powerful,

knife-like talons, harpy eagles are incredibly hard to find. Favouring
large tracts of uninterrupted forest in the tropical lowlands of Central
and South America, from southern Mexico southward to eastern
Bolivia, southern Brazil and the northernmost parts of Argentina,
one of its strongholds is the Darién region of Panama, one of the last
great wildernesses of Central America. This fabled, vine-knotted
jungle, navigable only on foot, by boat or on horseback, is at the
forefront of conservation efforts to protect the future of the
magnificent, prehistoric raptor. The Darién remains one of the best
locations in Panama – if not the world – to spot one in the wild. It is
also a place where to travel unaccompanied would be a sure-fire way
to meet a grisly end.

Closer to home, Mario tells me that Panama's biggest, baddest
bird has been seen in the Metropolitan Natural Park (Parque
Natural Metropolitano) in the capital city. He even pinpoints the
very tree on a local map. Harpy eagles need vast swathes of
undisturbed forest to live in, and the 200-hectare Metropolitan
Natural Park, with its abundance of different plants and animals,
250 species of bird and numerous butterflies would once attract a
pair, or two, of breeding harpies.

Panama is justifiably proud of its huge metropolitan jungle –
the largest tropical forest park within the limits of a Latin
American city. International business executives who fly in to
wheeler-deal in Panama City's banks and finance houses can't
believe their luck when they've got just a couple of hours to
spare, because Metropolitan Natural Park must be one of the
most easy-to-reach birdwatching hotspots on the planet. Within
minutes, a taxi can speed you from a board-level presentation in
one of the needle-thin skyscrapers on Avenida Balboa to bid
buenos dias to tropical kingbirds and streaked flycatchers among
the cecropia trees and slow-moving, mocha-coloured creeks.

A crack-of-dawn start at the Metropolitan Natural Park
guarantees a wildlife walk with rich pickings: a bird count of
between fifty and ninety species on a good day isn't that
uncommon. An impatient birder is looking for an endemic
yellow-green tyrannulet – his third attempt at searching among
the second- and young-growth forest, interspersed with scrubby,
grassy stretches. He reasons that, having managed to tick off a

lance-tailed manakin, rosy thrush-tanager, orange-chinned parakeets and a rare pheasant cuckoo, it is time, surely, for a yellow-green tyrannulet to make an appearance? He strides off, purposefully, binoculars at the ready, before I have time to suggest that Mother Nature probably doesn't work to a rota system. An assumption that she ought to rarely charts an easy passage to ornithological bliss.

I switch back to the Mono Titi trail, named after the tamarins that are easily spotted high up in the treetops, and immediately see a Geoffroy's tamarin peering out at me from behind a clump of vines. It feels good to be alone again after the unscheduled encounter with the impatient birder. Camaraderie is one thing, but when other people's selfish stuff gets in the way of my selfish stuff, I realise why it is so wonderful to travel alone. At times like this there are rich rewards for being a silent spectator. As a backyard birder who is still winging it, I delight in the serenity of simply watching birds go about their lives, beautiful and full of character. I still giggle at their strange calls, talk naively of their colours and plumage, marvel at the freedom of their flight and chuckle like a schoolboy at their silly names. I envy anyone who can talk of tits, boobies, shags and cocks without a smirk. I just can't. On my own, in a forest, I can laugh like a drain at the wildlife I see. Birds are fun. They make me smile. Snigger. Throw my head back in laughter. To me, birding and nature are about sheer glee and wonder. I don't get a buzz from counting and ticking lists.

Tempted by an enticing sun-chinked glade, twirled in spidery creepers, I dodge a shower of fresh faeces slung from the canopy by some roguish monkeys and wade into the leaves. At first, I fear I've stepped straight into a bee swarm, as a dark, stinging mass engulfs me. I shudder at the thought of flying, stinging insects, for angry wasps once stung me so badly in and around my eye as a child that my right iris temporarily lost all colour. From my milky white eyeball, the offending sting was eventually pulled out with tweezers by my headmistress, who then used a cup of malt vinegar as eyewash. I can still recall the agony as the acid was poured in. Today, it's just a mosquito cloud, as prickly, spiteful and smarting as a plume of billowing smoke – and a natural hazard on the hidden trails unmarred by the footprints of trampling tourists. I tug my sleeves down below the wrist, inch up my collar, pull my cap down over my ears and push on.

According to my map, I stand a good chance of sighting blue-crowned motmot, cocoa and olivaceous woodcreepers, thick-billed euphonia and red-legged honeycreeper in this part of the park. Bushy hedgerows are full of nut-brown Central American agouti, and I'm startled by a shy coati wrapped in ruffled ferns. A fleet of glass-winged helicopter damselflies swoops in amongst Panama hat palms heavy with pulpy scarlet fruit. For a while, I stand, silent and ever hopeful, beneath the outstretched arms of a giant ceiba tree. In years gone by, harpy eagles used to nest here, right in this very tree. I gaze up and hold my breath on the off-chance that they've decided to take up residence again. I know my prayers are pointless; the density of undisturbed forest is such that it probably hasn't supported a harpy nest for more than a decade. But, as I head back to the trail, I turn back to steal a final glimpse, just to double check.

Next on my list is Summit Municipal Park, a place known locally as Summit Zoo, although it is far, far more than a captive collection of creatures. In South and Central America, any ensemble of live animals runs the risk of being dubbed a 'zoo'– a confusion of words I've grown used to. This 250-hectare botanical garden and wildlife sanctuary, which sits inside the boundaries of Soberanía National Park about forty minutes from Panama City centre, was set up by the former canal company as a research facility for the study, propagation and dissemination of rare species of Panama's tropical flora. Over time, animals were introduced, initially to help the American servicemen new to Panama in the 1960s know what lay lurking in the jungles. The next step was an experimental breeding programme for endangered indigenous species. Anteaters, tapirs, big cats: you name it, they gave it a try. As I arrive, I nod salutations to a crowd of high-school students excitedly surveying a display board, clearly wowed by what they are about to see. An over-sized sun is hogging more than its fair share of sky space. Everything is drenched in hot, bright orange beams.

With a snap of his fingers, Miguel Miranda calls for a glass of ice-cold *jugo de piña con leche* (fresh pineapple juice milkshake) the moment I enter the Summit's air-cooled restaurant, embracing me warmly and noisily dragging a chair for me towards his table with a view. The smell of disinfectant hits the back of my throat; a pattern of damp orbits across the floor indicates that it is freshly mopped. With basic introductions complete – we share a former roommate as a friend and swap curious tales we've heard about one another – I gush thanks at him for meeting with me. Miguel is a Panama City mover and shaker, a journalist from Panama's exclusive club of influential families with gilded connections. Though he assures me that being here is 'his pleasure', his time, I sense, is as precious as gold. I ask him about his connection to Summit, and he admits this is his first visit. He picked it as a place to meet because he'd heard great things about the park's education centre: it has helped to shift all sorts of negative perceptions in young children about certain species of wildlife, and carries out conservation work with turtles and iguana, which were both once commonly eaten in certain provinces of Panama. The education team encourages children to value the natural habitat on the basis that they will one day be the politicans, educators, influencers and parents of future generations. For example, they are taught not to throw rubbish in the rivers, lakes and sea – once considered a convenient vessel that carried waste far away in its flow.

Miguel wishes that more tourists would visit. Most, he explains, come along when they've time to kill at the end of their trip, and arrive disappointed because they've been expecting a slick London Zoo experience. He raises his eyebrows. I glance over to the shabby, peeling paintwork and rain-faded wooden fencing and nod in understanding. Government funding is limited, and the Summit gardens and zoo rely heavily on the fundraising and support of volunteers.

Miguel, who at a guess is in his early thirties, has recently returned to his native Panama after studying and working in North America. Today, back on home turf, a philanthropic desire is bubbling up inside him. 'Y'know,' he says, 'from what I read about this place, I'm impressed. I was born in Panama, but most of what is here is totally new to me.'Over a second jug of milkshake, we idle away an hour chatting over and around my travel plans. He suggests places I should see and people I should meet, and I tell him about the freelance writing jobs I'm juggling while I'm on the road: a travel guidebook to Panama, the first by a British author; a pitch for a National Geographic TV show; a variety of magazine travel features, inspired by talking with Mario, from island-hopping on the Caribbean coast to hiking the Darién in search of a harpy eagle. For each project, he scribbles down a list of names and numbers, including people from the tourist board, tour operators, hoteliers and an insider at the Panamanian government.

'Wow, Sarita, it's great that you are telling so many people about my country,' Miguel enthuses, folding up the scrap of paper and handing it to me. With his slicked-back hair and clear olive skin, he looks cool and businesslike, but sincere. 'Hey, you will soon know Panama better than me! And the jungle, wow. But, if you are serious about the Darién, follow me please. There is someone I think you should meet.'

Moments later, after a stroll along a hedge-trimmed path, I am practically face-to-beak with Panama's national bird. This time, the poster is introducing me to the world's largest harpy eagle exhibition – right here at the Summit Municipal Park. To say that I am surprised to find it here, tucked away among the Summit's foliage, would be an understatement. It must rank as Panama's least-promoted tourist attraction. After poring over photographs and video footage honouring the harpy, I approach the mammoth eagle enclosure. I still can't believe that it will contain anything other than a battery-operated replica. Possibly – if I'm lucky – with moving parts.

I peer in, and see that the compound is set up as a natural harpy habitat. The smell of unknown prey fills my nostrils. Mice, maybe? Fresh blood has an earthy aroma on wet green leaves. A sign on the pound says that the Summit serves as a base for harpy eagle conservation and education programmes Panama-wide. These long-lived, slow-reproducing eagles play a vital role in the overall health of tropical forests. As an 'umbrella species' – one whose conservation indirectly protects other species in its habitat – its survival ensures the survival of countless other lesser-known species in one of the most biodiverse ecosystems on Earth.

With its wingspan, tip to tip, equal to the height of an adult human male, the harpy is the largest raptor in the Americas, where it is endemic. Elusive and almost extinct, it uses powerful claws and a razor-sharp beak to tear flesh from bone. It has legs as thick as a human wrist and a locking, vice-like grip. Using 3D binocular vision to pinpoint its prey, the harpy hops and flies from tree to tree through dense forest cover. Find a harpy eagle today and you will most likely be in one of the world's last remaining wilderness areas, for harpies need significant stretches of contiguous forest cover to survive. Populations are sparsely distributed throughout an extensive range in south Mexico, Guatemala, Belize, Honduras, Nicaragua, Costa Rica, Panama, Colombia, Venezuela, Guyana, Suriname, French Guiana, Ecuador, Peru, Bolivia, Brazil, Paraguay and north-east Argentina.

Despite human encroachment into its territory, the harpy eagle is rarely seen and interacts little with humans. It is easy to see why it is dubbed a 'unicorn of the rainforest'. Panama has the largest concentration of harpy eagles in all of Central America, at an estimated 200 breeding pairs – its depiction on the Panamanian coat of arms has helped conservation efforts. As an apex predator at the top of the food chain, humans are all that threaten it. Hunters prize it highly as a trophy. But loss of habitat remains the greatest danger to its survival. Its future will be assured only when the escalating rate of forest destruction is brought under control.

A fresh-faced volunteer wearing a Summit Municipal Park badge joins us for the Harpy Eagle Encounter, a joint project with Zoo Miami and private enterprise that hosts tens of thousands of visitors each year. Lucia, a conservation student, is in her second week. She covers a few of the basics about the harpy's diet of, mainly, arboreal mammals such as sloth and monkey, adding that it will also feed on iguana and other mid-sized mammals and reptiles. She stresses that as well as needing large expanses of forest in which to hunt, the harpy also needs habitat that provides a proper place to rest, together with an abundant diversity of prey. 'This combination of conditions is increasingly difficult to find together in one place. That's why it's rare to see them,' Lucia says. 'Your best bet is to go to the Darién – they still breed there in the wild. But, hopefully, this will do for now?'

I turn my head to where she is pointing and see a set of claws as big as hobnail boots gripping a rocky ledge. In view, an information board in garish colours illustrates how the size of a mature harpy compares with a human male. I squint at it, eyes darting back and forth between the board and the claws before me. Lucia steps in. 'A harpy eagle can grow up to forty-one inches,' she informs us, sizing me up. 'At a guess, I'd say this one is just twenty or so inches shorter than you. They can reach a weight of twenty pounds: more than a truck tyre.'

Judging by its feet alone, the resident harpy is one big, mean beast. It would be easy to feel nervous about this meet-and-greet. But I don't. I'm tingling all over. It's not every day that an opportunity arises to meet one of the world's most feared raptors – and such an iconic, keystone species – when you've simply popped out for a milkshake. I just wish there wasn't a strong steel fence between us.

'Let's come back later when it gets fed,' Lucia suggests. I hesitate, reluctant to leave, in case I miss anything. 'There's lots more to see,' she cajoles. And there is. We meet two baby two-toed sloths, which were brought to the rangers after being found by the roadside, motherless, starved and dehydrated. They are making good progress: gaining weight slowly and growing stronger each day. I zone in on an injured tamandua, a species of anteater, now almost fully recovered after being hit by a car. Between protruding ears, his small, beady eyes stare out of a tapered head with a long, tubular snout that sniffles in a constant twitch. With thick, bristly fur, he looks good enough to scoop up into my arms – until, that is, he unleashes a powerful musk from his anal glands. It is eye-watering.

Rapidly, I move onto another pen containing a rehabilitated hawk that is almost ready for release into the wild after being nursed back to health. It had ingested lead from a carcass, its digestive system so efficient that the poison was quickly absorbed into its bloodstream, affecting its nervous and circulatory systems. By the time it was brought to the Summit Municipal Park, it could barely breathe, was having seizures and required round-the-clock care. I meet emaciated howler monkeys, tortured ocelots and a sickly boa constrictor. All have been seized from poachers, abandoned by pet owners or rescued from the wild with life-threatening injuries.

We stroll the park's gardens and marvel at bushes filled with birds that are seemingly oblivious to human presence. Thick clumps of well-scattered trees allow easy viewing of several giant cowbirds, which look far too big to be sitting on the same tree. Like a weightlifter with a pumped-up torso, this peculiar species has a small-headed appearance, like a pea on an elephant. I'm more taken with an impressive grey hawk that holds our gaze from a low perch on a mossy branch. He has the air of a dignified aristocrat besuited in a grey three-piece. I feel I could look at him for hours. We enjoy up-close encounters with a shy, solitary, coppery-brown squirrel cuckoo, which hops energetically from branch to branch in a forensic search for bugs and flies, and a colony of playful chestnut-headed oropendolas with buttercream beaks. But my eyes turn towards the harpy enclosure. I am itching to get back, hopeful for more than a glimpse of eagle toes.

The winged assassin doesn't disappoint.

When chunks of rabbit meat are thrown into the enclosure, I get a true sense of the harpy's formidable size and beauty. It is utterly mind-blowing, with vast wings audibly swiping anything in its path as it moves, twisting and turning to 'hunt' the prey down. In a single pounce that is so swift and perfectly choreographed it stuns us all, it strikes the meat at high velocity, ripping into the bleeding flesh with the five-inch, blade-sharp claws powered by thick, strong legs. Of the fifty species of eagle in the world, this is one of the largest and most powerful. With an intimidating stance and petrifying dark-eyed stare, this harpy is a mesmerising force of nature. Its black-and-white battle-dress plumage features a menacing band of black 'war paint' running from chest to neck, and the double crest of dark grey feathers on the bird's head, which rises when it is threatened or alerted, serves to magnify its size.

These carnivores and diurnal (daylight) hunters wait in silent stealth before pouncing on their prey in short bursts of speed. Owl-like discs around the eyes pick up sound waves with staggering accuracy over large ranges, enabling them to pinpoint prey at different distances without using sight, under tree and plant cover. Reaching up to fifty miles per hour, they are high-speed killers, brutal and unmatched. A harpy's call is primal, a penetrating screech that echoes through the forest. Like other birds of prey, it can fly only with prey weighing less than one half of its body weight. However, this harpy looks as if it could snatch me up by my shoulders and fly far away without breaking into a sweat.

Yet harpy eagles aren't just brawn and brute. They are mono-gamous, mating for life and giving birth to a single chick every two or three years. The average harpy union, at around fifty years, is longer-lasting than most marriages in the so-called developed world. At around five years old they reach adulthood, at which point their white and light-grey feathers darken – a sign that they are ready to mate. Once they've paired up, they look for a nesting site at the highest point in the tallest trees of the forest. Working together to gather hundreds of branches to build a nest, they snap off suitable boughs using their mighty talons. This mammoth construction project results in a nest that spans around six feet in diameter and more than a foot in depth – big enough to accommodate two grown men.

After laying one, sometimes two large white eggs, the female sits on her nest for around fifty-five days, with the male sharing in the incubation when the mother needs a break to stretch her wings, hunt or eat. Despite the hard work of their parents, it is usual for only one egg to survive. Parenting duties are shared until the chick is around three years old. As I stare at this mighty bird's robust frame, it is hard to imagine that it was ever the size of a small mango. Harpies grow fast, though, and this one will have reached full adult size in less than half a year. At this point, falteringly, it will have fledged, shaky and awkward, before mastering the skies with the same lightning precision as her folks.

Long-living harpies can survive for around seventy years in their natural habitat, although in captivity it's usually just a third of that. At the time of my visit, this particularly impressive specimen was in its forties; it died about seven years after my visit. By this point, it had become an emblematic symbol of Panama City, and of Panama itself. To me, it will always be that steely-eyed poster star.

Lucia is about to go off duty, so she bids us a shy *hasta luego*. She enjoys working in Panama City, having been raised in Chicago by Panamanian parents. Miguel tells me she is part of a growing number of international volunteers who sign up for placements at the Summit Municipal Park. Some give a day while they're passing through, others stay for months or years. Some, like Lucia, have conservation experience. Others are plumbers, electricians or good at general maintenance. Limited resources, as Miguel points out, make every skill welcome.

Miguel pops into the administration office to shake everyone's hand before we leave, introducing me as a 'very famous travel writer from London'. Like a spice mill, he peppers the rather bland room with zest and zeal. The whole place is energised, fizzing and buzzing by the time he finally leaves. A generous donation and a pledge to return to lend a hand one day are his parting gifts. I pipe a farewell to the harpy eagle and vow to myself that the next one I see will be in the wild. Miguel has stayed at the Summit much longer than he intended and is now seriously late for a meeting. So our parting is a hurried exchange of email addresses and a promise to stay in touch by phone during the next few weeks.

'I'm sure your boss will go easy on you when you explain that you've been waylaid by a harpy eagle, Miguel,' I call after him as he waves from his highly polished executive car.

Like many of Panama City's privileged upper classes, he has a full-time driver, who is tasked with whisking him from A to B. Me, I am heading off in an eight-dollar-an-hour taxi to spend the night in an old 1960s' military-communications base – once I've shaken the driver's crumpled form awake. Slumped and dishevelled, with one hair-matted arm hanging awkwardly out of the window, he is lying forward using the steering wheel as a pillow, mouth squashed open. Climbing in the back, I slam the weighty steel door shut with a satisfying clank, sending the stationary vehicle into a mighty judder. Within seconds, the driver has unfolded, straightened and unwrinkled with eyes wide open, twisting the key hard into the ignition. '*¡Vamos!*' he croaks, patting his fringe flat before accelerating out of the car park.

We are on our way to one of the world's most famous wildlife-viewing sites: a five-storey octagonal tower topped with a giant white golf ball that rises out of the jungle canopy in Soberanía National Park. Built in 1965 by the United States Air Force to house a souped-up radar system, Canopy Tower once played an important part in guarding the Panama Canal. Around twenty years later, it became part of a network of radar systems used to detect drug-carrying aircraft in Central America. When this role ended, in 1995, the tower fell empty before it was transferred back to the Panamanian government under the terms of the Canal Treaty. A few years later, businessman Raúl Arias de Para – an avid wildlife enthusiast with solid eco principles – set about transforming the site into a centre for Neotropical rainforest observation.

The rainforest atop Semaphore Hill, within Soberanía National Park, just thirty-five miles north of the flyovers of Panama City, is visited by many congregations of migratory birds, which choose it as a place of rest part-way through their epic flights. All the four major North American flyways – the Atlantic, the Mississippi, the Central and the Pacific – overlap in Panama; the huge number of migratory birds on the isthmus is due to them merging into what is often described as a 'bird funnel'. Canopy Tower, partially hidden by dense, undisturbed rainforest, makes the most of this location, poking up from the thick, leafy mass, its famous viewing balcony at treetop height. If real-estate value was tallied on birds and animals alone, this place would have a mega-billion-dollar price tag.

The full magnitude of Canopy Tower's splendour only hits home once you've left. When the conversion of the site was first completed and the guests were rolling in, I was invited to review the new venture. Stupidly, I tagged an overnight stay there onto the end of another trip, arriving jet-lagged after several long flights and airport delays. It was an all-too-brief visit. I was furious with myself. How dare I occupy a room here while in no fit state to revel in the sheer joy of eyeball-to-eyeball encounters high in the forest canopy? So magnificent, yet all I could do was sleep. I was sore about missing out for months.

So today I am returning in better shape. And, in truth, Canopy Tower has shaped up too. Carving such a venture from raw jungle involves a steep learning curve, especially when aiming for minimal carbon footprint and habitat disruption. It has been one huge adventure fraught with challenges. The once-windowless shell of gun-grey corrugated iron is now a fetching shade of aquamarine. A sign on the gate still bears the military crest and states: 'This is a US Military Defense Site. It is illegal for persons not possessing a valid US-issued identification document to enter.' Raúl Arias de Para has worked hard to further develop the concept: food is largely organic; waste is removed from site; soap is biodegradable; water is recycled and the tower relies on hilltop breezes rather than power-sapping air conditioning. A handful of bright, comfy suites has been added to the tower's standard, cheaper bunk rooms and dorms, positioning it nicely for eco-comfort without comprising on its character or appeal to shoe-string nature nuts.

I am greeted like an old friend by the guy on reception, a talented amateur wildlife photographer whose work I admired on my last visit. When I'm handed a key to my room, I squeak with glee: it's called the Harpy Eagle Suite. Situated roughly at mid-canopy tree level, around five and half metres high, two gigantic window panes dominate the room to frame a living, breathing piece of artwork: a rustling, chirping, squawking cacophony of tanagers and tityras backed by trees, leaves, moss and bark. The views are even more spellbinding from the wide balcony that rings the nine-metre-high geo-tangent dome as Canopy Tower's famous observation deck. From here, I can almost shake hands with a troop of noisy black howler monkeys manically swinging through the branches. After fumbling for my binoculars, I realise I'm resting against a high-tech telescope. In perfect detail, I watch Geoffroy's tamarins scratch and nibble, before training the scope on a collared aracari, which, seemingly, surveys me back. Coloured a little like a tiger, in red-orange and near-black dark green, this exotic-looking fruigivore is a favourite of mine; I welcome its sighting like a prodigal son. The aracari stares at me with a big yellow eye; the pupil is as black as soot. A ragged sawtooth pattern on the cutting edge of its oversized toucan-like beak makes it look as if it is mock-snarling. A blue-headed parrot and then a great jacamar settle on a woody snag in a combined burst of colour that spans every spectrum of blue.

Sensing that it is time for dinner, I get ready to call it a day just as a flash of feathery electric-blue bedazzles the sky – my first brief encounter with blue cotinga. With sheer delight, I squeal discreetly, before realising that Canopy Tower has acoustics like a squash court. Even the quietest whisper can become a reverberating boom in this austere, utilitarian space. What the tiny cotinga lacks in size, it more than compensates for in colour: the lustre of its plumage is astounding. Though it disappears from sight, I can still hear the whistling of its wings, a thin, high-pitched sound about as loud as a steaming kettle.

With its exposed bolts, rivets and solid-steel grates, the Canopy Tower reminds me of my brother's old Meccano set. Or a shipping container. A succession of open doors, strung along a mesh-steel gangway, catch my eye. I peer in: they are a cross between student rooms and prison cells. Each one bare apart from a thin, single mattress and table set with a bendy-armed desk lamp.

Over an early dinner of meatballs, rice and vegetables, I write up my notes and chat casually to an all-male birding group from America's east coast. They are all wearing khaki. Other than diehard birders, there are a grey-haired husband and wife from Switzerland, a couple of lone backpackers, like me, and a larger group of serious-looking scientists with clipboards. They are, I learn later, from the National Audubon Society, visiting as part of a joint project with the Panama branch to help to conserve one of the western hemisphere's most important shorebird migration locations: the mudflats along the Bay of Panama. We chat away easily about our surroundings and experiences. Ted, a senior from Wisconsin, has already introduced himself. When I arrived, he heard that I'd visited before and took me aside, quietly, to enquire what the Canopy Tower's food is like. He has, by pure chance, quizzed the right person. I have all the gastronomic assurance he needs.

Cuquita Arias de Calvo, the Panamanian equivalent of a cross between Martha Stewart and Nigella Lawson, is Raúl Arias de Para's sister. And this celebrated TV chef and published author is an ambassador for Panama's fusion of Amerindian, Hispanic, African and Afro-Caribbean cuisine. My tastebuds know her culinary creations first hand, for I have met her twice and enjoyed her flavoursome dishes myself. Every foodie in Panama raves

about her menu at the Salsipuedes Restaurant in the swanky
Bristol Hotel in Panama City. She personally devised the Canopy
Tower menu and trained its chefs, ensuring that it isn't just
feathered thrills that provide the guests with sensory pleasure. Ted
is delighted, slapping me across the shoulders and dashing off 'to
tell Jim'.

After dinner, I fill up on the books around me. They are piled,
stacked and towering in the communal lounge, with even more
of them weighing down the shelves. I pull at a spine, drawing it to
me, hungrily studying its contents. Then I spot a more inviting
tome, so I slot the first book back in. This happens again. Then
again. Until I'm flitting from one end of the bookshelf to the
other. Scribbled inscriptions or nameplates suggest that this mix
of paperbacks and hardcovers have lost touch with their owners,
or have been donated by guests passing through. I discover old
National Geographic magazines, creased back copies of *BBC
Wildlife*, piles of dog-eared *Geographical* and *New Scientist*.
Pamphlets on treecreepers. Papers on avian disease. Maps of the
condor's range. Numerous field guides and travel books
representing the wildlife species and cultures of every corner of
the globe. Umpteen languages, from Arabic and Portuguese to
Japanese, Indonesian and Mandarin. I head to bed early, ready for
a sunrise start, having unearthed a guide to Central American
endemics – in Braille.

I wake to a dawn that is reluctant to break, so heavy rain and
low cloud are my companions over breakfast. I study the saturated
branches of the forest, hung with oversized droplets. Everything is
wet, from the moist rain vapour that is wilting my napkin to the
waterlogged trails and sopping puddles on the deck. A percussive
chorus of drips, drops and splashes is punctuated by the geyser-
like hiss of atomised rain. Precipitation has a hypnotic effect, I
find, in steamy heat. There are small, spherical cloud droplets,
larger oblate drips, bigger, flattened raindrops shaped like burger
buns and the largest parachute-like drips. Not one resembles a
teardrop. In the slow, sizzling wetness, some distort to take on the
shapes of faces, complete with drooping eyes and downturned
mouths.

Even the downpour can't spoil a Panamanian breakfast for me,
without doubt my favourite meal of the day. After squares of cake

made from the coffee grown in the rugged Panamanian highlands, I enjoy a delicious plate of just-ripe papaya, banana, mango and pineapple, before a dish of *huevos rancheros* (scrambled eggs with cheese, green peppers and chopped ham). A finale of homemade pineapple jam served with lightly baked, hot bread rolls provides the perfect distraction from the weather. By the time the tables are ready to be cleared, the skies are clearing, too.

The studious guys with the clipboards bring news of green and red-legged honeycreepers as they peel off bright yellow waterproofs. Only slighted delayed, the rest of us grab our scopes and embark on an amble along the soggy mile-long road down Semaphore Hill. Within minutes we spot antbirds, agoutis and several wood quail. We spend a magical half hour delighting in the flitting aerobatics of the hummingbirds at the feeders: two shimmering white-necked jacobins hovering back to back, like a couple of azure-pattened bookends, doing their best to avoid the scratching candy-pink feet and stabbing dart-thin beak of the altogether more rare bronze-tailed plumeleteers. A playful violet-headed hummer dallies in the midst of all the action, a soft blur of purple no doubt tipsy on the potent sugar cocktail.

I hold out for raptors. Ocean-to-ocean counts by the Panama Audubon Society have tallied well over 1.6 million migrating raptors passing over the Panama Canal on the way to and from their wintering grounds in South America. Each year, forty observers at nine points around the waterway monitor the skies in October and November: the highest one-day count totalled more than 460,000 birds. Panama is one of a handful of privileged countries where a million migratory raptors can be seen in a season; it shares this honour with Eilat in Israel, Veracruz in Mexico, Batumi in Georgia and its Central American neighbour Costa Rica. I have dropped back from the group, which is gathered round a mouse sleeping in a silky-skinned bundle in the nook of a tree. A high-soaring white hawk swoops down to perch in a hardwood bough just a few metres away. Proud, tall and straight-backed, with a chest as white as gloss paint against the dark green shadows of the forest, he returns my stare with his round amber eyes, so I drop my gaze. With a single movement of his broad, dark wings, the hawk takes to the sky again, surveying me like an ant in dirt once he is back on an aerial high.

Although Semaphore Hill Road is just a mile long, it can take four or five hours to walk it due to the sheer number of birds and animals. Time flies, and we all enjoy our gentle introduction to forest birding, which can be difficult and frustrating even for seasoned pros. Haphazard newbie birders such as me rely on chance and opportunity, and I've watched brows crumple like empty crisp packets when exasperation sets in. Hearing everything but seeing nought is a cruel twist of fate in the rainforest; sometimes, thousands of birds can surround you in the foliage, but not even a tail feather can be seen. This isn't a worry at Canopy Tower, where, with zero effort on our part, a red-capped manakin struts out in front us to perform its odd backwards shuffle across a branch, something akin to a Michael-Jackson moonwalk but double the speed. As a finale, the manakin slaps its wings and dips his head, as if clapping and taking a bow – a comical routine that has us doubled over in laughter.

During my three-day stay, I am bamboozled by the sight of more amazing birds than I ever believed possible. And that's not all. Up close I meet a six-foot bird-eating snake coiled like a giant Slinky around mossy branches, as well as several small troops of howler monkeys, a stoat-like tayra and an ant-snuffling nine-banded armadillo. The bird-crazy among my companions reach a state of fevered excitement, ticking off fifty or more species each day, from some particularly gregarious yellow-rumped caciques to numerous flycatcher species. By the stagnant pools of the old ammo dump ponds that lie a jeep ride away (they are a lot more picturesque than they sound), I stand a few steps from an enchanting pygmy kingfisher: the smallest of the New World kingfisher species and distinctive for capturing and eating insects in flight while swooping down for fish.

One day we explore Pipeline Road, a ten-mile trail synonymous with more varieties of bird than practically anywhere else in the world. Built during the Second World War on the east bank of the Panama Canal to ease the transfer of fuel between Pacific and Caribbean ports, the forested route now draws birding adventurers to Soberanía National Park from countries far and wide. Its extraordinary diversity of bird life is attributable to a mix of habitats: secondary and old-growth forests, swamps and streams. A sunrise start reaps untold rewards, kicking off with a dazzling red-throated ant tanager, whose vibrant scarlet plumage contrasts perfectly with the pale milky blue of the sky. Along the first part of the road, we spot a couple of cinnamon woodpeckers, their nut-brown crests melding into the bark of a tree stump. A thin 'kew kew kew' alerts us to a cocoa woodcreeper, its buff-streaked, liver-brown plumage and curved, long bill barely visible against dried-up vines and bracken. It is part of a small group playing hide-and-seek among the foliage. A slaty-backed forest falcon steals the show for me, appearing from nowhere in the rising mid-morning heat. Our eyes light up like headlamps at the noble stance of this rare raptor, which carries its long, rounded, white-banded tail like a regal cloak before heading off to higher ground. Three purple-throated fruitcrows, usually hard to pinpoint, dance in a colour-rich trio before our eyes. It is delightful, but unnerving, for birding to be this easy.

As the first to lie down, exhausted, in a springy patch of grass at lunchtime, I feel the flutter of the delicate wings of an electric-blue morpho butterfly against my face. We're joined by a wavy-haired Spaniard with eyes like bright buttons. He is so amazed by what he has seen so far that he can't imagine topping the morning's triumphs. Several of the list-ticking birders are worrying that they may soon run out of ink. As we collectively ponder the marvel of Pipeline Road, a semiplumbeous hawk makes a thrilling fly-past, its tangerine-coloured feet, beak and eyes as bright as the sun. Seldom seen soaring high like other hawks, this magnificent species prefers to streak across the forest just above the canopy layer, though rarely after first light. It swoops down to snatch up a lizard, not far from where we are standing. Surely, it can't get any better that this?

After lunch we labour across thick undergrowth, where conditions are sticky and hard going. Although two of our group decide to turn back, the rest of us force ourselves onwards, pushing back branches tacked with thorns as the hot, moist air sucks away our strength. At last, a magnificent golden-collared manakin provides us with a riveting reward for slogging through the unruly tangle, performing a series of aerial moves like an acrobat wearing a yellow scarf. Golden-collared manakins dance and snap their wings together behind their backs to win the attention of females – although the object of this one's intentions remains out of sight while we are around. At the nearby Summit ponds we giggle at the splish-splash antics of umpteen waterbirds putting on a show. A boat-billed heron takes a starring role, indulging us with a close-up of its kooky, penguin-like face while preening. On our walk back to the jeep, a collared forest falcon peers down at the forest floor from on high, so intent on a prey-pounce that it doesn't give us a second glance. With its short wings, long, banded tail and acute, radar-like hearing, this falcon is the largest of its genus, a slick predator that provides us with a demonstration of nature at its most primeval – and an easy target for our cameras.

Ted runs his fingers through silvery whiskers, giving silent thanks to an unknown higher power, his smile wide and bright. 'This is why we leave our warm, cosy beds before the skies have lightened!' he chirps to nobody in particular. He has twigs in his hair, snags in his neatly pressed clothes and his pale, cushioned sneakers are caked in mud. Pens, tissues and lengths of string are squashed into his multi-pocketed vest. He punches the air, which I sense is uncharacteristic. 'Boy-oh-boy-oh-boy,' he trills. 'What a day!'

On my final day at Canopy Tower, the threatening gloom closes in again and a four-hour tropical thunderstorm ensues, sending dramatic rumbles that vibrate the tower. But torrential rain cannot dampen our enthusiasm and desire. The khaki birders have by now clocked up more than 190 species between them, and even on this soggy, drab morning they have a Teflon-like resolve to add more. Riding high, they are even debating whether or not prolonging their stays will jeopardise their connecting flights and/or marriages. Ted is advocating a three- or four-day extension and has already haggled a deal. I may still be a birding debutant, but I too have experienced something very special at Canopy Tower.

Spending time so close to the wildlife in the jungle has been deeply enriching, reconnecting me with the nature that has captivated me since I first watched Tarzan on the family black-and-white television, aged seven. It was around that time that I started taking a blanket outside, draping it between two garden chairs and spending the night underneath. On family trips to the south-east coast, when my sister was two and my brother about six, I would jump straight into the cold, brown-green waters of the English Channel. Without adult supervision, I would swim as far as I could manage from the shore; my parents recall how I was just a dot in the distance. Preferring bare feet as I grew older, I would walk around my home town without shoes. Pressing wild flowers, collecting pebbles and watching for the swifts to return were true fascinations. Later, I could often be seen hitchhiking with a cat tucked under my arm to camp in the countryside, swim in rivers and sketch pastoral scenes. My spirit was unbroken. And I loved being me in an amazing world. Then something got lost along the way. I disconnected somehow. Forgot about where I fit into the world.

Now that the skies are dried out, I grab my pack. Plunged back into the humid forest, alone, with senses honed, I can just make out the sounds of lazy flapping. But it is not until I am in a clearing on Semaphore Hill Road that a fine white hawk enters my view. She soars, wings outstretched, before spiralling upwards. Then she levels and swoops in a sudden dramatic drop, down into the treetops: a fitting euphoric climax to a truly rosette-winning stay.

Elated, I allow myself a few moments of pure fantasy as I write up my notes by lamplight. Perhaps tomorrow will yield a harpy eagle. Today, I am in the Harpy Eagle Suite. Right now, I am sitting beneath a print of a fluffy-feathered juvenile on the wall. Yes, tomorrow I will meet a harpy. This fanciful notion carries me away into an imagined chain of events. Sheer will and determination has made many of my dreams come true. So why not this one? I dash out a quick email to my sister, Raichel, outlining my plans, pausing midway through to read the message back. My pulse races as I do so: it sounds terrifying. Raichel, six years younger than me and altogether more sensible, is no longer concerned for my safety − she knows I am competent solo − but now and then she worries I may not be sane. I toy with massaging the text a little, but I'm short of time and, anyway, Raichel is a master at reading between the lines. My index finger stabs the 'send' button and the text disappears. It's several weeks before I'm able to make contact again.

'Working hard, even here in the forest?' Ted questions. 'Not really, just getting ready to leave and thinking about what lies ahead. I hope to go to the Darién soon. Well, as soon as I can arrange it. Wish me luck!'

Later, as I heave the boot of the taxi shut on my muddy boots and luggage, the guy from reception is waving to me from across the car park. 'Everything OK?' I query as he nears me. 'Yes, fine. I just want to give you this.' He presses a large, old silver coin in my palm. It has a woman's face on it. And a name: Sara Sotillo.

'It's a special Sara coin,' he says. 'She is another Panama Sara – a strong woman in our history. Take it with you to the Darién for good luck. And *buen viaje*, Sarita.'

Sara Sotillo Guillén (1900–1961) was an educator and women's rights campaigner from Panama's Pearl Islands. She spent her whole life fighting to secure the female right to vote. She pioneered literacy standards in Panama and lobbied on behalf of the teaching profession for better pay and welfare. Tall and slim, Sotillo was characterised by neat black hair gathered and tied at the nape – much like I wear mine. She rejected all offers of promotion and office, preferring to remain independent and free-speaking. As the dynamo behind great social reform, she was honoured on a five-cent coin. But she never married or had children. At times, I fear this may be my fate, too.

Eyeballing an Eden

Panama
2004–2006

A thimble-sized cup of strong coffee does little to settle my stomach, so I take a swig of water and press the cold bottle to my brow. I'm unnerved by my throbbing head, for I am rarely ill. As a distraction, I needlessly but meticulously unjumble my camera straps, and smooth and pat them flat. There. All nice and neat. If only it were as easy to unravel myself and work out the reason for this confounding knot in my stomach. I check my tickets with a haunting doubt – something isn't right. Passport: check. ID: check. Phone: check. Everything is fine, I silently assure myself. I have no inkling then that a truly hellish day of travel lies ahead. The terrors still feed my nightmares.

There are several places in the world where it is essential to hire a guide. The Darién is one of them. Apart from disease, quicksands and wild animals, human dangers stalking the jungle with guns are always present. A speedboat bouncing atop the waves of the Gulf of San Miguel at seventy knots warns that drug-running cartels are moving around. Even the most intelligent, best-prepared and jungle-savvy explorer can become disorientated in the Darién's forested puzzle. In this terrain, egos are diminished. Everything is more powerful than you are. Being alone here isn't an adventure: it's all about survival. Getting lost would, quite simply, be fatal.

After several months in a cheery room in Cerro Ancon, my base for trips all over Panama to research travel features and gather material for a guidebook, I am ready to put an X on the map and venture into the Darién gap – where the Herculean harpy eagle flies. My head is full of possibilities: the encounters, the dangers, the astonishing wildlife. The flights are booked. The machetes sharpened. My arm is pumped full of inoculations. Night after night, I dream of jaguars feeding from my hand and pumas sleeping soundly at my feet. With an anteater on my arm, I take a midnight stroll along a moonlit path. When a spectacled bear tries to chase me down, I escape by hiding behind a tapir. Tribal cultures often see a message from an ancestor, spirit or god in a dream, or a meaning from one's own soul or unconscious. I see neither.

To be heading to this formidable, vine-knotted stretch of Panama's north-eastern fringes feels unreal, imagined almost, because I have been fascinated by the Darién since I was a child. Then, with a mixture of schoolgirl disbelief and wonder, I struggled to make sense of the forest captured in harrowing tales of perilous journeys and human survival. My teacher described a jungle almost too thick to pass through, so full of disease that those insane enough to venture there met a horrible, boil-ridden, mouth-foaming death. This feral place remains as intriguing to explorers as it was almost 500 years ago, when the first conquistadors sought passage, with their riches, to the Pacific Ocean. But I suspect that my Perthshire-born teacher may have felt a particular affinity with the Darién because of the role her homeland played in its history.

In the late seventeenth century, William Paterson, a Scottish merchant and founder of the Bank of England, led an attempt to set up a Scottish colony in the Darién that ended in a huge death toll and nearly bankrupted Scotland. The first expedition of the Company of Scotland, which was created by the Scottish Parliament to challenge England's dominance in world trade, set sail from Leith in 1698. After four torturous months at sea, the colonists – a mix of fiercely clannish Highlanders and less feudal, more civilised Lowlanders – finally reached a coastal strip of land in the Darién, later named Caledonia Bay. The frontiersmen had filled their boats with a cargo of wool, wigs, hairbrushes and Bibles, items that Paterson curiously believed would be invaluable to the indigenous peoples of Central America.

They claimed the bay as an 'earthly paradise' and founded a small town named New Edinburgh. But the reality of the Darién's inhospitable climate, terrain and wildlife soon set in, and the project spiralled into disaster and despair. Practising European-style farming in the thick forest was impossible, because as soon as land was cleared it became overgrown again. Tools snapped, ploughs broke and cuts immediately oozed with infection. Crops were swept away in the rains. Food supplies were extremely scarce, with barely enough for daily rations. Fights broke out, factions formed and many of the Scots, after burying their comrades, begged to leave the Darién's hell.

Eventually, English government obstruction and a spate of Spanish attacks forced the Scots to abandon the land they had tried so hard to tame. The dream of creating a thriving trading colony lay in tatters. By then, more than 2,000 men, women and children had perished in the mosquito-infested, fever-ridden set-tlement. The failure crippled the Scottish economy with debts of more than £400,000, around half of the country's available capi-tal. It triggered the dissolution of its Parliament, leading to the 1707 Act of Union with England: a humiliating end to Scotland's attempt to make its mark on the world.

At 3am, I am wide awake. Twenty minutes later I have a bag by the door. I have never needed, or wanted, an alarm to wake me, no matter how unearthly a time I need to leave my bed. Much like fingernails screeching down a blackboard, the nagging tones of a clock's alarm are utterly unbearable to me, an annoyance that sends my body into instant shock. Legions of travellers have survived for centuries without relying on a persistent beep to embark on epic sea voyages or set off on journeys of discovery. As soon as I started travelling, I wanted to do the same. When it's light, it's easy, wherever I am in the world. The sun rises in the east. In the northern hemisphere, a south-facing orientation gets more sunlight; in the southern hemisphere, a north-facing position yields more. So, unless I want a lie-in, I face east to catch the sun when it rises – often easier in a hammock than a hotel suite. I've learned how to influence my brain in order to control the time I awaken. I tell my body the time I need to wake up and the reason why (this seems to help), and repeat the instruction three times. It works – even if it is 1.25am. Of course, this makes it especially irritating if someone sleeping within earshot depends on an insistent, trilling alarm and continually hits the snooze button.

Opening the door onto the unlit street activates the yard light and sends several saucer-sized moths into a spin. I peer into the rain-filled darkness, scrutinising every foggy shadow. This is a safe part of town, high up above Panama City, but with rundown areas to the east, Cerro Ancon isn't without danger after dark. Turning my ear towards the main drag, I do an audio scan for a car engine. Nothing. Just the whine of insects and the rustle of trees. Catching a taxi in the early hours here is always a lottery. Will it turn up? Arrive on time? Be driven by a psychotic woman hater with a death wish? Only time will tell. Mastering early rising is fine, but the surety of making it to the airport on time rests with a guy I've never met. Experience has taught me that I can only plan – and hope. Every trip is the same, with an element of jeopardy. To add greater leeway, I routinely lie about my flight departure time to the taxi company. They always cut it fine.

The car arrives, finally, with minutes to spare, screeching noisily to a halt. The driver shrinks back with genuine fear in his eyes when I growl at him. Perhaps I resemble a psychotic man hater with a death wish? Mindful that he can jump back in his seat, slam the car into reverse and speed off, leaving me stranded by the kerbside, I sweeten the air with a compliment about the vehicle's upholstery – a sure-fire way to win over any self-respecting Panamanian cabbie. He smiles modestly, cranks the stereo up to maximum and tugs the steering wheel round in a maniacal loop. Farewell Cerro Ancon, with your lofty, flower-filled, early-morning walks. Hello Albrook 'Marcos A. Gelabert' Airport – and the Darién jungle beyond.

Albrook Airport is another piece of Panama's US military history. A former American Air Force base, it was built in the early 1930s to defend the Panama Canal. After the Japanese attack on

Pearl Harbor, greater numbers of troops were deployed to Albrook because the Canal was perceived as being under threat, and in the mid-1960s a shopping mall, complete with fast-food outlets, was added for the US servicemen and their families to enjoy. Today, the shopping mall is one of Panama City's busiest because it has been claimed by around a hundred cut-price outlets, discount stores and thrift shops, and is a major hub for buses and fleets of taxis. The airport itself is unimpressive, however, with an airless, pocket-sized lounge that serves both arrivals and departures. A string of tiny plastic seats – designed for minimal comfort – ensures that nobody hangs around for a moment longer than they need to, and the single cafe serves some of the worst coffee found in Panama.

When I arrive, the airport is deserted apart from a family of Kuna women. Their traditional robes in vibrant red, yellow and blue with reverse-appliqué bodices, their gleaming gold nose rings and attractive beaded bracelets brighten my mood. The youngest flashes me a white-toothed smile, which turns the navy blue line daubed across her forehead into a zigzag crinkle. I return the smile and gaze across to the window. Outside, raindrops are bouncing off the airfield in an otherwise motionless semi light.

'Wild times ahead, Sarita!' Hernan Arauz greets me in the lounge. With his well-worn backpack, binoculars, khaki jungle hat, shorts and five-pocket vest, Hernan is Panama's own Crocodile Dundee – albeit a dark-haired, suave and intellectual version. Panama's most esteemed naturalist and wilderness guide, Hernan has agreed to accompany me to Punta Patiño, the 60,000-acre nature reserve that is the largest privately owned protected area in Central America. Part of Darién National Park's complex of preserved lands, it will provide us with an all-important launch point for exploring the Darién's jungled depths.

The remoteness of the Darién has been its salvation. Few places on Earth boast such impassable knots of jungle. War, too, can be good for conserving nature: the prowling guerrillas that wield AK47s have kept out people who might otherwise have entered the forest to destroy it. While forests in the world's tropical belt are disappearing at a rate of more than an acre per second, the Darién rainforest is amazingly well preserved. It contains a mighty portion of the country's 10,000 species of plant, including around 1,200 orchid species, 675 fern species and 1,500 species of tree. Around fifty species of flora and fauna that are rare or endangered elsewhere thrive here.

A UNESCO-listed World Heritage Site and Biosphere, the Darién National Park contains an incredible diversity of landscapes, from sandy beaches, rocky shores and mangroves along the coast to countless wetlands, rivers, creeks, palm forests and more than half a million hectares of rainforest. As well as being home to several semi-nomadic indigenous tribes, it contains around 170 species of mammal, more than a hundred reptile species, eighty amphibians and at least fifty freshwater fish. It is rated one of the world's top-ten birdwatching sites; more than 530 species of bird have been recorded here, many of them endemic. They include the endangered great green macaw and the vulnerable great curassow. And, of course, an important population of near-threatened harpy eagles.

It is a rare trick to make a discovery in this world, but the Darién offers that possibility. It is here, from a jutting peak of Punta Patiño, that Balboa first clapped eyes on the Pacific before walking knee-deep into the salty water and claiming possession of the world's largest ocean in the name of the Spanish sovereigns. It is here, too, that new, exciting species are still being chanced upon every year – some by accidental luck and others after decades of meticulous research. More than ten new species of amphibian have been found here since 2009, including a spiky-skinned, orange-legged rain frog, three poison dart frogs and three glass frogs. Such discoveries are remarkable in this notoriously hard-to-access region, where thousands of species of plant, bird, animal, fish, reptile, amphibian and insect live unrecorded.

The Darién is where I hope to fulfil my dream of spotting a harpy eagle, a species that is especially hard to find. Nests are rare and thinly spread, and the birds themselves scarcely seen. My late Welsh grandfather always said that I was born under a lucky star. Today, more than ever, I will him to be right. I need every smidgen of fortuity right now. A twist of fate. Serendipity, perhaps. As preposterous as my ambition may seem, I would be prepared to cross my fingers, rub a penny, walk under a rainbow, carry a rabbit's foot or kiss a frog under a red Chinese lantern in order to see a harpy in the wild. So it won't hurt to put my faith in the ancient concept of planetary alignment and astral good fortune.

Hernan and I carry our bags above our heads to shield ourselves from ricocheting bullets of rainfall, and dash across the dreary grey concrete concourse, fast, crouched and low. Our plane is a small, twin-engined propeller aircraft not much bigger than a motorcycle sidecar. We throw our bags into its rotund grey belly and climb in after them, pulling ourselves up, with difficulty, onto the slippery lip of the stairless doorway more than a metre above the runway. With a row of seats wedged backwards against the cockpit and another row facing them, the plane can accommodate ten people – at a push. My boots are resting on a bare floor strewn with a spaghetti of different-coloured bungees that are presumably there to secure cargo. I bat away the tangle of toggles, pull-strings, cables and wires that are dangling in my face from the low ceiling. The 'flight deck' resembles a lorry cab. Sweet wrappers and empty drink cartons form a layer in the foot well, while the dashboard looks like that of a Ford Transit with one or two navigational extras.

I opt to sit facing the windscreen in the direction of travel. Hernan squeezes himself into the seat across from me; he'll be flying backwards. Stuffing is spilling out of his seat cushion, and as he worms around to get comfy, the catch on his fraying seat belt repeatedly springs undone. Even at a standstill on the asphalt, the aircraft is being buffeted by strong winds and heavy rains. I fix my eyes on a green rubber toy gecko suctioned to the inside of the cockpit.

The two-man piloting team climbs aboard in full uniform complete with neatly manicured, airline-issue haircuts and matching flight bags, as if they are about to fly an executive jet, not a grubby jungle puddle-jumper. But as they remove their jackets, ties and cufflinks and start fiddling with the flight deck, their shirts begin to crumple with radials of sweat. Our take-off is noisy but unspectacular, the loud, monotone throb of the plane in the rain making my head pound within minutes. But things take a dramatic turn for the worse once we are engulfed by the darkness of thick, thick cloud.

'Hold on tight, Sarita,' Hernan warns, grim-faced. 'This is gonna be bumpy.'

I stare out of the scratched acrylic window at a burbling mass of anvil-topped cumulus clouds, unable to spot even the tiniest chink of blue. Unlike the light, swirling fluffiness of clouds on a clear day, these swollen demons are as dark as Lucifer. With what feels like evil malice, they propel our plane sideways and downwards in terrifying jolts and judders. We plummet, regain control. Wobble, freefall and steady. Nose-dive, level again. Soar, drop like a stone, realign. I am a travel writer with half a million kilometres and hundreds of flights under my belt, but I have never known turbulence like it. This isn't a coffee-spilling rattler of nerves and filler of barf bags. This is a pummelling of deeply uneasy proportions, heightened by near-black skies and relentless rains. Hernan wipes his moist brow dry with his sleeve as I bite down hard on my lip. The next storm-force gust will surely flip us upside down, I reason, or knock us into a tailspin. Don't be silly, I counter. Aircraft are engineered to meet the stress limits for both positive and negative load factors and can take a remarkable amount of punishment.

Boom! A particularly rough shove propels me up out of my seat and my head collides with some sliding cargo. The engine noise alters as the engine decelerates and then resumes speed. With hands tight on the controls, the pilot is physically wrestling with the aircraft as it bounces around at higher and lower altitudes. We fly into a more menacing expanse of soot-black cloud. Uneasiness makes me feel sick. I sense Hernan is feeling the same, although I daren't check. From the corner of my eye, I can see that the co-pilot is in a sweaty lather. I am silently fighting a chest-tightening fear.

The pilot wipes his face with a handkerchief before tapping his microphone and thumping a dial. Both have clearly ceased to work. The co-pilot looks desperate, clenching his teeth and pleading to God, before muttering something to the pilot about meteorological devils. The pilot responds, as if quoting a memorised extract from a flight manual. I move my head slowly in a nauseous state and pop in my iPod earphones as a distraction.

R. Kelly's 'I Believe I Can Fly' is an upcoming track, so I poke the skip button. Cabin bells ding randomly and sudden wallops send us reeling.

As I cling, white-knuckled, to my seat, my mind flits back to a survival course I attended before travelling in the Australian bush. One of the sessions focussed on the safety aspect of travel, and the tricky questions to ask before you board a small boat, plane or train. For a plane such as this one, I was advised to enquire after the single-engine climb gradient upon take-off. According to the tough-guy outdoorsy type running the course, any pilot to be relied upon would answer reassuringly with an exact figure, which would be computed using the weather, temperature, pressure, altitude and wind conditions ahead, together with the weight of fuel, passengers and bags. The computation should also allow for aircraft capability should one engine fail. In addition, I should ask how much flight time the pilot had had in a twin-engine aircraft. I can remember the instructor looking us all squarely in the eyes and declaring that he would never place his life in the hands of a pilot with less than 500 hours of flight experience in the exact same plane. He would rather walk away and look for another flight. Other 'nice-to-knows' included the pilot's proficiency – hours flown within the past six months – together with the aircraft's engine history, including recent repairs, past malfunctions, oil consumption, and vibration and temperature limits. Oh, and it is always good, he urged, to get the pilot's ID card thoroughly checked.

I have, of course, done none of this.

I turn my head to face forward and study our piloting team: their faces are etched with obvious concern. They have no working navigation tools, communication equipment or altimeter instruments at their disposal. They are, therefore, flying blind. Drenched in sweat, they are crossing themselves quietly and mumbling in soft prayer. Perhaps I should have queried the weather conditions and the state of the aircraft before I boarded with a storm ahead. Oh, to be so wise after the event. Another heavy blow knocks us sideways, causing an involuntary gasp from us all. Then I sense a lightbulb moment, as the co-pilot reaches hurriedly into his trouser pockets and pulls out a scrap of paper that has clearly been through a washing machine. He holds it up to the light, muslin-thin and almost broken along the folds. It has a sketch and some notes on it in faded blue ink. This, I learn, is the 'manual back-up', which will help them to land at Sambu while we wait out the thunderstorm. Sambu, not our intended destination, is a small jungle outpost with a teeny-weeny landing strip. We have flown off course, disorientated by the relentless drubbing, and the pilot is keen to refuel. I anxiously finger a string of worry beads clipped to my bag,

We skate across the treetops and fly round and round in a ceaseless hoop. We are lost. Hopelessly without direction. Low atop one of the most formidable stretches of jungle on Earth. I worry about the mountains soaring high towards the heavens in a sharp ridge. We must be near them now.

Through an eventual thinning in the cloud, the co-pilot gauges a rough idea of our location. I wonder how, because all I can see is a never-ending carpet of dark green jungle and the occasional serpent-shaped, ochre-coloured river. Using the tatty piece of notepaper, he guides the plane over mist-cloaked mountain peaks through rainy torrents. A tiny clearing appears below, no bigger than a cinnamon stick; it is now or never, he decides, pushing hard on a lever for extra thrust. It is a clumsy landing that sends the plane into a skid. We slide sideways across the greasy track into clumps of thick vegetation. With a crunch, we grind to a halt. It is spookily quiet.

I peer out of the window, cautiously: the rain has eased a little. Though claustrophobia has never troubled me before, I suddenly feel desperate to climb out of the aircraft. My feet need solid ground. The plane's wheels are wedged in thick mud, but its fuse-lage appears not to have sustained any obvious damage. Though dented, the wings are also wholly intact. Relief sweeps over me, then I spot Hernan's nose twitching. He is sniff-searching for the tang of leaking kerosene, concerned about the risk of fire. Pulling myself up out of my seat, I blindly push a path to the door and beat my palms against it. Jet fuel can easily combust, and I've no inten-tion of becoming a fireball. With a final full-body shunt the door swings open. The smell of hot, damp air and fresh earth is a delight.

Sambu doesn't have an airport, just a tin shed with a shuttered, counter-style window. Pulling on my waterproof poncho, I slip and slide along a gloopy track to the shelter of the shed, while the pilot twiddles with fuel nozzles and tries, unsuccessfully, to get a signal on his cell phone. There is nobody in the airport hut, although a tinny radio is doing its best to fill the emptiness with the rhythms of salsa music. I sit on one of a line of upturned oil drums that appear to double as an arrival/departure lounge and swipe away at the confetti of mosquitoes that descends on me.

After about an hour, a round-faced airport official appears from the storeroom, rubbing his eyes, his faced creased with sleep lines after a siesta spent curled in a hammock. I greet him in Spanish and outline our predicament. He appears completely unfazed by our story, nonchalantly striking a match on a kerosene can to light up a cigarette. When he does respond, I'm initially unsure what language he is speaking: Darién Spanish is not the easiest to interpret, especially by an untrained ear. We muddle through, however, like two aliens from contrasting galaxies meeting for the first time on an intergalactic jaunt. I apologise endlessly for cupping my ear and asking him to repeat: *¿Como?* On learning that I am in the Darién to see its wildlife, he points to a patch of bare, wet mud. At first glance, it is smooth and shiny with the reddish-brown tinge of clay-rich soil. Then I spot the paw prints: deeply embedded shapes, filled with rainwater, so perfectly formed that they are almost cartoon-like. Hernan joins me to study them, sizing them up against his own size-nine feet. They are more than half his size.

Jaguars are found across Central and South America, in rainforest and woodland, dry prairie, desert, marshy swamp areas and flooded grassland. They are notable, like tigers, for being felines that can swim, moving through the river-ridded Darién region as solitary, opportunistic, stalk-and-ambush predators. Due to the destruction of their natural habitat, many jaguar populations have become separated from one another and they cannot move about over large areas or mix with other jaguars. This makes them vulnerable. They sometimes attack livestock, so they are often hunted by farmers protecting their cattle and pigs. Jaguars feed on practically anything they can, from caiman and sloth to peccary, deer and armadillo, biting down hard with their exceptionally powerful jaws to pierce the brain of their prey.

The word 'jaguar' stems from the Native American word *yaguar*, meaning 'he who kills in one leap'. Like the harpy eagle, the jaguar is both a keystone species and apex predator. Keystone species play a crucial role in ecosystems: they are usually predators with large ranges whose disappearance would have a negative domino effect, making it more likely that other species could become extinct, or endangered. Apex predators rank at the top of the food chain – they are not preyed upon by any other animal than man – and this also makes them highly important to the world's ecological balance.

Most jaguars are golden in colour with leopard-like splodges, although jaguars are distinctive because they have a black spot inside each tawny rosette. They have no defined breeding season and mate at any time of year. Gestation lasts for around a hundred days and litters are typically of two to four cubs. Mothers continue to feed and protect their young until they are about a year old, with jaguars reaching sexual maturity at around two (female) and three (male) years. Then, these loners of the wild set about finding a mate, leaving deep scratch marks on trees to let other jaguars know they are around.

Hernan moves towards a nearby hardwood tree and reaches up, standing on tiptoe to trace the gouged-out gashes that run vertically down the trunk from well over two metres up. This magnificent beast has stood up on its hind legs to full height and dragged its claws down to the ground. 'A big male,' Hernan grins. 'These tracks are fresh, maybe a couple of hours old at the most, and it looks like he has visited this tree numerous times. He's a regular – and probably still around.'

The airport official tells us, in almost incomprehensible Spanish, that this jaguar moves through the forest like a ghostly shadow, leaving the remains of carcasses in the undergrowth by the hut. While the average size of a male jaguar's home range can be as much as 170 square kilometres, he says, this particular big cat – which he dubs the 'phantom of the forest' – has stayed close by. It is bold, moving around freely with considerable stealth. So far it has been seen twice: once lounging elegantly on a fallen tree and another time slowly prowling across the airstrip in bold daylight.

'The third largest cat on Earth behind the tiger and lion,' he declares, measuring wildly with plump, outstretched arms. He's right. Adult males can reach a length of more than two metres, and can weigh anything up to ninety kilos. 'It is the largest and most iconic cat in the Americas today, found in eighteen countries in Latin America, from Argentina to Mexico,' Hernan says proudly. 'But we wiped out more than 18,000 jaguars each year for their pelts in the 1960s and '70s, so the largest feline in the western hemisphere has pretty much been eradicated from forty per cent of its historical habitat. You are sharing this space, right now, with one of the lucky survivors.'

I tune myself into the noises around me in the hope of hearing a jaguar's telltale roar, guttural grunt or meow over the rat-a-tat-tat of a generator and whiny insect buzz. I can sense that he is near, watching us maybe. Bemused, understandably. Curious, certainly. Sizing us up, for sure. Jaguars don't have lions' and tigers' reputation of maneaters, and there are few authenticated reports of attacks on humans. There have been a handful of incidents in which jaguars have killed people in zoos, but that is down to stress, not hunger. The number of jaguars killed by humans in retaliatory spite for lost cattle certainly outweighs human deaths-by-jaguar several thousand-fold. This doesn't stop me from almost leaping out of my skin at the sound of advancing steps through the creeper-thick foliage behind me. However, it is not a jaguar, but a group of a dozen brown-skinned locals with rope-led horses, axes, machetes and long, thin, wooden spears.

The jungle drums beat quickly in the Darién. Though it took a couple of hours of walking to reach us, these men have arrived to lend a hand. After roping the plane and laying branches on the ground, they tighten a lasso around the waists of each horse and man, refusing all offers of help. Each man stands at barely five feet tall and weighs less than 130 pounds, but has a taut, sinuous and robust frame in miniature. Intuitively, without a formal count, the men lean back tug-of-war style to maximise around a ton or more of tension. Applying identical leverage – an underhand grip with the arms fully extended – they pull hard on the rope. By holding their arms and bodies rod straight but not stiff and rigid, they transfer the power of their legs to the rope. It keeps them locked at a standstill for several minutes and the physical effort is clearly immense, yet the Indians waste no effort in huffing, puffing or hollering. In simply organising themselves, as if by telepathy, each instinctively knows what is required of him. No competitive squabbling. No dissent. Just teamwork. After about twenty minutes of harnessing their collective manpower, they give a final mighty heave to increase the resistance to a tipping point and the plane is pulled free. A neigh from each of the equine 'anchormen' echoes our human cheers.

Under sullen skies, I gaze over towards the pilot. His shiny, black slip-on brogues and navy trousers are caked in mud. His sleek tresses are now kinking awkwardly in the heat. His partner's hair is similarly wayward, although he will have less laundry because he has pulled off his socks and shoes. To the pilot, I comment on how efficiently the native peoples have worked together. He tells me that, a few months earlier, a plane landed here and sank so deep that the mud had reached nearly halfway up, sealing the doors so the passengers could not exit. When the Indians arrived, walking for several hours to reach the plane, they had to force open the windows with rocks to get the people out. The plane wouldn't restart, so the six passengers waded through the hot, boggy marshland with all their luggage.

By the time they reached Sambu village, they had muck right up to their thighs. They had to stay until another flight arrived that could take them, but because it was Carnival season that took four whole days. When the plane eventually reached them, it was four hours later than promised, so the tourists knew they would miss their connecting flights home. Once they'd climbed aboard, the aircraft door refused to close properly, but by this time they were so determined to leave that they braved the suction. Worried that decompression could rip out seats, they bound themselves together and attached themselves to the seats using bungee cords, luggage straps and ties.

When it is our turn to leave, the flight is, thankfully, less eventful. The weather is light and bright and clear. We reach La Palma, the capital of Darién Province, in less than half an hour, time I spend replaying the moment in my mind when an aircraft was rescued using old-fashioned horsepower alone. Inwardly I am groaning at the prospect of a two-hour boat ride, despite the clearer skies. Punta Patiño, our base camp during our stay, sits on the southern shore of the Gulf of San Miguel, a twenty-five-kilometre boat ride from La Palma. This gritty dockside settlement, a hub for supplies, trade and transport, is located at the mouth of the mighty Tuira river, which rises in the fresh springs of the Serranía del Darién range and meanders for a hundred miles before emptying into the Pacific Ocean. I remark on how the weather can change in an instant. Hernan nods: 'You don't need a weatherman to know which way the wind blows.'

We wedge ourselves into the only available seat in a flatbed truck that is waiting at the airstrip, engine running. Brown cardboard boxes branded as rice steamers are piled up in the back. That there is sufficient demand in the jungle for such a bulk order strikes me as implausible.

The jeep crashes over rocky ruts along a heat-hazy road that leads to the dock. Our launch is waiting. Hernan reflects on our flight.

'It is getting worse – the turbulence,' he says. 'Scientists say it is linked to climate change. If that's true, then it's going to be a bumpy future.' He explains that research suggests increased carbon dioxide levels will speed up the jet stream, leading to skies that are up to forty per cent more turbulent by 2050. 'When I first started flying by plane each week, I would unsnap my seat buckle as soon as the ascent was over,' he adds. 'Now I keep it fastened throughout the flight.'

Jet streams, the fast, mile-wide winds that whistle round the planet at the same altitude as airliners, have certainly been shifting in recent years. Over Europe, this was blamed for the UK's washout summer of 2012 and a succession of cold, frozen springs. When I travel around the globe, I witness first-hand the shifts in seasons, which are shrinking in number and variety. Rainfall is more erratic. Winds more violent. And unusual weather, such as storms, drier spells and fluctuating temperatures, is more frequent. Corals across the entire region are being bleached by warming seas. Millions of people who depend on rivers fed by Andean glaciers face the possibility that their primary water source may vanish entirely within the next decade or so.

'Temperatures are climbing and sea levels are rising,' Hernan continues. 'The world will be a very different place for our children and grandchildren – unless we act fast.' Central and South America, for example, has woken up to the threat that climate change may wipe out coffee crops due to a rapid rise in the occurrence of plant diseases. At the rate at which temperatures are rising, it is also likely that the Andean glaciers will disappear entirely, impacting upon water supplies and hydropower generation.

Numerous unprecedented weather events in South and Central America in recent years have altered the perception of climate change. Intense rainfall in central Venezuela; devastating floods in the Argentine Pampas and Panamanian Highlands; severe hailstorms in Bolivia; elongated rainy seasons in Paraguay and Uruguay; the Amazon drought in Brazil, Peru and Colombia; a trend of extended dry seasons in southern Chile, south-west Argentina, southern Peru and western Central America. Now ordinary people feel the impact, which on a simple, human level is perplexing and freakish. Sixty Latin American coastal cities are highly vulnerable to rising sea levels.

Hernan and I are still collectively pondering the ways in which our own lives have altered due to the effects of global warming, when La Palma town comes into view. Rivulets of perspiration roll down my neck as I gaze up at the tumbledown single-storey, zinc-roofed houses clinging to a steep slope set behind a narrow walkway. Blue, pink, yellow and white: each house is colour-washed in a different hue to form a ramshackle rainbow. Shutters swing off hinges and the wooden door frames look like pulled pork. It seems as if the entire higgledy-piggledy row could tumble into the water in the next stiff coastal breeze.

In years to come, I will spend more time in the grotty B&Bs of La Palma. Today, however, we are just passing through this one-street waterfront town. An archaic piece of red tape requires that anyone travelling into the Darién fill in a form here – in triplicate. It serves as a 'check-in' with the police at La Palma and also registers you with the border guards. A fine idea, perhaps, but nobody has a pen that works. In the little wooden shed on the jetty, I am given the third degree. The police are paranoid about anyone who claims to want to see birds and wildlife. They think me deranged. It is at least thirty-seven degrees Celsius and my face is florid in the airless heat. So I look as if I am deranged. Eventually, a pen is summoned, so I sign the wad of papers before me and head to the launch.

Our boatman, a skinny Afro-Panamanian Dariénite, grabs our bags and slings them into the wooden craft, issuing us with an assortment of life jackets from which we each pick our best fit.

The sun is radiating strong, skin-searing beams, so I pull my cap down tight to screen my pale forehead. We chug out slowly from La Palma at a sedate rate of knots, with warm sea breezes in our hair. Our route will take us out along a large, mangrove-fronted river to the Pacific Ocean. We'll sail between some small islets, around a jungled spit and into the coastal Darién. Numerous seabirds circle the boat as we navigate the river, but have disappeared by the time we enter open, deeper seas.

Suddenly, in by far the most dramatic and fast-moving meteorological turnabout I have ever encountered, the calm, sun-sprinkled waters transform into death-defying waves. Hernan and I have barely exchanged a smiley thumbs-up when a roaring wind rips the tarpaulin roof off the boat in single swipe. Then, as if the power has been cut, the sky turns charcoal-grey. Giant black puff-balls bubble up from nowhere, and for a torturous three hours we are tossed helplessly around by a merciless storm that soaks us to the skin. Seawater swamps the deck, drowning our luggage and reddening our eyes with its painful sting. Our only option is to travel with them closed tight shut. Giant, rolling whitecaps crash against the boat and I fear we are about to capsize or be dashed into reefs by the swells. Cavernous sea tunnels up to three times the size of the boat rise on each side, so that we are entirely dwarfed by water.

Each time the boat bottoms out after cresting a large wave, the impact is excruciating, as if we are being smashed against concrete slabs. I double over at each body blow, forced into the brace position. My hands grip my bag to my body for fear it will pitchpole over the side. Like a floppy-limbed crash-test dummy, I'm flung from bow to stern, feeling as bruised as a boxer's punchbag. Pelting rains quicken. Thunder rocks the air. Shards of rose-hued lightning illuminate the sky. Lightning is dangerous: I know this because I interviewed an expert once for a magazine article. An abiding memory is that 24,000 people die of lightning strikes each year. That's more than a busload every day.

As conditions worsen, violent waves pound the boat with ever greater rage. A dislodged box piled high with corn, mango, pineapple and plantain is swept away by a giant curtain of water. It parts high above us like an angry theatrical drape, swishing from side to side in a terrifying torrent. I am too petrified to do anything other than stare ahead. A morbid notion pops into my head. It is extremely unlikely that anyone will know to look for my body, should I be washed out to sea. Only a few people know I am here. My friends, family and travel-writing colleagues know I am in Central America. Some, such as my little sister, could possibly pinpoint Panama at a push. But it will take weeks or months for them to realise that I haven't been in touch. I'll be food for the Pacific's bull sharks by then.

I anchor my feet against the seat and study the strain on our boatman's face. The sheer force of the waves is making control of the vessel an obvious struggle. In dark, heavy rainfall he leans into the wind. Panic rises in me as a massive wave overtakes the boat, filling it with water. It drowns out the engine with a choking splutter and I cry out for help. In the howling wind, my voice is thin and pitiful. We are in open seas some distance from the shore, so it is utterly futile. I am certain that it is just a matter of time before a wave knocks me overboard, and I shift my weight to the bottom of the boat to lower the centre of gravity.

After rollicking around at the storm's mercy for what seems like forever, the boatman manages to coax the engine back to life. Relieved, I exhale. It takes an eternity to inch our way blindly around the cape, but I am, at last, buoyed by the sight of land. Hernan is quiet and serious but calm. By the time we reach the sands of Playa Patiño, I am clinging to him under a scrap of plastic sheeting, willing the end to come. In an instant, the storm relents. Like that. Gone. Our boatman stops gunning the engine and we glide into shallow waters as mellowly as a pleasure boat. Hernan manages a weak smile, but my stomach is churning. With joints locked and spines stiff, we jump ship into the warm, knee-deep waters of the Gulf of San Miguel for the slow wade ashore.

Punta Patiño, a jutting spit high above the water, is Panama's largest private reserve, owned by ANCON, the environmental non-profit organisation, and run by its sister company, Ancon Expeditions. ANCON has spent almost two decades nurturing large swathes of the reserve to better preserve its red and black mangroves. A large tract of secondary jungle has been planted by an army of volunteers. Recent rains have added a hundred per cent humidity to the forest trails, so they are slippery, overgrown and as stifling as a Turkish hammam. I don't care. I almost press my lips to the ground.

Singing birds and monkey sightings soon help us forget our nautical nightmare as we trudge up the sloping trail to the Punta Patiño Lodge, our wringing wet clothes glued to heavy limbs. Feeble sunshine does its best to warm up moody skies in constant twilight. The lodge's tousled-haired cook greets us. While he is preparing a simple meal of grilled chicken with plantain and rice, Hernan and I each gulp at a bottle of sickly sweet fizzy pop. Never have warm E numbers tasted so sublime.

Together, we marvel at the view from the terrace, sighing with contentment. Across dark green treetops lies an arch-shaped bay edged by deserted sands. With our stomachs full, it is time to contemplate our options. Hernan dissuades me from a boring early night. Instead, we stomp down to the beach to explore pug-holed sands. Littered with springing, scuttling crabs and the rain-smudged prints of crab-eating raccoons, the beach is scattered with a zillion frothy swirls of sand that remind me of teeny-weeny cupcake toppings. Each tells us where a crab has burrowed: the pattern is made when the crab emerges from its hole to sift sand for the tasty detritus wedged between the grains. From a smooth, yellow boulder we gaze out to sea. Though the storm has long gone, the air is still bloated and heavy. Close to shore, a brown-grey crab-eating raccoon scours the sand holes. Its bushy, ring-patterned tail points skyward as it frantically shovels for crabs; near-black 'bandit mask' eye markings lend this guy the look of a stuffed plush toy. As the light fades, a torchlit path yields sightings of owls and night monkeys. An orchestra of cicadas, mosquitoes and tree frogs serenades the stars.

Back at the lodge in my cabana, I peel off damp clothes to wrap myself in towels and flop onto the bed, exhausted. It's been quite a day. It feels good to be alive, and I'm elated to be in the Darién, a fantasy fulfilled. But suddenly I feel a long way from home. Something spinning like a casino chip on a poker table interrupts my melancholy. It is the Sara Sotillo coin, freed from a pocket, moving across the floor at increasing speed until a final shudder sees it fall face down. I lean down and pluck up the lucky talisman, pressing it tightly into the flesh of my palm. 'Thank you,' I whisper. Today it has more than done its job.

* * *

The sound of heavy paws on the roof of my cabin wakes me in the morning. When I peer out to see what it is, I am greeted by a jaguarundi, one of Central and South America's oddest-looking felines. With its lustrous black coat and tapered, otter-like tail, it has the strange, overstretched slender frame and small, squashed head that marks this species out from other big cats. It twitches its short, rounded ears at me and examines me closely with its close-set amber eyes, sniffing the air. Then, with the precise pacing gait of a domestic cat, it leaps down from the rooftop and disappears silently into the surrounding forest.

I wrap my hiking boots in a waterproof bag, seal it, then dig out my rubber wellies for the varied terrain that lies ahead. Punta Patiño contains a mix of habitats including mangroves, sandy beaches and marshlands that attract nesting pelicans and seabirds. It protects dozens of threatened species of flora and fauna, such as crocodiles, deer, green iguanas and harpy eagles. I stuff a scope, sunscreen, pen and notebook into a small day pack and grab a couple of bottles of water. When I gather up last night's clothes, discarded in a heap on the floor, I am punished for my slackness. They are teeming with small black ants. After a cold rainwater shower and a stroll around the gardens, I meet Hernan on the veranda and breathe in the mesmerising view. Unlike yesterday, it is clear, bright and free of cloud. Cobalt-blue waves lap serenely, languid with no sign of fury.

I quiz Hernan on the history of the Punta Patiño Lodge and learn that it was once a lumber plantation. Today, its kitchen, restaurant and terrace enjoy jaw-dropping views across the gulf, where timber mills once stood. Ten simple, wooden cabins have hammock-slung verandas and mosquito-netted bunks, with private bathrooms that use recycled water. We gather round a map, and Hernan points to where we walked last night: the reserve's Ramsar-listed Wetland of International Importance – 13,805 resplendent, frog-filled hectares in the fertile marshes of the Pacific watershed.

The larger Darién region encompasses more than 8,000 square kilometres of protected area, including Punta Patiño nature reserve on the Pacific coast and the 575,000-hectare Darién National Park, which stretches across almost the entire Colombian border. The gardens of the Punta Patiño alone contain some sixty-eight species of bird, four of which are endangered and five under threat. In among the forests, mangroves and waterways it is possible to spot tanagers, common black hawks, brown pelicans, frigatebirds, terns, American oystercatchers, Amazon kingfishers, blue herons and spotted sandpipers. Humpback and pilot whales can be spotted from the lodge's treetop terrace, and caimans lurk in the swampier mangrove forests nearby. Other reptiles include iguanas and crocodiles, while fifteen species of mammal include twelve threatened with extinction. Pumas and jaguars prowl in neck-high grasses that are home to snakes, monkeys and ocelots, and shy gray foxes lurk among the trees.

Our spirits are high as we feast on a plate of sweet juicy mango, papaya and pineapple.

'It's gonna be great today, Sarita,' Hernan promises, draining the last from a cup of coffee. 'Bring your scope, we'll see some amazing stuff. Who knows, we may even spot a harpy eagle. I'm gonna try my best for you.' I know we will need good fortune to steal a glimpse of one, and Hernan has instructed me to search the upper canopy continually to be in with a chance. But he assures me that we will see crimson-crested woodpeckers, with their blood-red punk Mohican hair, Gothic-looking black-chested jays, whose sooty heads are daubed with flashes of blue, and lots of scaly-breasted hummingbirds – almost impossible to spot in their green-grey camouflage until they break cover at speed for a sugar fix. It'll be a tough day's hike with the ground so wet, he warns. But once I learn that I'm staying in the same cabana that Sean Connery once occupied – the former James Bond star has been a supporter of attempts to excavate the site of the failed Scottish Darién scheme – I feel inspired to tackle the jungle with true 007-style grit.

Hernan is true to his word. Our day is mind-blowing. A large tract of virgin forest that remains largely undisturbed by humans is riddled with vast termite mounds and thick with towering ferns, oversized palms and beer-belly trees. In the morning alone, we are rewarded handsomely for delving into these untroubled reaches. First, we spot a three-toed sloth, descending a tree on its weekly toilet break, dangling in an ungainly manner on a thickly leafed branch before plopping noisily towards the ground. Even as one of the most prevalent tree-dwelling mammals in Central and South America's rainforests, sloths are difficult to spot. The three-toed variety spends all its time high in the tree canopy, feeding on the juiciest foliage and, basically, just hanging around. Moving very slowly, almost noiselessly, blending into the crowns of the rainforest trees, it is a constant in the rhythm of the rainforest, existing with just the right amount of light, warmth and moisture to munch away in a territory of just a few hundred metres. Long, sturdy claws help it to hang or sit nestled among the branches, looking to the untrained eye like a clump of decomposing leaves or a shaggy, moss-covered bough.

The pooping habits of the three-toed sloth are one of the great curiosities of the jungle. Its once-a-week toilet break is the only interruption in an eat-sleep-eat routine, and involves an arduous – and dangerous – slog down from the leafy heights. Sloths are vulnerable on the ground, exposed and easy prey. More than half of all recorded sloth deaths are caused by attacks at ground level, so a simple crap can cost a sloth its life. It also expends around ten per cent of its daily calorie intake on the climb up and down the tree. The two-toed sloth, incidentally, prefers a 'bombs-away' style of defecation, lobbing its poo to the forest floor willy-nilly from the treetop spot in which it chews, sleeps and eats. Two-toed sloths are less fussy eaters and will forage a wider area, so they may be less concerned about alerting predators to their ever-changing locale. One thing is for sure: when the faeces hits the ground, everybody knows about it. The poo of a sloth – unlike the odourless creature itself – smells really bad.

Hernan explains that, despite obvious similarities, two- and three-toed sloths are in fact very distant relatives, separated by forty million years of evolution – almost as long as dogs and bears have been different species. Of course, animals all over the world, including humans, are continually adapting to their environments: the fish-shaped mudskippers that spend most of their time out of water; the Dumbo octopus, whose flappy ears allow it to feed while floating along the bottom of the ocean; the vulturine fish eagle, an African cousin of the golden eagle and goshawk, which has turned vegetarian and now rips the life out of palm oil trees. Strange that evolution could alter potentially lethal toilet-break behaviours.

'Some scientists say that the three-toed sloth leaves a trail of faecal deposits to fertilise the trees it needs for nourishment,' Hernan theorises. 'Others think it has something to do with a symbiotic arrangement with a moth that lays its eggs in the dung. But I reckon it's sloths' way of letting sloths of the opposite sex know where to find them. Nature calls, so leave the poop there as an invitation to a night of passion. It's kind of romantic, eh, Sarita?'

We giggle, childishly, and I joke that I'll give it a try next time I'm in London and need a date. We paddle across a shallow stream, which Hernan tells me gets swollen in the rainy season. On an earlier trip he saw a sloth swimming by, moving through the water with ease. Sloths are surprisingly capable swimmers, taking to the water when the forest canopy is flooded or interrupted by a river or lake. Their oversized stomachs and relatively light body weight helps keep them buoyant. We spot a four-foot caiman the colour of centuries-old tree bark yawning on a mudflat and a cute-faced red-tailed squirrel spiralling around the upper section of a leafy trunk. Despite the restricted view offered by the dark, thick forest, we see too many birds to take in with a single pair of eyes. In a couple of hours, Hernan — unobtrusive and armed with a retractable laser pointer — helps me to pick out more than thirty species. A collection of inquisitive trogons in a rainbow of brilliant hues follows me Pied-Piper style using a mix of hops and flaps as I meander along trails of vivid crimson, pink and yellow blooms.

Surprising a little group of coatis by the river, we hide among the ferns and watch the omnivorous, ginger-coated members of the raccoon family nibbling on shoots and leaves with their sausage-shaped snouts. We limbo under giant spider webs that glisten gold in the sunshine, and follow the rough trail that leads through old-growth forest to reach a mammoth cuipo tree. Instantly recognisable by the rings that mark the reddish-grey bark near its crown, which sprouts at the top of a trunk that can reach sixty metres high, the cuipo is an endangered species in the tropical rainforests of Central and South America.

'These plants shouldn't be in bloom yet, it's too early,' Hernan says, shaking his head at the bright red-and-orange blossoms that would usually mark the start of the rainy season. In recent years, unpredictable seasonal weather has made the wettest months wetter and the drier months more prone to heavy rainfall. Nature is confused by the changing climate. Hernan teaches me how to harvest water from the tree by cutting a piece of the root, cleaning the bark off one end and tipping it into my mouth. Its thick stem, which bulges at the base, is superbly adapted to store and conserve water. Used as an emergency source of drinking water by tribal people journeying the jungle, it tastes starchy and earthy, like the water from a pan of boiled potatoes.

An adventurous 'Indiana Jones' afternoon is curtailed all too soon when we spot the sunset. We've cut our way through dense forest, climbed rocky slopes, catnapped in a hammock and bathed in shallow rivers after high-humidity, strenuous hikes. The isolation of this place from the outside world is utterly invigorating, as are its ever-present dangers. I feel vital and alert thanks to the scorpions lurking in rotten trees, flame-coloured coral snakes hiding in the bushes and orb-weaver spider webs that I almost walk into face first.

'The Darién is Panama's foremost theatre of life,' Hernan enthuses, as he tiptoes towards an ant swarm. With a machete the size of a gatepost by his side and a pistol packed on his hip, he is primed like a ninja warrior, with ears trained on the faintest sound. I'm thoroughly enjoying being with such a top-notch guide. He isn't just a fountain of knowledge, he is also excellent company: bright, witty, erudite and strong. The son of the late anthropologist Dr Reina Torres de Arauz and the explorer Amado Arauz, Hernan is a veteran of numerous trans-Darién expeditions, including the first one transmitted over the Internet, he has an innate affinity with the jungle that few possess. Most travellers, like me, struggle to get a true sense of their orientation in the Darién, due to the jumbling effect of the intensely dense forests. The sheer effort involved in moving half a mile can also cause even the most cavalier of travellers to feel out of their comfort zone. Initially, I wonder if I'll ever shed my clumsy awkwardness and find my jungle legs.

In the many days that follow, we fall into a gentle rhythm, rising early before the full weight of the humidity can be felt. We eat breakfast overlooking the mist-draped Gulf of San Miguel, setting off on each expedition once the sun's orange globe has begun to erase the swirls of cloud. We delve into the Sendero Piedra de Candela (Flintstone Trail), so named because of the sparks created when a machete strikes the reddish quartz of the boulders. In intense heat, we weave through tropical dry forest along a gentle two-hour loop, snaking through bird-filled secondary-growth coastal forest gloriously alive with hawks, jays, woodpeckers, toucans, hummingbirds and tanagers. We also take a boat out to an expanse of darker primary forest that is altogether more foreboding, slicing through fallen tree trunks, gushing streams and chest-high grasses.

Cutting a trail is laborious and physically exhausting, so I am pleased that the vigorous training regime I put myself through to boost my strength and stamina before the trip is paying off. But it isn't all about being in shape. Surviving the jungle requires good mental health, too. I know I need to hold my nerve and have the guts, self-assurance and determination to face tough challenges. It is important to me that I can hold my own, whether I'm carrying a backpack across muddy terrain in terrible weather or dealing with bugs and dangers in the jungle, where the biggest threats are often the tiniest and hardest to see. With Hernan's help, I soon learn to avoid the leaves that cause oozing infections and recognise the sharp, thorny branches that can almost sever a limb. With assistance, I can start a fire, or certainly keep one going. I have also become pretty good at chopping wood. Fishing with a spear is trickier than it looks, but I've scored some decent successes. I still struggle to hear and see what Hernan does, as early as he does. I resolve to be less dreamy and more tuned in.

Around us, the warning cries of birds and small mammals alert Hernan to the presence of a predator close by. He spots new puma tracks and piles of fresh puma scat, and I jump nervously at every snapping twig. The puma is a slender, agile cat with powerful forequarters, neck and jaws that serve to grasp and hold large prey. An obligate carnivore, it is capable of sprinting, but hunts more commonly as an ambush predator, stalking through brush and trees before leaping powerfully onto the back of its prey and delivering a suffocating neck bite. Pumas weighing up to seventy kilos roam close to the Punta Patiño Lodge. The one that is stalking us, swapping between being in front of us then taking a spot behind, is probably around the same size.

Suddenly, Hernan raises his hand, silently grinding to a halt. A pile of puma droppings lies at his feet. They are fresh – alarmingly so – and full of grey bristles that indicate a large peccary kill. Hernan scrutinises the neck-high grass that surrounds us, his ears pricked and eyes narrowed. I hold my breath. A puma is more likely than a jaguar to attack a human. Goosebumps prickle my skin, but I hold my nerve. As we hike deeper into the leafy depths, I feel small, vulnerable and rather low down the food chain. Hernan quickens his pace, senses heightened. He waves his machete around, Sinbad-style. 'I'll make a shish kebab out of him if he pounces on you, don't worry.' He laughs. For comfort, I slip my knife from my belt and rest it in my palm. We march on for several hours, a silent shadow ever present.

One day, we trek the five-hour trail that takes us to the small Afro-Colonial town of Punta Alegre (Happy Point) – a gloomy outpost, despite its sunny name. It was founded by the descendants of slaves brought to Panama from Jamaica, Trinidad, Barbados, Martinique and Guadeloupe to help dig the Panama Canal. Cheerily painted wooden boats tethered along the shoreline are bright and welcoming, in sharp contrast to the scowls of practically everyone we pass. This surprises me, because scientific studies have proven that living close to trees or in forests brings most people happiness. Trees filter air pollution, bestow beneficial psychological effects and help people live longer, healthier lives. Although the full magnitude of tree benevolence isn't properly understood, one famous US study in the 1970s surveyed patients following gall-bladder operations and found that those whose hospital rooms had a view of trees recovered more quickly than those looking out at another building. So, where's the anger and hostility in Punta Alegre coming from, I wonder? I hear the tooth-on-edge screech of a chainsaw and all becomes clear.

Recognised globally as an important centre of endemism, the Darién is highly valued for its biological diversity. But it is under threat. Since the Pan-American Highway was extended in 1988 from Panama City to Yaviza – the wild-west style town in Darién Province where the 48,000-kilometre road stretching from Alaska to Argentina tails off to a slither of crumbling asphalt – the population of eastern Panama has doubled. Every acre of forest is being eyed up as potential pasture by a rapidly expanding farming sector that has already left some horrifying scars. Fifty years ago, seventy per cent of the Panamanian landscape was covered by forest. Today, it is just over forty per cent. So far, the deforestation has eaten about eighty miles into the outer wooded swathes of the Darién, and although largely confined to the north of the region, the damage is savage.

The farmers, sombrero-clad migrants and cattle ropers from the central provinces of Los Santos and Herrera, have torn down large chunks of the forest. They hail from the strongholds of Spanish settlement in the folkloric heartlands of Panama, where farming has been the lifeblood for well over 500 years. When these windswept grassland savannas became sought by luxury condo developers and golf-course architects, affordable land became rare. Farmers protested. Families struggled. Communities became poor and fractured. Unrest unsettled Panamanians countrywide, because farmers, as the custodians of Panama's breadbasket, have an almost heroic place in national culture. In a bid to appease the firebrand farmers, the government offered them a deal. If they were willing to leave Los Santos and Herrera to try their luck at farming in Darién Province, each would be sold a piece of land for less than the price of a cup of coffee. The farmers had no choice. To stubbornly refuse would result in their families starving. So they snapped up the offer with a mix of recklessness and reluctance, and set about working the land.

Moving lock, stock and barrel into unfamiliar terrain on the ragged edges of the Darién's dark tangle of forest proved too much for some. Those that stayed spent months slashing down virgin jungle, selling the trees for lumber and setting fire to anything left. Where ancient trees once stood, flat, rootless, barren soil remained, causing one Panamanian newscaster to liken the Santenos and Herreranos to *hormiga arriera*, or leafcutter ants, which can destroy entire trees with powerful, razor-sharp jaws that vibrate a thousand times a second.

The tale would be nowhere near as harrowing if the farmers' agricultural endeavours had thrived. But they did not. Removing the root structures that once held the soils in place led to the rich layer of decaying, nutrient-laden vegetation being swept away in the first heavy rains. Once a crop had failed, the farmers abandoned the impotent land, moving their families and livestock a few miles away to clear-cut more jungle and try all over again.

Isolation, certainly, has spawned a deep suspicion of strangers in Punta Alegre, where the tempo of life is measured in minuscule degrees. However, the children of the town feel no such reserve: they grab our hands excitedly to lead us across the rubble-strewn sands to a giant wormhole. They have been watching it for hours, patiently waiting for an appearance. They have even organised a rota to cover lunchtime in case a head pops out.

We pick up the trail from the side of the beach under glowering skies, and are back under the tree canopy by the time the downpour starts. It turns the air to warm steam as we climb over moss-clad tree trunks, marvelling at lunar-like termite mounds patterned by anteater claws. With ears perked and eyes squinted, Hernan seeks out the soaring silhouettes and graceful glides of every avian form. He is uncannily perceptive, pointing out birds that haven't even registered on my radar: a skill honed by years of parsing birds from impenetrable foliage. 'Quick! Wow, listen. Listen.' Hernan hisses in rapture as the maniacal call of a snake hawk resonates in the trees above. 'He's been in the Darién too long,' he jokes, twirling a finger close to his head to indicate the bird's madness.

With his gentle voice rich in sentiment, Hernan tells me more about the role his parents played in Latin American ecology. His mother lobbied to secure the place of the Darién National Park on the UNESCO list of World Heritage Sites. She also founded seven of Panama's museums and wrote many of the articles in Panama's constitution. Panama's National Academy of History declared her the most prominent woman of the twentieth century: a fine intellectual and a formidable protector of the nation's cultural heritage.

His father, now a retired academic, led many expeditions into and across the Darién when he was younger. Amado and Reina Arauz were part of the crew that achieved the first vehicular crossing of the Darién Gap – the hundred-kilometre break in the Pan-American Highway – during the dry season of 1960 in two custom-equipped Land Rovers. Negotiating unmapped rainforest using rough, machete-cut trails through steep hills and over 180 rivers and streams – many of them without bridges – took four months and twenty days. They set the precedent for other explorers to venture into the Darién, including John Blashford-Snell, who led the British Trans-Americas Expedition along the Pan-American Highway in two Range Rovers between 1971 and 1972. In 1973 the Briton Ian Hibell became the first cyclist to cross the Darién Gap, followed by Robert L. Webb, who made the journey by motorcycle in 1975.

Hernan has clearly inherited his parents' adventurous streak, as well as their fascination with Panama's storied jungles. When he reached his thirties he swapped a successful diplomatic career to work as a naturalist guide, following in his father's footsteps. As a young father himself, Hernan introduced his daughter, Luisa, to her first bird – a yellow-backed oriole – when she was three years old. By her tenth birthday she had visited most of Panama's protected areas. She is also lucky enough to have seen a harpy eagle at Punta Patiño.

On an overgrown section of the trail, we round a blind bend and hear the sound of tusks gnashing. Hernan's eyes widen in alarm at the sight of a large herd of white-lipped peccaries. The ugly dark grey hogs are among the most dangerous found in Neotropical rainforests; they easily feel threatened and will protect their herd with a fiercely violent charge. With fat heads and long snouts, they have coarse, bristly hair and rough manes that run from head to rear, where the gland that gives them their unique scent is located. By rubbing these glands against tree stumps or rocks, peccaries make sure that everything within smelling distance knows where they are. The musk odour is particularly pungent when they're riled – you'll smell an angry peccary before you see it. Solitary peccaries are rare, posing little threat to humans. But an entire group is speedy, aggressive and agile. Initially they seem unaware of our presence. Then they stop dead in their tracks, cracking their teeth furiously. They've got wind of us. Standing three abreast across the trail, the peccaries are clearly agitated, turning to face us head-on. In a highly charged stand-off, they square up with chests puffed out, snorting loudly. Fearless.

For around thirty years or more, stories have been shared throughout the Darién about a 400-strong pack of white-lipped peccaries that terrorised the forest, becoming almost as feared as those other dangerous roamers – the left-wing guerrillas from Colombian rebel group FARC (Fuerzas Armadas Revolucionarias de Colombia). Hunters would tell of gnawed rubber boots after climbing trees to escape the menacing charge of the herd. According to one story, a hunter and a jaguar shared the same log for hours as they waited for the herd and its asphyxiating musky smell to pass by. Hernan motions me to drop down into a crouch. We silently retreat, leaving the trail unobstructed. The air is thick with pheromones as the dozen-strong herd moves through, snarling, grunting and gnashing at us loudly as it passes.

Back at the lodge that night, after a moonlight-bathed dinner of grilled sea bass, we sharpen our machetes and strap on headlamps. Everywhere is vibrating with a buzz of nocturnal activity as we embark on a dimly lit march through swampy forests. While we jump across a string of stepping stones, our flashlight beams pick out the eyes of several crocodiles glowing in the dark. We are in deep marshland and I breathe easier once we make it safely to the other side. As we stroll back along the sands, we spot the unmistakable silhouette of a big cat crouching by the shore. We move closer and see that it is a jaguar eating a large crab or turtle. It turns momentarily, flashing its orange eyes in the dark to acknowledge our presence before continuing to feed on its kill. An hour later, as I climb into my bunk to write my journal, my heart is still pounding with excitement. I fall asleep with visions of the eye-shine of wild beasts in the night.

The next day's dawn start enables us to hit the right tide on the Mogue river in a motorised dugout canoe. Our plan is to visit a harpy nesting site, and we've both woken up excited at the prospect. While we're drinking a mug of strong coffee and getting ready to leave, a message reaches us – the trip is off. The nest has been destroyed by trophy hunters and the birds have not been seen for more than twenty-four hours. As he relays the news to me, Hernan's face is almost ashen. My deep disappointment is palpable. I feel sickened to the stomach.

'What happened?' I ask, gently.

'Nobody is certain,' Hernan says. 'But the nest was found totally smashed up this morning, and the eagles have disappeared.

They may just be someplace else, of course. But trophy hunters were seen in the area yesterday, so it doesn't look good.'

Despite the news, we set off, keen to see the site for ourselves. We load up the boat with everything we need for a few days downriver. A large medical pack is balanced on top of a tray of fresh mangos, the fat amber globes shining invitingly in the sunshine, twice the size of any I have seen. Next to them is a gun, a shovel, two pairs of wellington boots and a part-filled sack of rice that is already splattered with bird poop. Within minutes of our departure, we spot a flock of blue-gray tanagers, no less beautiful in their delicate, pale silver-blue plumage for being two-a-penny in humid lowlands. On a hot, sticky, gloomy day there are few things more uplifting that the sight of a pair, or small group, of these pretty little birds: to watch them foraging for arthropods together is like watching the sky dance. Equally abundant in the canopy along forest borders are yellow-rumped caciques, highly social black birds with bright splashes of yellow on their wings and rumps – as if they have fallen into a yellow pot of paint.

After an hour or so, our boat drops us at a muddy riverbank and we both scramble up, pulling ourselves upright on some rope-thick trailing vines. As we push through thick tree cover to where the nest site had been, my fingers are crossed tight. Hernan leads the way, eyes and ears peeled, and I am hoping, really hoping, that the nest is there, that someone has made an honest mistake. The filtered tropical light of the forest canopy all but hides the top of a towering 200-foot tree where the harpy nest was seen. We crick our necks but cannot see it, so trudge on further, pushing our way through a mass of tightly bound leaves. Hernan's machete is hacking at fallen branches; we both have faces turned to the sky. When we stumble upon scattered debris our hearts sink into our jungle boots. Twigs, branches, fragment of bones, tufts of fur and scraps of skin across the forest floor tell us all we need to know. The nest is no more.

I wander aimlessly around the tree, achieving little. Hernan picks among the rubble and plucks out a grey harpy feather. I tuck it into my pocket.

'The harpies may have eluded us today, but the Darién has more to offer,' Hernan encourages me. 'Let's see what Mogue brings.'

Back in the boat, away from the oppressive heat of the jungle interior, we are fanned by a gentle breeze as we continue our steady voyage through the wilds, inching our way past riverside anteater and tapir trails riddled with swarms of Aztec and leafcutter ants. Our motorised dugout canoe, carved from a single tree trunk, emits a low hum as it cuts through the weed-tangled waters like a sleek torpedo. We duck under trailing boughs dotted with roseate spoonbills the colour of Zinfandel wine. An osprey demonstrates its fishing supremacy, plunging feet first into the river to pluck out its prey before emerging in graceful triumph. As we glide past a giant spider sitting in a web the size of an armchair, a trio of white-faced capuchins shakes the treetops above our heads to the persistent squawk of a flock of noisy macaws. It is a voyage straight out of an extraordinary adventure novel. This feral stretch of eastern Panama contains some avian species not seen easily elsewhere in the Darién, such as the golden-headed quetzal, with its bright red underbelly, jade wings and fetching gilded skullcap. It is also the harpy eagle's realm.

As we near the mouth of the river, where the strong current creates a whirlpool effect, we see that a small dog is trapped in the corkscrew waters, his paddle growing weaker with each spinning spiral. A profusion of sharks feeds around these fertile, sediment-rich waters – especially when the currents have gathered power after heavy rains – and Hernan instructs the boatman to venture into the tumultuous swirl, leaning out over the side to reach the drowning dog. 'Hold on buddy,' he calls to the mutt, whose head is now barely above water. In a single tug, he frees the dog and plops it like a slimy newborn calf into the centre of the boat. It sits shivering in shock, scrawny and frightened, with skin stretched taut over a bony frame. It is clearly dazed by its miraculous rescue: it could have been days, or weeks, until another vessel passed that spot. Big, expressive eyes give thanks to Hernan as the lucky canine moves, gingerly, to lie on his feet. Its tail is wagging – and little wonder.

We follow the curvaceous line of the river, which is framed by a tight binding of creepers and palms. Our moods mellow and relaxed, we marvel at large flocks of ibis and wave to Emberá tribesmen spear-fishing in the murky shallows. On the river's broader stretches, our driver sweeps the boat from side to side so that we can capture wider views on camera. I click away at a panorama of extraordinary beauty, not daring to trust recollection alone but willing myself never to forget.

The Emberá people are one of three indigenous groups, alongside the Kuna and the Wounaan, living in the Darién region. They migrated from settlements along the tributaries of the Amazon to Colombia's Chocó region in the sixteenth century, traversing into Panama's Darién forests to escape the Spanish conquistadors. As is the case with many indigenous peoples that have no written language, the history of the pre-Colombian Emberá remains ambiguous. Hunter-gatherers and fishermen, their constant movement and wide dispersion of their communities throughout the most remote parts of the rainforest made accurate anthropological studies near-impossible until recent years – Hernan's mother was awarded her PhD for research into Emberá women. Semi-nomadic, they moved through the Darién's impenetrable mass, erecting small riverside settlements and hunting monkeys, peccaries and wild boar with blowpipes, poison darts and long, sharp spears.

The extension of the Pan-American Highway, carved out of the jungle in 1979, has had a significant impact on Emberá history. While the road offered communities access to the modern world, it ended their reliance on hunting and gathering. Drug trafficking and guerrilla activity caused large numbers of Emberá to migrate away from the Colombia border region to safer land on the Panama City side of the Darién. The nation's other major cut-through, the Panama Canal, displaced as many as 50,000 indigenous peoples, many of them Emberá. In recent years, the number of Emberá in the Darién has dwindled to around 31,000 from ten times that figure in the pre-Hispanic era. Their numbers are hard to pinpoint with accuracy, despite census attempts, because the effects of deforestation are pushing them deeper into the wilderness.

In order for the Emberá to have greater clout in national politics, they joined forces with the Wounaan people, who also originate from Colombia's Chocó region, to create the Comarca Emberá-Wounaan, a semi-autonomous indigenous region, in 1983. The government recognised them politically, and this brought about structural change in each indigenous community, with decision-making committees replacing single chiefs. In 1998, the smaller Wounaan population separated from its Emberá neighbours as an independent entity.

Despite the conquistadors' efforts to influence the Emberá's religious beliefs, traditional dress, medicine, dance, music and spiritual celebrations, the Darién communities have retained a strong grip on their culture. They practise a kind of hybrid religion, mixing what they have selected and rejected from the Church with non-Christian celebrations and customs. It is not uncommon to see Emberá children wearing silver crucifixes round their berry-brown necks as they traipse through the jungle to a pagan ritual.

After snaking along the inky-green river for about an hour we arrive at Mogue, a mud-and-thatch community of around sixty Emberá families. Tucked behind the twisted spires of a black mangrove forest, the settlement sits within scenery of near-magical beauty that its seclusion serves to heighten. Along this slender slip of jungle-trimmed river, the Emberá have, to a large extent, managed to resist the bait of modern civilisation. Despite being pushed further and further north during the past quarter century, and having been gifted a temperamental satellite phone by government officials, the community is granted almost total isolation by the remote headwaters of the Darién. Visitors are welcome by appointment, but otherwise asked to keep their distance. Not that people pass by here often. Access along the muddy riverside trail is restricted by the ebb and flow of the tide. Boats that get this wrong can be marooned on mudflats for several hours – although this is no real hardship when there are herons, kingfishers, ibis, caiman and numerous species of snake to watch in the mangroves.

On a sloping, grassy clearing surrounded by thick, spouting jungle, about thirty bare-footed, bare-chested girls and women are waiting to greet us. Many are holding infants and young children daubed with markings of a purple-black pigment derived from crushed jagua fruit. The women guide us to a communal meeting place at the centre of the clearing, set high up on a bamboo platform and accessed via a tall wooden ladder. With no two rungs sharing the same depth or shape, scaling the ladder requires a high degree of brow-furrowing focus – although I later watch an old guy easily twice my age ascending with ease, despite having a large, hairy hog strapped across his shoulders. At the top, I look out over the simple huts scattered around. Though smaller than your average residential garage, each is home to an extended family group spanning two or three generations – being clustered together in this way shares chores, enriches kinship, and ensures the safety and protection of the family. In the hottest months, most family groups operate a shift system at bedtime so that each person gets some space and sleep. Mogue's youngest resident is a newborn girl, who arrived yesterday; its oldest a withered elder who thinks he may be eighty-eight.

With straight black hair, big brown eyes and wide smiles, the Emberá have kind, open faces that draw me in. The Spanish-speaking regional chief (cacique), a smooth-skinned, softly spoken guy in his mid-thirties, explains that they are a deeply spiritual people who embrace an ancient mythology as well as Christianity. This community is strong and healthy, he says, thanks to the traditional medicine practised jointly by a spiritual man and a herbalist, using plants, roots, nuts, berries, bark and sap from the surrounding forest. They use conventional medicine, too: a visiting auxiliary from La Palma medical centre visits monthly and offers a paramedic service for emergencies.

For special celebrations, such as our arrival at the village, the Emberá women wear skirts fashioned from lengths of brightly patterned fabric wrapped around their waists. Decorative beads adorn their necks, while faces and arms are inked with juice markings in geometric designs. Men wear loincloths, while children rarely wear clothing at all until they are two years old. Babies are often covered head-to-toe in the jagua stain from birth to keep evil spirits at bay. I watch the women craft intricate beaded necklaces and try my hand at making a basket out of tightly woven palms. The men have become adept at carving wood or tagua (ivory nut) using customised screwdrivers and filed-down penknives.

I accept the offer of a walk round the village's botanical trail to learn about the Emberá's plant-based medicine – not realising that for an elderly Emberá a stroll is a lung-busting three-hour hike. I struggle to keep pace with my nimble-limbed guide as he skips along the forest's needle-thin paths. Reaching into a knotty braid of vegetation, he plucks out a handful of bark strips and a thin, black, stringy root, and motions for me to smell and taste. He explains that the almond-tasting bark soothes aches and fevers, while the rootball, with its strong, clove-like aroma, is used as a numbing agent for native dentistry. The plant, *Clavo huasca*, also doubles as a powerful aphrodisiac and treatment for male impotence. When the root is boiled in a particular way it is known in Spanish as *rompe calzon*, which, roughly translated, means 'bust your britches'.

Medicine men have supernatural powers from birth, according to Emberá beliefs, with the innate ability to communicate with the spirits in the matter of health, illness and cure. They use medicine sticks crafted from dark hardwood, which develop a sheen from generations of handling. Different sticks are used for different maladies, depending on the guidance of the spirits. Everybody's life is controlled by an animal spirit, which lives on their back from birth. As they grow older and attain more wisdom, the spirit moves up to the top of their head – hence why elders are the most respected members of the community. Healing rituals often involve incense and the chanting of ceremonial rhythms around a small fire. Mashed grasses, herbs, roots, berries, saliva and flowers are frequently used. After drenching my machete-blistered hands in a herb-infused ointment, the Emberá women help to guard me against illness by covering my skin in berry-dye patterns using a two-pronged bamboo stick.

Dinner is a basic meal that Hernan whips up using the provisions he packed: two gallons of fresh water, a bag of rice, some salted crackers and a few cans of tuna fish. After helping to wash the dishes in a bowl, I join the Emberá women on a tree stump, where a trio of brown-skinned toddlers climbs up to perch on my lap. A small boy with seal-pup eyes hands me a fist full of droopy wild flowers. The others, two shy, angelic-faced girls with grubby chins, curl their tiny bodies around my legs and nuzzle their soft cheeks against my bare knees.

Darkness falls as if controlled by a celestial dimmer switch, the daylight disappearing within seconds to give way to the night. It is so dark that it is beyond black. My hammock feels still and cool above the bamboo platform, and I am soothed by the snuffles and gentle snores of the livestock penned beneath. In England, where my expensive bed has an air-sprung mattress and fluffy duvet, I suffer from chronic insomnia, waking several times during the night, tossing and turning for hours, unable to stop the mental rehashing of the day's events. Minimising sleep-disorder triggers has had little impact. I clear my mind using meditation. I avoid all stimulant-based medications. I eat tryptophan-rich foods, such as warm milk and turkey. When I do aerobic exercise, I allow ample cool-down time. To improve the air circulation in my bedroom, I keep it free from debris, and cover mattresses and pillows with allergy-proof covers and natural fibre bedding. I make sure that my slumber zone is free from the smallest diffusion of light or noise. Yet, despite all this, I suffer with body-wracking sleep anxieties that make it impossible for me to sleep soundly through the night.

In this jungle, on a suspended bed in an open-sided hut, I zonk out with minutes. The vociferous crowing of Mogue's loudest rooster isn't an early-morning annoyance but a full-throated and rhythmical fanfare for a bright, new day. As it resonates across the silence in echoing triumph, the village begins to stir. Cold rainwater from a bucket splashes away the last bit of slumber. After coffee and oatmeal porridge, our guides are ready to lead us out into the deeper forests upstream.

We trek through sparkling, icy rivers chilly enough to numb my toes through my thick rubber boots. We climb giant boulders up to high plateaus to shower in cascading waters. Twisting paths take us past rocks deeply etched with ancient petroglyphs, through beautiful fruit-filled forests as dark as caves. At a small inlet, flocks of capuchin monkeys herald our arrival as we collect a pirogue to paddle further upstream, where we stop among delicate, pale yellow orchids to eat a meal of cold rice and yuca, a knobbly root vegetable indigenous to the rainforest. Then, with hammocks tied and mosquito nets assembled, we settle in for the night. Each of us has a torch and a machete under our pillow. I scribble in my tatty journal until my eyes begin to water in the rapidly fading light.

Since learning how to sling a hammock properly I've rarely had a bad hang, and tonight, after a day trudging slippery trails, my bed feels especially cosy. Few people realise that when

Columbus discovered the Americas he also discovered the hammock. After he brought it back to Europe it was used extensively by sailors at sea, who preferred it to sleeping on a cold, hard, dirty deck. During the construction of the Panama Canal, the net-shrouded hammock became an integral part of the US military physician William Gorgas's plan to eradicate disease. Incidents of yellow fever plummeted within weeks of the 'hanging bed' being introduced.

It is the Maya, however, whom we should thank for the invention of the hammock. Constructed using plant fibres and tree bark to a design that has remained unchanged for a thousand years, the hammock is still much used in the tropical regions of Latin America and the Caribbean. Scientists believe that the swinging motion synchronises brainwaves, allowing people to fall asleep more quickly. It is also claimed that it is easier for adults to achieve a deeper state of sleep in a hammock, like children who have been rocked to sleep. For me, a hammock is a hygienic, flexible and space-saving way of ensuring somewhere comfortable to sleep when I travel. It can be slung in just a few minutes, with differences in height, distances between anchor points and the angle of the hang all influencing its shape. I have never toppled out. I don't feel scrunched up. With practice, I can now wriggle round without forming an unruly bundle. And in the morning I can sit up, bleary eyed, without twanging my nose on the overhead rope. I don't need a king-size divan to sleep long and deep.

In the Darién, as I'd expected, a riot of flying and crawling insects moves across and around us all night. Because of this, we don't light the lanterns that often keep vampire bats at bay. But we have worked through a whole list of other safe-but-sure steps before daring to attempt to fall asleep. Once we're satisfied that the hammocks are tied high enough to allow jaguars, pumas and white-lipped peccaries to pass underneath, we check that the nets are sealed to keep mosquitoes at a distance – essential in this malarial hotspot. Then we rub the ropes with a citrus and diesel mix to help deter red ants, scorpions and spiders; the killer bees and horseflies don't like this either.

Often, I have only just climbed into my hammock when a small, inquisitive furry thing pops up briefly to say hola. Tonight, in the wee small hours, it is a flabby frog as weighty as a kerbstone that lands on the netting with a thump. It wakes me, just as a bat decides to pay a visit. Worried that it may want to suck blood from my forehand through the netting, I swipe it off with a forceful backhand and wrap my head in a blanket. Despite these nocturnal shenanigans, the jungle's constant rhythms are as comforting as a lullaby. Even with a large amphibian sprawled above my knees, I get a decent night's sleep.

After a glorious tangerine sunrise and a breakfast of scrambled eggs, I watch the younger of our Emberá guides catching fish for lunch. It is a near-perfect morning: bright, sunny and not too humid. The forest is umpteen shades of glossy green. First, the guide binds a machete blade to a stick with a length of woody twine to create a spear. He holds it, rolls it, twirls it and throws it into the air to feel its weight. It should handle well, becoming a seamless extension of his own forearm. Then he steps silently into the shallows of the river, careful to create the barest of ripples. Standing motionless for an eternity, his spear and arm held at shoulder height, he casts the skinniest of shadows, like a ribbon of trailing vine. Only his lungs are moving. He spots something swimming under the surface of the water, but still he doesn't move. Only his eyes narrow. Then, in a swift, fluid motion, he powers the spear into the water with a brutal stab. For a moment, I wonder if he has impaled his toe: the point of impact is inches from his foot. But he has pronged a big, flat, grey-blue fish – one of the 116 freshwater species recorded in the Darién to date.

We spend the rest of the day delving into wild, primeval forests crammed with unfolding Neotropical drama. A mud-coloured boa gulps down a rodent in a single swallow in front of our eyes; a fledgling plover takes flight from a mossy bough. A streak of brown fur tears out of the bush and hits me squarely on the shin. I shriek, fearing the worst, but it's only a gopher. We pull ourselves up through ancient gnarled trees, sharing jokes about the velociraptors that hide behind them. Our guides, utterly baffled by our version of evolution, confess that they fear we are suffering from dementia. To them, stalking jungles far away from home in pursuit of a bird is madness. Maybe they are right.

The younger guide accepts that as modern guardians of the harpy eagle, the Emberá need better to understand the threats of the world. After all, it isn't just Panamanians that kill harpies. He listens to Hernan talk about climate change and nods gently, offering opinions about pollution. We even discuss the much-debated plans to build through the Darién Gap, but realise we must first explain that it marks the only break in the road linking Alaska with Argentina. Hernan details its role in acting as a bio-barrier against diseases, such as foot-and-mouth, which is absent north of Colombia, and screw-worm, a parasite that eats the living flesh of humans and animals. This is clearly news to the Emberá, who frown in palpable concern, understanding that disturbing the ecosystem will help it spread northward. Yet when Hernan attempts to explain Darwin's theories, both guides physically recoil. Their heads have no space for this weird mumbo-jumbo. They shut their eyes to block it out.

Our companions also become edgy when we stop to look at snakes. Almost a hundred species of snake hide within the Darién's abundant foliage, marshland and forests, including giant anacondas and the fer-de-lance – Panama's deadly, venom-fanged viper. Just a glimpse of a tail is enough to have them reaching for their arc-shaped blades. Many indigenous tribes of the jungle revere and fear snakes in equal measure. The guides tell us that serpents are often the main characters of Emberá legends, representing good and evil in mythological tales both ancient and modern. Parents warn children against roaming too far in case a snake attacks them, while the main fear of hunters at night is a snakebite. A few years from now, a friend in Panama City will ring to tell me that a boa constrictor more than five metres long has swallowed an Emberá man whole in the Darién. Hernan and I step carefully around a camouflaged boa constrictor coiled peacefully in the middle of the trail, his scales mimicking the deep leaf litter around him.

The early morning is magical – dreamlike and ethereal – and we wake up to a symphony of birdsong. Dozens of species form the jungle's chorus of joyous exaltation, rich a cappella harmonies filling the air like a rousing hymn. This incredible song accompanies us for most of the morning's trek. Hernan pinpoints individual voices in the choir, calling out when he hears the familiar hoot of a whooping motmot or the four short, rattling trills of a black-cheeked woodpecker. We keep up a steady stomp, stopping when a particularly ear-catching bird grabs our attention, or to take a drink.

Our Emberá guides drink nothing all day and refuse all offers of bottled water. Yet they continue to stride through the fierce humid heat, barely breaking into a sweat. Experience has taught me to reject the advice of most guidebooks – including my own – on the subject of drinking water in the tropics. Unless I am happy for my hands and feet to swell, my pores to pour with sweat and my clothes to rot, I find it better not to drink much at all during the day. Each morning starts with a big mug of warm water, after which I sip small mouthfuls of bottled or coconut water. It is likely that the Emberá's reluctance to take on liquids is also related to local superstition about the body's sensitivity to hot and cold. Adding cold water to a hot body is believed to send it into shock, but I've yet to meet a Panamanian concerned about chronic dehydration.

Many of the beliefs that strike fear into the Darién's indigenous communities are related to fearsome creatures. A winged dragon with the head of a jaguar is believed to drag its prey up a hill to devour it – this is why the Kuna and the Emberá people always pass quickly over the forest's myth-steeped serrated ridges. Equally loathed are the one-armed beasts that have a hook instead of a hand and tear out people's hearts, and the Madre de Agua (water mother), who hides under whirlpools and pulls fishermen down to their watery graves. A child-stealing witch known as La Tuluvieja, a hideous hag who has a single, sagging breast and hides her face with long, straggly hair, is believed to take her victims back to a dark cave, spraying the trail behind her with breast milk to make it too slippery to pass. Hernan points to a distant forested hill where she was once seen, and I sense the hairs on the back of our guides' necks bristle.

On the gently sloping slog back to Mogue, the humidity is energy sapping and we are forced to trudge extra miles to avoid parasite-filled swamps that our guides fear will swallow us whole. At a crook in the trail, we stop to marvel at wispy white orchids and notice deep gashes on a tree bough strung with bromeliads. The marks are old and have been gouged by the sharp, pointed claws and talons of an adult harpy eagle during years long passed.

* * *

'Quick. Now. The tide, Sarita!' I hurriedly push my scattered belongings into my pack and pull the zip tight. Our tidal window is closing, so the dugout needs to leave now. Just a few minutes could leave us stranded. All the villagers have turned out to bid us farewell, including the trio of children that has become my permanent shadow. They gaggle together and hand me a harpy eagle naively carved from hardwood, and I draw each one into my arms for a goodbye cuddle. Before jumping into the boat, I hand out the last of my colouring books and crayons, and snap a few last photographs. Though we share no language and come from very different worlds, we inhabit the same planet. Their smiles will travel for miles.

The water is dangerously shallow as we speed along the river. The engine churns up the ankle-deep water and showers everything with a sludgy spray. Back at Punta Patiño, we take a last walk to the butterfly-scattered wetland for a final rummage around the mangroves and reedy pools for a capybara. The world's largest rodent is at its northernmost range in Panama, a common sight nuzzling among the marshy vegetation. Standing almost a metre tall, looking like a cross between a guinea pig and a hippo, it is hard to miss – yet I almost manage it. With very little noise at all it moves through swampland towards me and seems unconcerned by my presence. That is, until I decide to take a photo and pull my camera from my pack.

That night Hernan and I toast our trip with a can each of *Malta del Baru*, a fizzy molasses-flavoured drink named in honour of Panama's volcano, as a rose-red sun begins to plummet in a lilac sky. We reflect upon our trip, flicking through dozens of digital photographs, collapsing in laughter when the camera reminds us of a hammock-invading giant frog and fresh piles of puma crap.

Before we leave the next morning, I take advantage of Punta Patiño's square metre of mobile-phone signal, marked by a piece of blue tape on a tree. By standing on tiptoe and holding the phone in the air, jutting my face skyward at an awkward angle, I can call friends in rural England from this most unworldly Middle Earth. I try, but fail, to convey my location and its vast wealth of wonders: it sounds as if I am boasting, or drunk.

Our boat takes us to back to La Palma airport via the poop-splattered island of El Morro, a ragged spurt of wave-splashed volcanic rock that hosts numerous seabird colonies. We spot a bare-throated tiger heron, then several magnificent frigatebirds, with their large, bright red throat sacks inflated. I laugh out loud at El Morro's comical blue-footed boobies, which are marching around, army style, their feet lifting up and down in a showy seduction attempt. The females do a grand job of appearing disinterested, but I am totally wooed. On the plane back to Panama City, I replay the trip over and over again in my mind. I think back to when I first heard of the Darién, at school, more than three decades ago. Did this feral land, with its large tracts of untamed forest, the longest and widest rivers, and the tallest trees, live up to my expectations? Yes, and more besides.

We didn't see a harpy eagle, but we came close, I'm sure. The lowland forests of the Punta Patiño have yielded several active harpy eagle nests over the years, as have those near the village of Mogue. Were we merely unlucky, I wonder, or was I fooling myself that it was even possible? As I gaze out of the aircraft window at the late, golden-pink sun, I pray for the harpy eagle and hope that the empty nests don't mean the sun is setting on this endangered species. And I can't help but wonder, as I finger the feather in my pocket, if this is the closest I will ever get to the mighty winged beast itself. I am already pledging to return to the Darién, moments after leaving. Illogical as it is, I reach inside my jacket to squeeze the Sara Sotillo coin for extra luck.

Meeting the Wounaan

Panama
2008

Although I feel anxious at what lies ahead, it is imperative that I don't show it. Fear is every bit as repulsive as cocksure arrogance to this ancient forest community. It sickens them. Fills them with anger and, ironically, frightens them to the core. Fear breeds fear here. It upsets the equilibrium, warns the people that there is harm around them – usually at the hands of strangers.

In some of South and Central America's ancient rainforest tribes, the unborn child is believed to have a purpose before it leaves the womb. Once born, it is already equipped with the requisite imagination, drive and determination to attain its goal. All it needs to do is accept guidance.

I wonder if I was born with a predetermined intent; a destiny? My sensible, analytical mind would say no; my heart, otherwise. My horoscope on the day I came into the world concurred that 'I strive for worldliness and a spiritual oneness with nature'.

I certainly felt a strong desire to travel from an early age, as if my purpose was in some way prearranged. During my gestation, my legs were continually on the move. I needed wriggle room almost as soon as I was born, as if itchy feet had set in. I walked early, relishing my newfound freedom, giggling and shrieking as each small footstep took me forward, developmentally, in leaps and bounds. It was, at ten months old, my first move towards independence.

I was born on 14 November 1967 in Kingston upon Thames, Surrey, arriving impatiently just before midnight with a protracted wail that my parents, John and Gill, swear didn't stop for several months. When I born, Kingston was considered to be part of Surrey; today, city planners have decided that it is in Greater London. It is located about twelve miles upstream from Westminster Bridge in the heart of the capital, and is just around the corner from the All England Lawn Tennis Club at Wimbledon, home of the world's greatest grass-court tennis tournament. The name Kingston means 'royal manor' (derived from Cyninges Tun, or Cingestune); the Queen granted it Royal Borough status in 1965. I used to wonder if this was why my parents named me Sarah (meaning 'princess' in Hebrew), and my mother did little to dissuade me, suggesting to me on numerous occasions throughout my life that Prince Andrew, just a few years older, was perfect husband material. Coincidentally, I also shared my birthday with his other brother, Charles, the heir to the throne. Today, Kingston is one of London's poshest suburbs, full of mansions set behind formidable gates equipped with video-entry systems. For the record, we didn't live in such a place.

Apparently, I came into the world covered in dark brown fuzzy hair (lanugo), which lent me a primate-like appearance. Home was a council house opposite the nineteenth-century County Hall building. The whole neighbourhood had been badly shaken by a flying Second World War bomb in 1944. Our terraced home was earmarked for demolition while we lived there, eventually being razed to the ground in the early 1990s. I remember 'discovering' a derelict air-raid shelter behind our home; I must have been aged about four, and delighted in my rubble-strewn den, with its crumbling stairs and heavy door. Kingston was once the site of dozens of such shelters, some large enough to accommodate several thousand people. Mine was full of old newspapers, ripped and water damaged. I clearly recall a headline that read: 'There are more birds in the world than people'. It is a fact that has fascinated me ever since.

I was born into a decade of cultural and political change across the globe. More than thirty countries in Africa gained independence between 1960 and 1968. Revolutions and conflicts in countries including China, Cuba and Greece characterised much of the decade. The world population hit more than three billion, the average cost of a house was £2,530, a Manchester United season ticket cost £8.50 and a loaf of bread five pence. The 1960s saw the test flight of Concorde and the arrival of man on the moon. The world began to shrink as package holidays took off and British people started swapping traditional seaside resorts for more exotic climes. Flights became cheaper and more frequent; foreign lands more accessible. Little did I know how much those early cut-price deals would eventually shape my world.

By the time I started primary school, I had set my career compass on being an adventurer and had a fascination for wildlife and precious stones. I would stalk bugs and scrutinise grubs. I'd gather ceramic fragments from the garden and, after examining them under a magnifying glass, declare them rare fossils. With a bunch of drooping daisies in my hand and a marmalade sandwich in my pocket, I'd embark on a bear hunt or butterfly safari, my mane of thick dark hair flying in the wind. On spotting a butterfly in my urban jungle, my skin would start to prickle, adrenalin pumped into my bloodstream and an adventure would begin. Birds weren't of any real interest. Suburban London didn't offer anything eye-catching, so I largely ignored the scraggy, brown-feathered worm pullers that foraged on our patchy grass.

My dad, a besuited civil servant by day and rock drummer by night, assumed the role of expedition leader. By this time, my mum had given birth to my brother, Jeremy. Our favourite stomping grounds – the leafy parks of south-west London – seemed like untamed wildernesses to me. We'd pack a picnic, whatever the weather, and venture to Ham Common, a sprawl of tufted riverbank meadows and scrub that seemed permanently dotted with butterflies and wild flowers. Even better, we would head off to nearby Bushy Park, one of London's Royal Parks, where I'd run across carpets of pine cones, hide in woodlands and collect handfuls of horse-chestnut blossom in May. The landscape of this sixteenth-century Royal Park, a gift to King Henry VIII from Cardinal Wolsey, seemed otherworldly to my young eyes: a vast patchwork of deer-filled parkland, gardens dotted with fountains, wide avenues of soaring trees and mysterious medieval remains. Occasionally I would spot a rabbit or hedgehog, but my excitable shrieks put paid to any potential encounters with the water voles, woodpeckers, kestrels and tawny owls that called Bushy Park home.

Shortly after I started school, my sister was born: a baby as blonde as I was dark and my brother was ginger haired. We left the traffic of London behind to move to Letchworth Garden City in Hertfordshire. The world's first Garden City, it was founded in 1903 following the residential planning ideals of Ebenezer Howard, who urged developers to merge the best of Victorian architecture and amenities with the beauty and health benefits of the countryside. He wrote that 'human society and the beauty of nature are meant to be enjoyed together', and in Letchworth, residents were able to do just that. The town's residential and industrial zones were carefully separated, so the prevailing winds would take smoke away from housing. Handsome properties, influenced by the Arts and Crafts movement, nestled within large areas of greenery and broad pavements.

My mum's family all lived in Letchworth. She'd been born there and schooled there, and had left only to go to teacher-training college in Kingston, where she met – and married – my dad. It was lovely to be close to all my cousins and spend proper time with my maternal grandparents. I was especially fond of my grandfather, a distinguished Welshman with impeccable manners, who always wore a suit. He was a popular local councillor: everybody knew and respected Jack Talbot, which is why there is now a street in Letchworth honouring his name. My grandma, as far as I'm aware, didn't ever work, other than for the war effort. She was a complete eccentric and seemed blissfully content in her odd little world of mouldy sandwiches, made-up songs, missionary work and nightly episode of *Crossroads* (a mundane television soap opera renowned for its wobbly sets). During the school holidays we would spend time at Norton Common in the heart of the town, picking blackberries and elderberries, and marvelling at the cuckoo pints and butterflies.

We didn't stay in Letchworth long, so I barely got to know my new classmates before I was settling into a small Bedfordshire village called Henlow. A highly confident child, I had no problem making friends. Our new home was on the edge of the local sports field in the heart of the village. Apart from having a pavilion and a children's playground, the field also adjoined the resplendent parkland belonging to a Grade II-listed Georgian mansion house. These grounds contained streams, rivers, bridge-straddled lakes, hay-filled meadows and small thickets of bluebell woods. The name Henlow is believed to derive from the Old English *henna hlaw*, meaning 'hill frequented by wild birds'. I vividly recall being startled by squawking and fluttering as I played hide and seek among the hawthorn, crab apple and spindle trees, hearing woodpeckers and spotting the occasional blue flash of a kingfisher.

The mansion, then a rather exclusive beauty school, was remodelled as a health farm and is now a spa. Before land was cleared to extend the building, it was almost completely obscured from view by beech and horse-chestnut trees. The most daring of us would climb over fences bearing 'Private Property' signs to paddle in streams, play Pooh sticks and swing like Tarzan from a rope hung on a giant oak tree. We'd leapfrog over rickety stiles, roll in grassy meadows and stuff handfuls of wild flowers in our pockets. My mother, waving me off after breakfast on a Saturday morning, would issue me with a written list of 'treasure' to bring home at teatime. Favourites were a brown feather, a speckled stone, a daisy chain, a bark rubbing, a twig and a heart-shaped leaf. All the children would join in, from toddlers to teens. We never dreamt of returning home until the list was complete.

Living in Henlow was idyllic. I had a huge natural playground and was allowed to roam free. I made dozens of friends, excelled at the local school and idolised my teachers, who, unhindered by bureaucratic red tape, would hold classes outside in the park on the sunniest days, swap textbook maths for bird or butterfly counts, and encourage us to take charge of lessons and be creative. My parents seemed happy, too, even though we were living on top of one another in a two-up-two-down Victorian mid-terrace. Money was extremely tight: the mortgage my father had taken out to buy our first family home was keeping him awake at night. We lived a simple life without luxuries, sweets or holidays, but I can honestly say I barely noticed. Clothes were always hand-me-downs, and we got most of our toys from church-hall jumble sales. We wore everything until it was threadbare; nothing went to waste. My mum cooked up vegetable dyes from onion skins and beetroots to give second-hand clothes a new lease of life. She even turned my scuffed brown winter shoes into much-needed summer sandals by cropping off the fronts to form peephole toes, and painting the shoes white with leftover household emulsion.

Our house was one of crowded chaos among books, crayons, paints and instruments. My musical mother allowed us to bang drums, clang bells, strum guitars and attempt to play the violin (badly). Murals adorned the walls; our bedrooms were papered with patchworks created from wallcovering sample books. After tea, my sister would do handstands against the sofa, while my brother tortured his action figures with pins. I'd busy myself with great lumps of clay: grey, wet and gloopy. My mother, eager to see it transformed, would await a wonky sugar bowl. I can still recall the thrill of unveiling a perching barn owl, its feathers textured with meticulous detail using a hard-bristled toothbrush. Her pride was obvious as she positioned it on top of the kitchen counter to dry overnight. It was morning before she realised to her horror that the toothbrush was her own.

Once, I returned to school to discover I'd been chosen to be involved in a BBC concert at the Royal Festival Hall in London. My job was to create a collage of painted autumn leaves as a backdrop for the performance. In the whole of my life so far, it was one of the most exciting things I'd been part of. I was so proud and honoured. It made the local paper, and we listened to the recording of the concert in class, gathered round a battered transistor radio.

We learned French, staged outside plays and were taught about reptilian beasts, from crocodiles to dinosaurs. I became captivated by images of prehistoric winged creatures with vast wingspans and deadly talons – the origin, no doubt, of my later fascination with harpy eagles. I was given key roles in school performances, be they musicals, nativity plays or recitals. I was top of the class (in everything apart from mathematics and PE). My life was absolutely amazingly wonderful. But then.

My parents divorced. Today, this might not be as big a deal as it was then. In the mid-1970s, in a leafy village in rural Bedfordshire, there wasn't another child I knew whose parents weren't together. To say it brought my world crashing down would be an understatement. Everything I knew, lived with and trusted seemed to disappear in a single moment. My father was devastated, betrayed and hurting. My mother off to pastures new. My sister and brother, too young to grasp what was happening, simply accepted what was told to them. I felt permanently nauseous with a burning rage that woke me with a jolt early each morning and festered all day. Numbness, anxiety and grief eventually gave way to delinquency. I purposefully failed tests at school, simply so that someone would notice me. I screamed, fought, raged. I was only ten, yet nothing in my life would ever be the same again.

The only place I felt any happiness was in my daydreams, so I lost myself in those, creating elaborate voyages that transported me to faraway lands. My other favourite pastime was playing in the garden, creating imaginary civilisations in piles of mud, chasing butterflies, picking buttercups and daisies, or joining the other village children to build dens from bales of hay. When my playmates told jokes they'd heard on television, I'd have no clue what they meant – we didn't have a TV. Yet they were fascinated by my knowledge of different hedgerow flowers. They'd spend hours with me, studying ants and bugs with quizzical intensity. On rainy days the local children would often end up at my house, being taught how to make rose-petal soap, press wild flowers and sew lavender sachets. Dad would collect me and my siblings at weekends, to spend Saturday afternoons swimming, gathering conkers or visiting the local bird reserve.

Once the divorce had gone through, I waved goodbye to my friends in the pretty little village and moved to a council estate in a market town eight miles away. It may as well have been another planet. To cope with the culture shock, I retreated into my own little world. My imagination, fired by a collection of brightly coloured maps and a shelf full of encyclopedias, powered my epic voyages. I would daydream for hours of mysterious lands and the exotic people and animals they contained.

* * *

Entering a tribal community, such as that of the Wounaan people, always has risks attached. Whatever you know of your own world is of little use or comfort, because almost every societal rule, cultural value and superstition is alien. While I am no stranger to encounters with remote jungle tribes, every new meeting is quite unlike any other. Each community is wholly unique. On each occasion I am 'sized up', character-profiled in an instant. Knowing this, I stay calm and do my best to emit positive vibes. But, in many respects, this is futile. The criteria used to assess me are something I have zero influence over. I am what I am, or at least what I am considered to be. Am I friend or foe? Any smidgen of suspicion that I am anything other than the former and I will be cast out, unceremoniously and without courtesy.

Clearing my throat or rubbing my sun-sore eyes could alert tribal people to the dangers of contagious infections, foreign parasites and alien bacteria. Pink skin, especially that reddened by the heat, could suggest a terrible illness. Even my touch, the unfamiliar softness of fat, clammy Western hands, could be a dangerous transmitter of serious ills. In years gone by, entry to the Kuna community was denied to a scientist with razor rash for fear of a contagion. My freckled complexion may well not pass the test.

Intruders are alarming and rarely to be trusted. That's what the panic of suspicion tells the tribe. A powerful sense of dread can secrete from anxiety, like fraying wire before a power outage. Terror can spread throughout a tribe at machine-gun pace, bubbling up in an explosion of hostility within minutes. It is horrified, trembling fear, not spite or hatred, that can cause a community to take up arms in unified opposition. The people are scared beyond belief.

So I am always ready to be greeted by a crowd of men armed with sharpened spears. Prepared to be chased away by angry, axe-wielding warriors; accepting that I may be spat at and told never to return. Yet I am also concerned that I could be shot at, or killed, even. Fear of outsiders, and the death and disease they bring, creates a very real threat, one that I am mindful of as I approach the thatch-topped huts of the Wounaan village.

The Wounaan place great emphasis on the aura, believing that it provides a visual narrative on the past, present and future life of the bearer. Auras are completely invisible to us, but they are a tangible presence to many indigenous peoples, who commonly see them as colours, figures and occasionally sounds. Protecting themselves from people with harmful energies is just as important as keeping warriors with weapons from entering their village. One of the reasons they don't invite visitors in is the potential fear of an outsider's reversed aura, which sucks all it needs from others and leaves them weakened.

The properties of my aura, and how they sense it, are all important. If I look wrong, or have the wrong colours around me, I won't make it past the entrance. My eyes, or rather shadows within them, could reveal the dark secrets of my soul. The energy I carry – invisible to me but evident to them – could confirm the hidden animal instincts of a dangerous inner psyche. Thankfully, mine is considered a positive, luck-bringing light. My aura hangs like a gorgeous haze all around me, purple with hints of gold and red. I know this because some of the women tell me later. Apparently, the colours suggest a unique connection with God. The aura is so strong, they remark, that everyone around me can actually feel it. I wish I had their eyes to see it too.

It takes less than an hour for the significance of my aura to become apparent. All tensions are eased and a level of trust ensues. After I meet the elders and listen attentively to an introduction by the most senior member of the community, I am taken out to meet the people. The dozens of young children who are tugging at the hands of their parents, eager to run to my side, are set free. They run, shrieking and laughing, into my arms, coiling their small brown limbs around me. Waddling up at the rear of the pack, the youngest clings to my ankles as the warm, swaddled body of a cooing baby is placed in my arms. Children are perched on my shoulders, toddlers climb into my lap and others hug each hip. To them, the hues of my aura are a promise of kindness, compassion and nurture. To the parents, they confirm a heart of empathy, that I am well connected with worlds other than my own and take on the feelings of others. The earthy golds signify that I am grounded, with an affinity for soil and nature. The bolder colours assure them of my sensitive, bright and cheerful character and capability for bestowing great love. The elders can see a fragility and broken connection within me as a result of childhood trauma – my parents' divorce, I assume.

My visit has been arranged through a complex network of introductions in order to give me time to learn a little about the Wounaan people. In return, I will offer English lessons, help with chores and pay a nominal daily amount into the community purse – about ten US dollars. For this, I hope to be allowed the perfect mix of time to observe and opportunities to integrate.

More and more children are freed to rush towards me; they emerge from dark doorways with their arms outstretched, running at full pelt. Some yell unintelligible greetings at the tops of their voices, squealing with glee as I ruffle their hair. We hold hands and share embraces while they twiddle with the buttons on my cargo pants. For the next couple of hours, the children rarely leave my side. They climb over me as I rest on my haunches in a swept-mud clearing under the shade of a thatched roof, sucking on slices of mango. Then, as I move around the village, they trail after me in a noisy crocodile of chatter, pointing out dogs and livestock and teaching me random words of Woun Meu.

Historically the Wounaan lived in the Darién jungle and on the Pacific south coast of Colombia. Yet, with domestic migration and the blurring of traditional borders, Wounaan culture can now be found in riverside jungle locations throughout Central America. In order to survive, the Wounaan have joined forces with the Emberá people, a different indigenous tribe, with different languages and different customs, but one that shares similar societal values.

Like many traditional rainforest settlements, the Wounaan village on a tributary of the Rio Gatun, about an hour from the soft sands of the Caribbean, is an elongated circle. At the time that I visit, there is talk of opening up the settlement to a select number of visitors each year. I suspect I may be a guinea pig, which is an unfortunate analogy, as many Central and South American communities still eat these fluffy rodents, roasted on spits. Set back from a small tributary, alongside a thick, orchid-covered grove behind a muddy riverbank, the village is laid out in a clearing tucked behind a curtain of jungle. The village centres on the Men's House, which, as it sounds, is an all-male gathering hut where political, spiritual and administrative associations meet on a daily basis. Another house is where the entire community gathers for the many meetings and rituals that mark all aspects of life in a Wounaan community: birth and death; the onset of menstruation; the first hunt by the boys upon reaching adolescence.

Houses are rectangular thatched huts, open on all sides. Several families live together in each house, sleeping in hammocks slung from the rafters and cooking over open fires along the sides. Everything needed to support family and communal life takes place within the clearing. Friendship ties are often as strong as blood. Domestic kitchens, children's spaces and weaving areas, separate from the houses, are arranged around the clearing and, set back on the periphery, various buildings are used for workshops. The men skilfully carve wooden animals from tagua nuts, the mahogany-like fruit of the vegetable ivory palm: crocodiles, turtles, dolphins and eagles as shiny as waxed doorknobs. The women collect fruit and firewood, and wash clothes with river water close to, or inside, the houses. Livestock and food stores (smoked meats, nuts and vegetables) are housed within the centre of the village, where they can be protected. In recent years the community has cultivated large gardens, where manioc, peppers, bananas and many other fruits and vegetables are grown.

The strength gained from safety in numbers lies at the very heart of the community. Everyone is involved in everything, from sacrosanct rituals to daily pastimes. The village is run democratically by an elected committee, chaired by a chief. Decisions are made collectively and every family has a vote. At the last count, the village had around a hundred residents, according to the people I ask. I struggle to count more than fifty, suggesting that certain families are shielded and afforded privacy due to age, health or other factors.

Break the law and the community will decide your fate, from a term of incarceration to a public flogging. Like many other tribal communities, the Wounaan have their own judicial system, often incorporating traditional sentences that enforce a programme of societal amends. In some cases the focus is on reconciling aggrieved members, or compensating victims, not punishing offenders. Generally, the shame and remorse of wronging your 'family' within a tight-knit community is prevention enough.

When I awake on the first morning, I squint at the brilliance of first light as it pushes its way through the rainforest canopy. My hammock is swaying gently under a roof of palm fronds and there is a line of cherubic, honey-brown faces watching me. The children, who have been studying me sleeping, giggle at my wayward bushy hair, nudging each other in shared amusement. When I ruffle it up even further, they burst into peals of laughter. I grin at them, and they take this as an invitation to climb aboard. We swing, pendulum-style, for at least half an hour until the momentum causes the hut to judder.

For several days I spend almost all my time with the children, aged around six and younger. We draw in the dust with sticks, play throwing games with a ball I make from old scraps of cloth bound with packing tape – piggy-in-the-middle is a favourite – and do lots of colouring with packs of crayons that I produce from my backpack.

Under the tutorage of some of the women, I learn to harvest palm fibres and weave them into small baskets (canastas). Soon my prime role is to gather palm leaves each day, once the men have removed the leaves from each stalk and stacked them neatly together on the ground. As part of the all-female group, I help strip off the spiny edges of the palm to extract the weaving fibre – a job best suited to a loose-limbed contortionist. Using a toe to hold one end, we peel away the fibres in thin strips in a tricky, almost yogic sitting position. With my soft Western toes, cramp is inevitable. My big toe spasms constantly and painfully for about two hours, stopping only when I unfold my legs. Once the fibres have been extracted, they are carted off to be dried and coloured with natural dyes from big inky vats. Then the weaving can commence.

There's an amber-red glow from the kitchen all day long, the women rallying round to keep the embers burning beneath a metal cauldron supported by a tripod of branches. It is hard work in sweltering heat, yet the Wounaan women are nimble, efficient and uncomplaining. Before the sun is up each morning, their work has already started and they rarely have time to rest until they sleep at night. I have it easy, as they won't hear of me helping them with the daily chores until I have eaten. So I cherish some extra time with the children, breakfasting in the early sun on slices of pineapple and mango, juice running down our chins.

I have been given a place within the group. But I am watched closely, continually scrutinised for the 'good' and 'bad' things I bring to the community. Other than assessing my character and interpreting my life story, the community will respond to my ability to respect their heritage. Customs and conventions should be observed. Traditions honoured. Behaviours admired and beliefs valued. Getting these explained to me is all important, to ensure that there is no cross-cultural misunderstanding. The Wounaan value modesty, humbleness, honesty and an ability to listen. Women shouldn't stare straight into a man's eyes, or be alone with a man at any time. There are also numerous protocols around who is served food first and umpteen more that govern the community's many tribal rituals – although, thankfully, they know that it is unrealistic for an outsider like me to comprehend these.

Most crucial to understand are the rudimentary cultural beliefs that are so susceptible when there is a collision of two unfamiliar worlds. Great unintentional hurt could be caused by many things in my backpack: my camera, my magazine, my knife, my radio, my watch, my flashlight. A camera lens pointed at their faces is an intimidating threat to 'capture' their image – and soul. Suspicion of wristwatches and mobile phones prevails; technology is confounding and impossible to put into context. Conservative behaviour is approved of; loud laughter and ridicule frowned upon. Glossy fashion magazines containing pouting models might as well be hardcore porn.

Travellers such as me – Westerners journeying solo or in small groups, far away from home – are considered weird, foolish even. It is unfathomable to the Wounaan that a person would leave friends, family and possessions voluntarily to travel thousands of miles into the unknown. The presumption is that you are antisocial, unloved and unacceptable. If not, why aren't you with everything that is life giving?

My gender always perplexes the tribes I encounter. It challenges all their societal norms and, because of this, often provokes trepidation. After the initial shock has worn off, it tends to work in my favour, implying that I am not an aggressive force bringing harm to their door. Still, the idea of a female travelling alone is utterly inconceivable. As a tribal woman, I would only be alone if I'd been banished for a terrible crime or act of witchcraft – adding to the suspicion, lurking not far from the surface, that I have been cast out by my own people. In a community such as this one, you are never alone. Not even to wash or to sleep. Solitude is considered dangerous. Collectivism and togetherness create a bigger pool of wisdom, energy and power.

Being a writer lends some credence to my reason for being here alone. But the people don't understand it or like it. However, I'm quiet and hard-working and have been able to learn through gentle enquiry to avoid upsetting the dominant characters within the tribe. By gently melding into the background, and enjoying the process of observation, I have learned much. Luck has played a big part in my acceptance here. Arriving at a time considered auspicious by the community has immediately boosted my status to good-luck talisman. If I'd turned up just as the rivers ran empty, or a fisherman had drowned, my presence would be considered a bad omen. Inwardly, I pray that the crops won't fail.

Nothing happens without a reason here; everything is interlinked. The presence of a visitor is tied in some way to the good vibes of ancestral spirits or the relationship with Mother Nature, governing future harvests, weather patterns and food supplies. In short, everything – drought, illness and life itself – hangs on you. For example, it is a big deal for me to be allowed to 'invade' the river, for this is their natural life force, crucial to their survival. Only once the trust has deepened am I left alone at the river's edge. I am also monitored to ensure I that do nothing to damage the harmony the tribe enjoys with the spirit world. This could be anything that may offend the divine creator, from harming an animal to doing something that might impact negatively on soil fertility.

In the afternoon, once the ingredients for dinner have been washed and chopped and the bright cubes of squash and plantain placed in covered pots, I am usually free to write for a few hours. I wash my hands in the river in an attempt to rid them of the smell of dry-cured meat – the tribe smokes most of what it hunts and stores it in sealed containers that look like big black dustbins. Not only does this eke out the food across the leaner seasons; it also helps store it up for big community feasts, such as puberty rituals. Basic jungle food is well within my comfort zone, usually fried plantain, rice, yuca, eggs and sometimes fish. However, to welcome me on my first day, the women opened a dustbin to pull out one of the fattest rodents I'd ever seen. The community rarely eats meat, and this was cooked over the fire in my honour: a rare treat. It tasted like well-grilled, dry spare ribs without the sauce – the occasional tuft of coarse hair, tooth and chewy gristle not diminishing the gourmet splurge.

Each day, I venture out to the bathroom in the trees, which seems only to be used by me; I never see evidence of anyone else's usage. I dig a fresh hole and cover it over with a mix of ash gathered from the embers of the village's many fires and dark, sun-dried soil harvested from the depths of the jungle. Ash eliminates the odours of newly deposited waste and keeps flies and harmful microbes from entering and contaminating the forest. Once I've raked it over and marked it with a stick, I leave nature to work its magic. The system helps to keep the community free from diarrhoea, a leading cause of infant mortality and illness in the jungle.

Families have always disposed of their waste in the forest, a system that has worked for thousands of years. But at the time of my visit, there are plans to consider a more viable option. Government land quotas to indigenous groups have resulted in families living in closer proximity now than they used to. An overlap of human waste deposits at the village is causing rumbles of real concern due to fears of water-source contamination. The community has started to move its waste deeper into the jungle after news arrived of a sister tribe, around one hundred miles to the west, whose creeks and rivers were poisoned after a rainstorm washed toxic human waste into them. Since then an eco-toilet has been installed in that village, with a tin roof, tiled concrete floor and strong, wooden frame. Urine is separated into a plastic funnel connected to a perforated hose, and fed to the garden's plants. Faeces are deposited in a recycled hundred-kilogram rice or flour bag and covered with ash. After drying out for six months in a dark, cool location, they are used as covering material for new faeces. Several charities are involved in projects to install ecological dry toilets in jungle communities all over South America and beyond. The Wounaan hope that their village will be next.

Even in the quiet moments when I write, I am rarely alone. A green lizard pockmarked with orange likes to hide among a pile of books and poke its head out to watch my every move with attentive, bulging eyes. On other days, four-year-old Chiciliana drops by. With her glossy, dark brown hair, smooth, round cheeks and eyes like shiny conkers, she looks very much like I did as a child – although much, much cuter. As I sit writing up my notes, propped against my backpack, she stands behind me, twiddling with my hair and curling it around her fingers before smoothing it down and starting again. If Chiciliana is busy with her chores, a bad-tempered brown chicken visits to terrorise my bare toes. Chiciliana usually chases it away, so it only drops by when it is sure I am alone. It eyes me maliciously with black beady eyes and flaps at me, aggressively, should I dare to ignore it. I squeeze on my boots if I see it approaching, but it pecks at my feet ferociously. One day I have had enough and catch it perfectly under my toe in a fifty-metre volley. It lands on its feet, turns to glare at me and seems to consider revenge. Then it changes its mind. The crankiest chicken on Earth and its vicious beak give me a wide berth.

The community wants me to continue my work with the younger children, so I drop my kitchen chores and spend more time with the toddlers. I adore the children and love the constant challenge of finding new games to play. Naturally resourceful and practical, the children relish arts and crafts and have an amazing box of materials at their disposal. We make big pieces of hanging art using every child's handprints. We draw pictures with stubby sticks in the soil, adding to them daily. Led by Chiciliana's older brother, the children dash off to gather pebbles, fern sprigs, seeds, leaves, berries and kernels, which they arrange into pictures – often depicting the village and its occupants – then press firmly into the ground. We sing songs and play music using seed-filled containers, oil cans and tribal drums.

Then, I almost blow it. After a few weeks, my camera is still unwrapped and I'm itching to capture the gleeful faces of the children around the village. Without fully thinking it through, I venture to ask Chiciliana's mother, Lila, about having free reign to take photographs. Immediately, I wish I hadn't. Faces are stern. Uncomfortable. Hurt. I am beside myself with regret almost as soon as the words have left my mouth.

Having earned a place in the gathering party for healing plants and helping with meals, I am no longer an out-and-out outsider. Even the older folk nod hello now, proving a level of acceptance that once I could only dare hope for. On learning that a meeting has been called to discuss the subject of photography that evening, I feel a sense of dread. It is a communal session, to which I am not invited, which convinces me the offence I've caused is serious. The debate will, I'm certain, focus on how best to ask me to leave. I am so cross with myself. Why couldn't I keep my big mouth shut? I knew before I arrived that the tribe was sensitive to photography. All I had to do was respect that. Who am I to ride roughshod over an age-old sensitivity?

Culturally, I feel clumsy. Inept. Relatively recently this community believed that taking a photo of a person gave you magical control over them. Would they now think that I was rejecting their beliefs as nonsense, a fallacy or Third-World voodoo? I am dismayed at what I have unwittingly conveyed. Chewing my fingers down to the bone is the only distraction. My attempts to clear my head by writing fail miserably.

After several hours, late into the night, the meeting closes and I am summoned to the communal hut. Inside the building, just a few of the elders remain. I hope this is a good sign. 'Come, sit,' the Chief in the centre beckons me in heavily accented Spanish, his voice soft and deep. 'I need to tell you something.' I perch on a wooden bench by his side and wait for his elongated pause to come to an end. Just his presence has a hypnotic effect on me. I wait, hardly daring to breathe.

'Sarah, please, think of the humpback whale, which journeys more than 9,800 kilometres from Brazil to Madagascar. Or the fragile globe skimmer dragonfly that completes an 11,000-mile round trip from India to Africa. The 4,300-mile monarch butterfly migration from Mexico to Canada is another amazing journey. On land, think of North America's caribou, a terrestrial mammal that migrates farther than any other at around 3,000 miles in a year. Then, of course, there are the million or so wildebeest in Africa. Oh, and the legendary journeys of the leatherback sea turtle, which can spend almost two whole years travelling to its nesting site. Think, please, of the tiny Arctic tern that migrates on a zigzagging route between the Arctic and

Antarctica, the longest migration of any animal, at more than 44,000 miles.'

He pauses. Clasping his hands together. His oratory is spell-binding – and statistically precise.

'We don't fully understand how birds stay on track during these travels of hundreds or thousands of miles, of course,' he continues. 'But we must admire these masters of navigation for their excellent sensory skills and surety. When birds migrate, heading east or west, north or south, it is an act of faith. An act of faith! For most there is no turning back. Think of that. They leave everything behind and trust what they will find.

'Tonight, we were reminded what it is that our migrants bring to us, when they arrive. We learn from the new.' He shoots me a knowing look. 'They bring flashes of exotic song and fresh energy into our daily lives. They remind us that we are part of a wider world. A wider world! You, Sarah, have also made such a journey, a migration thousands of miles to eat at our table. We must let you rest, get the most from your journey, and prepare you for your travels back. After all, like a migrant bird, you visited us on a wing and a prayer. Who are we to block your tracks?'

A bubble of emotion steals my voice away. I gulp a meaningless response.

'I speak for the entire community,' he says. 'Please, take your photographs. Seek permissions where you have to from individuals. There will be those who say no. Respect this, please.'

I blink back tears and whisper heartfelt *muchísimas gracias*. It doesn't seem enough. He smiles and turns to leave, signalling the other elders to follow. I thank each one as they pass me. They nod, silently.

Back in my hammock, as the blackness closes in, I bury my face in my pillow and weep with sheer relief. That night my dreams are filled with Arctic terns, wildebeest and humpback whales all attempting to reach South America. I reach out to a globe skimmer dragonfly, but it evades my touch. My stomach feels as if it is full of fluttering monarch butterflies. I greet the morning like a new horizon, bright and full of hope.

From that day, the Wounaan elders seem more comfortable with my presence. I also sense a greater willingness to invest in my understanding of how the community works and thinks. In particular, the Chief has ensured that he is at hand to answer any questions I care to ask. More than that, he now takes the time to sit and quietly natter with me, or we may simply walk and talk.

Everything that jungles have revealed to me over the years has nurtured a fascination with natural health remedies. Matching symptoms with the abundant vegetal cures that flourish around us feels so right. When Lila asks if I'd like to spend a morning with the medicine man, Wen, preparing treatments for daily health conditions, I struggle to sleep the night before. In a small, palm-roofed hut with a wooden table and several dozen bowls, he explains the botanical powers of individual plants and the multitude of ways in which they are used, ingested or applied. He has a complex understanding of medical conditions, human biology, and the relationship between plants and people. Without a computer system, dispensary or shelf of medical texts, he regularly treats more than fifty distinct diseases. Unhurried and gentle, he mixes practical medicine and spiritual therapy with considerable healing prowess. An hour of holistic therapy in his hut leaves me rested, restored, bright and well.

Wen is patient, accommodating, accessible and wise. When I re-read my copious notes after each stroll through the jungle, I marvel at how well we communicate in broken Spanish. Within my inky scrawl are case notes about treatments for all sorts of gastroenterological complaints, endocrine diseases, haematological disorders and rheumatologic conditions. I've learned so much about the curative properties of the shoots, nuts and fruits in the surrounding forest, and how they are used to make pastes, poultices, infusions and ointments to treat and ward against all manner of maladies. The greatest gift a tribesman can give an outsider is some of the unique knowledge he possesses: the skills he has acquired from forefathers, the command he has of tribal history, the mastery he demonstrates in the medicinal powers of the jungle.

In recent years Wen has treated rising numbers of neurological diseases, from migraines and insomnia to tremors, together with a greater number of kidney complaints, cystitis, prostate problems and impotence. Bronchitis and asthma are two of the common chest and respiratory illnesses he deals with. Gynaecological conditions and fertility issues are a medical priority, as are treatments for all forms of cancer. In his company my brain feels like a spaceship orbiting new, unexplored planets and delving into galaxies full of promise and awe-filled wonders. Wen assesses the physical, mental, emotional and spiritual parts of each patient, and how those parts relate to one another and to the animal, mineral and plant kingdoms. I challenge the notion that this health system, which interconnects with the circular rhythm of life and the various seasons of nature, is primitive, while the Western world's super-slick version, founded on science, is superior. Counselling, a relatively modern Western phenomenon, has been part of shamanic medicine for centuries, often in the form of small groups. A symbolic object, such as an eagle's feather, is placed in the centre of a circle of people, and when a person wishes to speak, they pick it up.

One night a girl goes into in labour. Although I don't fully understand the nuances of what's happening, the baby is coming early, and fast. The women gather and several of us are given jobs to do. It takes a while for the penny to drop, but I've been assigned to help with the birth. I'm stunned, as I have no experience of childbirth. At all. Not unless you count watching it on television hospital dramas, but even then I probably shut my eyes. Because of my travel career I have missed out on the pregnancies of friends and family, even those of my two younger sisters. Children seem miraculously to appear while I am away. Suddenly they are at school, going through their teens, getting married – and all of it has passed me by. I love children, but I haven't felt maternal. Not even the slightest ache. I rarely played with baby dolls as a child. I was too busy sketching butterflies, befriending beetles and adding to my pine-cone collection. While my friends were planning weddings and anticipating parenthood, I was stepping over tahr goats halfway up Himalayan mountains and avoiding saltwater crocs in the Australian bush. So, my suitability for a midwifery role? Well, I doubt I am up to the job. The tribal elders insist that I am. They clearly think my age is synonymous with experience, as it is in their culture.

With four other women I take a bath in the river, change into clean clothes, cut my fingernails and bind every strand of unruly hair up on the top of my head, tight. Strangely, I feel calm. I've done a good job of convincing myself that it will be like helping a cat deliver kittens. Natural, instinctive, requiring minimal fuss.

The mother-to-be, Leida, is a sweet girl of about seventeen. Her pale face peers out at me from behind an enormous, bloated belly that her tiny frame struggles to carry. New babies enter the world in the middle of nowhere all the time, I reason – although this one is premature. Because the other women have performed this role before, I step back to follow their lead. As she walks, Leida grabs at my arm, involuntarily almost, and I can see her whitened knuckles. Sweat is pouring down her cheeks and her chewed top lip is traced with blood.

Slowly, a female elder, the three other women and I help guide her to a sheltered clearing of soft tufted grass and pretty flowers. Leida assumes the squat position but almost topples over, she is so front-heavy. We steady her, she grasps my hand and sighs. No screams, no grimace. Just a slow, controlled succession of breaths. My palm holds hers tightly. Beneath her, a more or less clean towel awaits the arrival of her baby. There is a strange gush, like an emptying water bottle, and I am staring at a miniature body. A plum-sized head shot with dark hair reminds me of a prickly pear. One of the women cuts the cord, while another ties it with a strip of palm fibre that she shortens with her teeth. Intuitively, Leida lies down on her back so that the placenta can be delivered. At the instruction of the eldest woman, I join the mother, lying at her side. The baby boy is positioned across my chest so that his head is resting on his mother. She reclaims my hand, her palm hot and wet, and looks down to smile at her son.

Just like every other labour in the village on record, hers lasts for around four hours and is silent and peaceful, without a single scream or curse. The medicine man, happy not to have been called upon, rushes back to the village to relay the news. In a Western maternity unit this premature miracle of nature would have been pulled from his mother's breast for jabs and injections. In the jungle his first memories are centred on his mother and the glorious wonder of the natural world.

While Leida rests, her arms wrapped round her wrinkled offspring, I absorb the scene: it is so serene that it is almost biblical. Other than the occasional contented squawk or snuffle, all is quiet. With eyes screwed shut, tiny hands clenched into tight balls and chin upturned, the baby boy appears as small as a baby sparrow in a nest. Around him the orchids are a vivid yellow against the backdrop of glossy green trees. The eldest woman points to a regal-looking raptor perched on a bough and we gasp collectively at the auspicious symbolism of its presence as a divine connection with God. A yellowy owl butterfly flutters by: another symbol of hope and new life. We shriek in disbelief and delight. Amid the peachy fragrance of a sweet afternoon breeze, we draw together in an embrace and share a whispered prayer to Pachamama. 'Mother Earth, our home, our family. We love you, for giving us our lives.' We wipe away tears of joy. Closing my eyes, I feel every sense in my body tingle.

We help Leida and her baby son – now wrapped in a traditional palm-fibre scarf – back to the village. Less than two hours later, the new mother is washing clothes by the river. In my wildest dreams, I had never imagined that watching a woman giving birth could be so moving. So empowering. So peaceful. So free of fuss and drama. No intravenous drip, medical gowns, beeping monitors, austere hospital staff, elective caesarean or numbing pain relief. I have witnessed a magical part of nature, just as a cocoon bursts open, an egg cracks to reveal its chick, a seed sprouts a young, green shoot. Beautiful. Simple. Just like bringing life into the world should be.

Something stirred within me that day that never went away.

Mangroves and the Moonchild

Panama
2008

I feel better connected to womankind as a result of being around many inspirational females: they teach, mentor, effect social change, care with compassion; they are wise, funny and smart. Their no-messing, straight-talking critique of my personal life resonates with me somewhere deep down, haunting my dreams and troubling my subconscious with a nagging twinge of doubt. Yet my hopes of penetrating this tightly knit circle are only partially realised. However much I work alongside, interact with and spend time with them, I am always on the outside, peering in. A misunderstood creature from another land.

Before their divorce, when I was aged about seven, my parents scraped together enough money to buy a cheap and very old car – the first in my lifetime. As soon as it pulled up onto the drive, it opened up all sorts of possibilities. Occasionally, we'd leave Henlow's hedgehogs, moles and deer behind and visit my paternal grandparents on England's south-east coast. Here, I got the chance to explore unfamiliar sand-and-shingle terrain, hear the relentless screeching of gulls, discover the leathery grey-green leaves of sea kale and become a lifelong collector of seashells.

However, in a cruel twist of fate, it turned out that I, a would-be road warrior, suffered from chronic motion sickness (kinetosis) that prevented all early attempts to travel. I could fill a sick bag before our beloved Morris Minor Traveller had fully reversed out of the drive. The dizziness, nausea and relentless vomiting were debilitating – I later learnt that motion sickness is caused by a conflict between what the eyes see and what the balancing inner ears sense. My stomach would lurch and my head would whirl, be it on road, rail or sea. The violent sickness would last for hours and hours. There was nothing I could do except hunker down, face grey and sweaty, unable to move an inch. I would pray for the motion to stop, but when it did, I'd still be bedridden for days with a shaky queasiness and pounding head.

It felt so unfair. I despaired. I wailed. My parents encouraged me to try self-help techniques: fixing my eyes on the horizon; counting back from a hundred; using music as a distraction. It failed to make a jot of difference. Doctors suggested travel-sickness pills, but they just seemed to make me vomit more. Smelling salts, barley sugar, sitting on a sheet of brown paper – I tried them all. Ginger supplements, ginger biscuits and ginger tea helped, but only a little. Bracelets were ineffective.

On an ill-fated class excursion to the Natural History Museum in London, the coach had to stop over a dozen times because I was so sick, and we arrived home hours later than planned. A polite letter to my parents outlined the dilemma the school faced when considering my participation in future outings. I got the message. I wasn't welcome. So a decade of school trips and holidays passed me by.

Then, when I was seventeen, I discovered magnetic acupuncture therapy. A friend of a friend knew a guy who wanted a chance to unscramble my manic neural receptors. He stuck a few needles in me, used a set of magnetic pressure straps and, kapow, I was cured. At long last, a wide, wonderful world opened up to me. I was propelled onward, as if life had grabbed me by the scruff of the neck and given me back my purpose. Illusory voyages of pure fantasy became plans for great global adventures. I bought a rucksack and a few more maps and never looked back.

I arrive in Carti, in Kuna Yala, a few days after a funeral. The whole village is in a reflective mood: part celebratory, for the afterlife and the joys of reincarnation, yet also sombre about the emptiness that a passing leaves behind. I, too, feel troubled. It seems that my trip has been a wasted one. A harpy nest, parents and eaglet had been reported in Kuna Yala territory, but on my arrival nobody can provide any information. Its very existence is denied. All doors, metaphorically, are slammed in my face.

The autonomous home of the Kuna people stretches like a fraying scarf along Panama's Caribbean flank, a scattering of 400 coral islands and a skinny strip of coastline reaching from Colón Province to the outer fringes of the Darién. Often characterised as aloof and stern faced, the Kuna are fiercely protective of their identity, separating themselves from outsiders in order to minimise any dilution of, or influence upon, their culture.

Some of the pinprick islets are large enough to accommodate a handful of families, and one of these communities has been persuaded to let me stay, having taken part in the BBC2 documentary series *Tribe* – the experience was a positive one for the village, and helped pave the way for my arrival. It is my first experience in Panama of a fiercely matriarchal society. When my plane touches down on a patch of grass the size of a village green, my luggage is hauled out of the hold by a striking Kuna woman of advancing years and miniature stature who barely reaches my chest. With puckered skin of reddish-brown, her hair covered by a red-and-gold scarf, she bears the spirited expression and trim agility that I associate with Kuna women.

Short and stocky, with small hands and feet, the Kuna have eyes of soul-piercing intensity. They appear almost bottomless, as if they could swallow you whole. A Kuna gaze can draw you in with impelling magnetism, a commanding power that can just as easily push you away with a single, dismissive blink. These long-lived hunter-gatherers have fascinated nutritionists for some time, for they have no history of obesity, suffer from low levels of cardiovascular disease and cancer, and appear immune to anxiety and hypertension. Studies suggest that this is due to their high intake of fish and unprocessed carbohydrates, and to their outdoor life full of sunshine and exercise. From the Kuna, I have also learnt that a chocoholic life in my latter years may be medically beneficial, because the dark stuff not only soothes the soul but also sharpens the mind. They eat a lot of cacao, which is known to increase blood flow to the brain during problem solving, thanks to the antioxidant flavanol. There is no history of Alzheimer's Disease among the Kuna.

My home will be with Ada and her husband, a fisherman. Straight away, she lays down some ground rules. I am to be useful, make myself scarce at times of sacred ceremonies, wear modest clothing and leave the men alone. I must take on chores and work hard beside her and the other women, a level of immersion I am thrilled to take on. Kuna Yala's sisterhood is formidable. At barely five feet tall, the women are wiry and muscular, with nimble fingers that I swear could snap steel. Quietly spoken and conservative in nature, they care little for drama or theatrics. Blatant displays of emotion are frowned upon; raised voices and temper tantrums rare. A long, hard and petrifying stare is the usual way to convey anger in Kuna Yala. That, or vigorous sweeping.

Kuna women are rarely seen without a broom and a machete. They rise at sunrise to chop trees for firewood and harvest manioc and maize. They cut bamboo, prepare and cook all meals, wash clothes, keep their houses clean and care for the children. They also make all major decisions, manage commercial trade, handle community finances, and arrange the festivals and celebrations. The women own everything; run the society. And the men? They have a much more simple life. They fish at sunrise, make repairs to fishing nets and clean the wooden dugout canoes. Then they stay very much in the background for the rest of the day, lazing around in hammocks for hours before going out to hunt at night. By contrast, the women work all day, barely pausing to rest or eat. However early I rise in the morning, the women always beat me to it. I honestly wonder if these superwomen ever sleep at all.

Each community has a distinctly different character: some are warm and welcoming, others closed to outsiders. All are formed of low-level thatch-and-bamboo huts of a single room, behind an open porch. Here, a brewpot bubbles all day long over glowing logs, sending swirls of light grey smoke up into the sky. Meticulously cleared dusty pathways turn to slop after heavy rains, but form wide, flat 'pavements' around each 'neighbour-hood' – some are just a couple of families; others part of a community of thousands. Piles of chopped wood, neatly stacked, denote each family's cluster of homes. This is where the Kuna women stand, machetes by their sides, as they debate the price of coconuts – still a commonly used currency across the islands.

Under the guidance of Ada's mother, a twinkle-eyed elder of indeterminable age, I learn to stoke the fire so that it will only turn to ash at sundown. I gather firewood, prepare vegetables, and keep paths, communal areas and huts swept clean. Ada and I haul baskets loaded with clothes down to the river for washing, rubbing them over smooth stones and rinsing them in the tepid shallows.

In the late afternoon, it is time to hand-roll a batch of the long cigars that the Kuna smoke at festivals. They degrade rapidly in eastern Panama's high humidity, so they're made to order before each celebration by dexterous female volunteers. Cigar making requires a degree of artistry that looks easy in the hands of skilled craftsmen. Too gentle, and the cigar will be loose and floppy; too hard, and it will be overly tight. The women moisten tobacco leaves to make them supple enough for manipulation. They then delicately de-vein each leaf, tugging the stem away from the middle. The cigar roller places the filling – sun-baked flakes of tobacco crumbled between a strong thumb and forefinger – on the first wrapping leaf, handling it with care to avoid blemishes, and presses it together in her hands. She folds it over itself to form a cylinder, repeating the process until the whole cigar is wrapped, leaving a narrow passage through the centre to ensure a good draw. She then binds it together and snips off the end. The finished cigar has an earthy smell, like dried grass cuttings. About the length of a rolling pin and a little narrower than a cricket stump, it is designed for all-night puffing, wedged between two yellow-stained palms.

On one occasion I am allowed to lend a hand in the brewing of the Kuna's potent hooch: a lethal concoction with a pungent smell made from fermented maize. It is made early in the morning, usually before 5am, by a team of designated chicha masters. They chew woody stalks using liberal amounts of spittle – which nobody seems to mind – whose naturally occurring enzymes break down the starches, a similar method to that once used to make Japanese sake. The stalks are boiled in water, cooled and poured into large earthenware jars, then stored in a chicha house, with carved wooden dolls and burning incense of cacao beans placed around them to keep bad spirits away. After about two weeks, the mixture is fermented – news that spreads like wildfire from person to person throughout the village. By now the crude concoction is strong enough to stupefy an elephant within a few minutes.

Chicha isn't drunk for refreshment. It is consumed with the aim of getting totally and utterly slaughtered. Intoxication is part of Kuna culture at times of celebration: a Kuna proverb states that getting to know God comes only from getting drunk. In theory, the consumption of chicha follows a well-defined procedure: who drinks when, the shape of the cup and the number of cups consumed are governed by tradition. In practice, after a few hours, everyone is completely inebriated and has forgotten who, what, where and how.

At one of the Kuna's celebrations, big vats of chicha take centre stage, but I politely decline a swig. Nobody asks why, and I suspect the Kuna simply assume I'm a lightweight. In fact, I have abstained because I am a newly pledged teetotaller. My life has always involved lots of social drinking; it goes with the territory of being a journalist. And while I haven't necessarily always liked the way it tasted, I have always loved the way it makes me feel. First, the sweet bitterness on the lips, then a numbing effect on the inside of the mouth, before the liberating warm surge as the liquor floods the bloodstream, filling every vessel and spidery capillary with pleasure.

If the first mouthful of wine is ecstasy itself, the rest of the glass is sheer bliss. It frees me. Eases every tension. Channels my thoughts. Helps me glow. Makes the sun shine within. I gulped it down and life felt good. Really good. My work rate accelerated; a creative rush could go on for hours and hours. I'd write with passion, energy and freedom – and an emptying wine bottle by my side. Looking back, I don't know when my drinking changed. Or why. It just did. One day I was a nice, happy social drinker, content with a glass or two at the end of the day. I'd slug an ice-cold beer at an open-sided, thatched-topped beach bar or share a salt-rimmed jug of Margarita on a sunny day. But then, uncorking a bottle on a routine basis lost its life-feels-good euphoria. I realised I was ever chasing the next sip. Nothing beats crisp clarity when you've got a mind that feels like a jumbled puzzle waiting to be assembled. One morning, shaken by a truth bomb, I decided to stop. And I did. Forever.

My abstinence goes unnoticed by the women of Kuna Yala, who are supping the place dry, their wee, brown-skinned hands wrapped around pint-sized drinking vessels from which they guzzle on great gulps of chicha. I rather enjoy being an onlooker, and not a participant, as it allows me to witness the seismic personality change that alcohol brings about. Jeepers, it's crazy. Before my eyes, these stoic, steady mothers and grandmothers are wholly transformed. Some are bawdy, others argumentative, but most are lurching and swaying unsteadily and crashing into walls. A damson-cheeked woman attempts to tell me something but is unable to move her lips. Another is squawking like a chicken. Yet, even as their eyes roll backwards, they continue to insist that their cups be refilled. All protocols concerning serving size are now forgotten. There is no steady, measured pace of consumption, just a drunken free-for-all. By midnight, the scene is shambolic. Many of the women are unconscious on the dusty floor. It is a husband's job to pick up his booze-addled wife and swing her over his shoulders like a sack of maize to take her home. After an hour or two's slumber, the women awake, gummy mouthed, and haul themselves out of bed. They then stagger back to the party, squinting like moles, to start the drinking all over again.

I am allowed only partial access to the medicine man in the community, spending a morning learning more about the rituals surrounding pregnancy and labour. Strong similarities exist between the Emberá and Kuna women: the medicine man works closely with one or two women who act as midwives. Every day, he gathers fresh herbs and prepares a tincture for a pregnant woman to swallow. She is also given instructions on the foods she must avoid. Her husband is told not to eat, touch or handle certain things that could harm the baby, and warned to stay away from asphalt, glue and tree sap in case these keep the baby 'stuck' inside the mother's womb. Contact with sea urchins and sharp thorns is also believed to impede labour. Problems during delivery are often blamed on the carelessness of the man.

One thing that surprises me is the great lengths to which the Kuna go to shield their children from the realities of procreation. This is quite different to many other tribal cultures I've encountered. When a baby is born, a fairytale is told of its arrival courtesy of a dolphin. And although girls are taught a little about the facts of life during puberty rites, they are often spared the details and not encouraged to be sexually aware. Children are even kept away from birthing livestock and domestic animals.

At the birth itself men remain at a distance, including the father and tribal medics. In the event of complications, the medicine man is summoned to sing a special song invoking the spirits who preside over the creation of new life. If the baby is a girl, the news is greeted with great joy and merriment – the first in a series of celebrations that marks the life of a Kuna female. At about three months old, the baby girl's nose is pierced during the Ico Inna (needle festival), when she is adorned with the gold ring that she wears for the rest of her life. Gold is coveted in Kuna society and the female is likened to treasure.

If the newborn is a boy, the reaction is much more muted. Following the birth of a daughter, the father is allowed to leave the matrilineal household to set up home independently with his wife. But after the birth of a son the father has to remain at his in-laws' home and isn't granted full authority over his child until he can convince his father-in-law that he is ready for parenting rights. One husband, I was told, still hadn't attained this status several months after his baby boy was born because his daily haul of fish kept falling short of expectations. Divorce is uncommon, but it does happen. In contrast to the endless legal wrangling so often linked with the end of a Western marriage, however, the Kuna husband merely gathers up his clothes and moves out in order for the union to be annulled.

Kuna daughters, like their female elders, are highly prized for the competence and manpower they bring to the community. Without exception, every Kuna woman is extraordinary: I have yet to meet one that hasn't impressed me somehow. Ada's daughter,

Lina, for example, is a strong, confident and talented girl who, in typical Kuna style, combines robust fortitude with artistic creativity – the true definition of 'beauty' in her culture. Keen to make a mark on the world, she was determined to plough everything into her education. After persuading her parents to allow her to read business studies at a university in Panama City, she pushed herself forward for a scholarship. She secured it against all the odds, but before telling her parents, she asked for additional funding so that her travel expenses and books could be covered, too. When she couldn't raise the money for school bags and equipment, she contacted the manufacturers direct and urged them to sponsor her. Only then did she tell her parents.

We meet when she takes a break from her studies to visit her family. She is candid, funny and exceptionally bright: her company is enlightening. No other member of her family has ever left Kuna Yala. They have never seen a high-tech mega city, have no first-hand experience of eight-lane highways, know little of air pollution. Living on an island with no roads, they have never been in an automated vehicle, other than a canoe with an outboard engine, and have yet to experience a traffic jam. They have never surfed the Internet, held a mobile phone, used a television remote control or seen a movie at the cinema. By contrast, Lina speaks several languages other than her native Kuna and Spanish, and has high hopes of learning Japanese. '*Konnichiwa*,' she says, hoping, I suspect, that I am able to respond like a native of Tokyo. With uncertainty, I try '*Ohayo gozaimasu*,' a casual greeting that I've plucked out of the dim, distant back rooms of my brain. She shrieks with laughter, her smooth skin crinkling for a second and her eyes widening with delight. She is clearly thrilled at my willingness to join in the fun.

Although Lina is wearing the traditional dress of Kuna women, I can see traces of nail polish on her index finger. Her blouse, cut from beautiful printed fabric, has short, puffy sleeves and *mola* – multicoloured appliqué panels – set into the front and back. Her skirt, the *saburete*, is a mid-length rectangle of vivid blue-and-green fabric wrapped around the waist, and contrasts with the yellow-and-crimson head scarf (*muswe*) draped over her short, black, poker-straight hair. Long strands of orange, yellow and black beads (*wini*) are bound around the forearms and calves. In addition to the small ring through her nose, her ears, neck and fingers glisten with yellow gold. The sunburst stain of the annatto fruit highlights her high cheekbones, while an inky line from the *jagua* runs from her forehead to the tip of her nose. Tucked beneath the many strands of beads, I spot a neon-pink friendship bracelet: a concession to her modern student life buried beneath ancient Kuna traditions.

Over a jug of fresh papaya juice, we play a game of chess. She wins, easily. This girl is good enough to give Garry Kasparov a run for his money. 'Sarita, did you know that if you place a single grain of sand on a square of a chess board, then two in the next, and so forth, by the time you reach the last square on the board it contains more sand than there is on the whole of planet Earth?' She drops this in as she packs the pieces away. I fold the board. 'And, did you know that if you fold a piece of paper, about the same size as the chess board, in half one hundred times, it will end up 800,000 billion times the distance from the Earth to the Sun. In fact, just fifty folds in half would be about 100 million kilometres, which is about two thirds of the distance between the Sun and the Earth. Amazing, huh?'

Yes, it is.

I try to keep pace. 'OK, did you know that bacteria split into two every couple of hours, so if a single bacterium did this for two whole weeks it would weigh as much as the entire Milky Way galaxy?' I'm laughing, and so is she. 'More, Sarita. C'mon – another!'

'What about this? In 1943, the head of the American computer giant IBM, Thomas Watson, a brilliant salesman, anticipated that the world demand for computers would be five. Not even one per continent. He believed this would be enough to serve the world.' 'No, really? What about the salamander, and how it can grow a new tail,' she ventures. 'We are so very close to understanding how evolution has somehow "switched off" the regeneration gene in other species. Once we work out how to switch it back on, the human species may be able to regrow limbs. Imagine what it'll mean to land-mine victims, casualties of war and people hurt in industrial accidents?'

A tiny plane buzzing overhead catches Lina's eye. She stands up, pushes her scarf back onto her forehead and shields her eyes with one arm. With her other hand she waves up at it, face beaming – a recognition that she, too, will be leaving soon. Though a deeply patriotic Kuna, politically active and forthright in her opinions, she is already a woman with a bigger reach. One who has wriggled free from parochial life. Later that day, as we canoe between the gleaming, flag-strewn yachts that occasionally venture into Kuna Yala's clear blue waters from all over the globe, I sense her readiness to rejoin the world outside. Distance has given her the space to figure out what frustrates her about her homeland. First, she confides, while she applauds the entrepreneurial spirit of the Kuna people, she fears this will be their downfall. Everything has a price nowadays, even the natural world. For a quick buck we will trade it all away, she laments.

'We have lost almost fifty per cent of our wildlife in just a few decades,' she says. 'Our waters are almost empty, our jungles are almost bare and there are fewer birds in our skies. We have sold all of our sea cucumbers to the Japanese for sushi; our lobsters and coconuts go to the Colombians; our fish, shrimp and sea urchins are flown to Panama City in big iceboxes each morning. As a society that has its moral codes and religious beliefs bound up in sustaining Mother Nature, we should be facing this dilemma head on. We are not sustaining the very thing that holds us together. We are failing ourselves.'

Showing a care and appreciation for nature is a vital part of courting acceptance in Kuna Yala, because it knits into the very core of Kuna beliefs. That I share in this love, despite being an outsider from a polar-opposite world, connects us. The world is a dual civilisation to the Kuna, containing the 'world of spirit' and the 'world of subsistence'. The former surrounds and resides inside every material thing, underpinning the world of subsistence and giving it power. Spirits are believed to dwell in sanctuaries on rich, fertile land that isn't farmed but kept forested and intact. To violate these sanctuaries is to cause the spirits to rise up in rage and bring harm to the community.

To the Kuna, the Earth is the body of the Great Mother, who, in union with the Great Father, is the creator of all plant, animal and human life. The Great Mother instructs every living thing of its duties. For example, medicinal plants are given their role in curing illnesses and certain animals are told they are to be used by the Kuna for food. Trees are considered to be at the heart of all life: they renew their energy by taking up water through their roots and the Great Mother drinks their sap for strength. They protect the Kuna people, and provide health-giving cures and fruit for the animals. To exploit the trees of the forest would be to abuse the Great Mother, and Kuna beliefs expressly forbid this. They also insist that nature must be treated with respect, flattery and compromise, as if it were human. As a result, Kuna communities take from nature only what they need.

Ada and her daughter watch over and protect me. But the Kuna have learned to keep all potentially harmful intruders – me included – at arm's length. I attend community meetings, even though, so far, I can only utter the word for fish (*ua*). Outside the extended family I am rarely spoken to directly, and not just because I don't speak the Kuna language of my hosts. The younger generation can speak Spanish, but most wait until their elders are out of earshot. This is a mark of respect for those Kuna who fought the Spanish and the rest of Panama to protect their own culture and escape outside influences on religion, language and societal rules. Outsiders have continually sought to change the Kuna, to teach them new beliefs, strip them of their identities and get them to raise their young as Latino Catholics. I understand why they are guarded around me. The battle is still being fought.

The Kuna are no strangers to warring. When the Spanish arrived in the sixteenth century, the Kuna were living in what is now Colombia, only later did they move westward towards the land now known as Kuna Yala. After tensions with the conquistadors, they journeyed the thick, jungled Darién, where they fought with the Emberá. Although some Kuna remain in the Darién today, most continued onwards, finding respite in the fertile offshore Caribbean islands to the east of Panama. They remained a unified force against all efforts by the Panama Government to suppress their traditional customs. In a short-lived yet successful uprising in 1925 – the Tule Revolution – they proved themselves a force to be reckoned with. Led by

Chief Nele Kantule and supported by the American adventurer and part-time diplomat Richard Marsh, the revolt resulted in a treaty awarding the Kuna a degree of cultural autonomy, a greater political voice and designated land.

Social politics has a strong tradition in Kuna culture. Today, almost every tiny, palm-trimmed island is a separate Kuna community with its own political organisation. As important as politics and governance are the powerful oratories, spiritual songs and ancient stories of the Kuna people. Overseeing all of this is the *Saila*, a trusted community elder who recalls the legends and laws of the Kuna and administers political affairs. At meetings held in a *Onmaked Nega* (Congress House), the *Saila* chants, delivers sacred verse and recounts ancient parables. At the very top of the Kuna General Congress – made up of representatives from each community – are three *Saila Dummagan* (Great Sailas). Officially, the number of Kuna in Panama is recorded as 60,000, although this accounts for individuals and smaller, dispersed communities across the nation. Around fifty communities make up Kuna Yala itself, totalling about 35,000 people.

To journey around Kuna Yala is to witness a near perfect, almost cinematic vision of a paradise idyll. Flawless, luminescent beaches strung together with lush palms encapsulate every travel-brochure cliché. From the thatched-top hut (*palapa*) that Lina shares with her mother and father and two uncles we set off in a dugout canoe, entering narrow jungle channels overhung with trees filled with huge flocks of ibis. 'Don't make a sound,' she hisses. 'Otherwise it'll get really messy.' As instructed, I stay mute. It isn't until the return trip, later in the afternoon, when an engine backfires on a boat further along the river, that I realise why. The firecracker bang resonates across the water and surrounding jungle, propelling hundreds of terrified birds into the sky. Large flocks of airborne ibis can produce a heck of a lot of poop when frightened, and the scene soon resembles an explosion in a paint factory. Everything gets covered in a downpour of glossy white. Branches, leaves, palms and boughs are draped in oozing, oily slicks that have formed floating dollops on the surface of the river. It hangs from rocks and melds into mud in slow-moving, elongated white drips.

Thankfully, on this occasion, we have escaped the line of fire. The two Canadian fishermen in the boat ahead aren't so lucky. We watch them remove their faeces-splattered spectacles and sun hats and attempt to mop themselves clean of the fishy white deluge. Lina points at a big-beaked black bird in the distance – it looks like a great ani. She tells me they are known as 'naughty birds' in Kuna Yala and believed to be the reincarnation of nosy or interfering neighbours. As we laugh at this apt characterisation of such a bold, noisy bird, it joins in with raucous guttural gobbling.

Using a sharp, slender knife, Lina shows me how to cut strips of woody twine to rope palm fronds together – a valuable life skill on these islands, where almost every piece of household furniture, from sleeping mats to walls and roofing, relies on woven palms and string. We bundle up the fish we've caught by using the end of a pointed spear to prong them one by one. We pull up at many uninhabited islands – some are smaller than a football field – to escape the sun under tufted garnishes of coconut trees while watching a rainbow of fish in the Caribbean waters. We drink coconut water from fallen fruit while discussing the shrewd business acumen of the Kuna and the commercial policies that exist across the islands.

Each year the Kuna fix the price of coconuts and agree not to undercut one another. Coconuts are like gold to the Kuna. They use every part of the plant for cooking, eating, drinking, firewood, tools, household implements, building materials and shelter. Until the late 1990s they were the archipelago's official currency. Annual harvests of 25–30 million coconuts are not uncommon. Today the Kuna use them to barter with Colombian traders in preference to selling them to 'Panama' (as the Kuna refer to it in remote terms). In return, coconut merchants bring jars of coffee, canned goods, clothing and fuel to Kuna Yala each week, arriving in large, painted wooden schooners.

Just like the price of coconuts, the Kuna also settle on a charge for tourists entering each island community and pledge to protect their culture. As accomplished merchants, they are easily irked by anyone who tries to cheat them – the motivation for the famous charge made for taking photographs. A Kuna woman spotted a mass-produced postcard in a Panama City souvenir shop bearing her image and discovered that it had been sold to tourists from all over the world. She reasoned that someone was getting rich off the back of it, but it wasn't her. With the support of the Kuna General Congress, the woman fought successfully for compensation and a change in the law. Now, every photographed subject has the right to charge an on-the-spot fee before the lens cap comes off. It's usually a couple of dollars, but can be as much as ten.

Income generated by *mola* sales reinforces the islands' matrilineal status. The practice, which began in the early 1940s when a missionary purchased one as a souvenir, represents a vital part of the Kuna economy, and is a sector wholly reliant on its women. A trend for pitching for the tourist dollar on the largest islands, where cruise ships lay anchor, has seen new garish *mola* designs emerge, featuring Mickey Mouse, popular teen idols and pop stars. They're horribly tacky, but a mercantile triumph, and as self-determined economic success is highly prized in Kuna Yala, these modern interpretations of the islands' most famous souvenir are likely to continue.

Tourism makes up an important part of the Kuna GDP, together with the export of fish, coconuts and palm fibres to Colombia and the rest of Panama. The drug trade also passes through, providing occasional windfalls in abandoned cargo. In recent years, the narco-traffickers have scored some successes in persuading disillusioned Kuna youths to act as drug mules along the wilderness trails that connect Kuna territory to Panama City. The route is so established now that it is guarded by both the Panamanian and US Drug Enforcement Agencies. This is a source of great shame to the Kuna. To remind everyone, lest they forget, how important their heritage is to Kuna Yala's societal values, signs declare the following in Spanish and Kuna across the larger, populated isles: 'The people who lose their culture lose their soul.'

We paddle along a jungled stretch where the trees rustle noisily with monkeys. Lina slows her oar stroke, and I follow her lead. 'Look. There, Sarita,' she whispers, pointing into the leaves. 'Some of your cousins!' From the bushes several impish, creamy-pink faces peer through and stare at us. In Kuna Yala, these noisy capuchins are likened to sunburned gringos.

Mostly black with a yellow-white face, neck, throat, shoulders and upper arms tinged with a bright, blush-pink, the white-faced capuchin is the most savvy of monkeys. Living within large, mixed-gender troops of up to forty animals, it is distinctive for its use of herbal cures, rubbing certain forest plants, including vine leaves and citrus fruits, over its body, possibly as an anti-inflammatory agent or parasite repellent. Though diurnal and arboreal, the white-headed capuchin spends more time on the forest floor than many other New World monkeys, walking primarily on all four limbs. Females rarely stray from their social group, while males migrate to new social groups multiple times during their lifetimes – often every four years or so and in the company of other males who are kin.

Typically, troops occupy ranges that span up to eighty hectares. Where ranges overlap with those of other troops, aggressive encounters are common. Several non-primate animal species are known to follow troops of white-faced capuchins, such as common agoutis and white-lipped peccaries. If you look up into the sky whenever you see a white-headed capuchin troop you're also likely to spot several species of raptor that shadow them, too, such as white hawk, double-toothed kite and sharp-shinned hawk.

White-headed capuchins display remarkable adaptation to support their feeding habits, using branches and stones to smash mollusc shells and hard fruits, and throwing anything they can at predators or aggressors. They forage at all levels of the forest for fruit and insects, stripping bark off trees, searching through leaf litter and breaking dead tree branches. In Panama, they eat almost one hundred fruit species, testing everything for ripeness by smelling, tasting and prodding the flesh, then eating the pulp and juice and spitting out the seeds and fibres – they are important seed dispersers. Moths, butterflies, beetles, ants, wasps, caterpillars, flies and larvae make up the rest of their diet. They also prey on small mammals, frogs, birds and lizards.

Lina gestures to a pyramid of debris beneath the trees. It's a neat stack of crushed snail shells, thrown – with a high degree of accuracy - by snacking capuchins overhead. 'They're so clever! They've worked out that they can use twigs, or rocks, like a vice to hold the snails steady,' she explains. 'It's a way to ensure the tasty morsels don't roll away.' As several more creamy-pink faces poke out through the trees, the noise from the rest of the troop behind them is immense, the echoes of squeals, coughs, calls and barks ricocheting around the forest.

Shrieking, leaping and shaking branches, the white-faced capuchins are as easy to watch as a kids' television cartoon. They swing from bough to bough in a blur of black, white and pink. Then it happens. A couple of male capuchin monkeys settle onto a fallen tree and move towards each other. We assume they are going to fight, or groom. But no. One sticks a long, filthy finger deep into the other's eyeball, between the eyelid and the eye. I wince. My own eyes water. The capuchin's eyeball is almost popped out, yet it doesn't move away or resist. Deeper and deeper the finger probes, up to the knuckle. I can barely watch. Although I'd heard about this behaviour, I never expected it to be so brutal. Having observed it at first hand, albeit from a distance, I can confirm that it is one highly disturbing bit of monkey business.

The capuchin's eye-poking ritual is considered to reinforce the strength of fraternal bonds. It says: 'I trust you so much I'll let you poke your finger in my eye.' It nurtures faith and confirms allegiances within the group. It isn't a quick probe, either: these pain-inflicting tests can last around an hour. Risking one's eyesight to gain some sense of trust seems like a big gamble to me. But it is one the white-faced capuchins seem prepared to take.

We search for great ani, scouring the mid-height branches of the forests on the banks for glossy blue-black plumage and purplish tails. It's usual to hear these boisterous show-offs before spotting them, and as we approach a scrubby patch of old-growth trees, a chorus of megawatt cackles tells us 'we're over here'. Lina imparts a few more words of native Kuna (*Dule Gaya*), and by the end of the day, I've mastered a few basics. I have asked many of the small children staring quizzically at my pale, flabby face *Igi be nuga?* ('What's your name?'). Lina claps her hands with glee when I say thank you (*nuedi*) for my lunch.

While we paddle back around an arc-shaped bay, I ask Lina about 'moon children', the largely unseen population of white-skinned children born into Kuna families. Kuna Yala has the highest rate of albinism in the world, with an estimated seven out every one thousand births being a 'moon child' – so named according to the Kuna belief that an albino birth occurs after the pregnant mother is exposed to the moon. In Kuna legend, the spirits give albino children the responsibility of shooting arrows at the full moon. Since the moon controls the tide, and Kuna people live on small atolls, the presence of albinos is considered a gift from the gods to protect them from rising waters. The reality, of course, is one of genetics: intermarriage is a hangover from when tribal laws restricted movements between different villages. Albinos are often born with eye and skin complaints, a reason why, in centuries past, albino children were considered bad luck in the Western world. In Kuna culture, no such stigma exists: quite the opposite, in fact. In a conservative society in which individualism is frowned upon, albinos are a rare, accepted deviation from the norm.

'They are viewed as gifted, strong, artistic and blessed with wisdom,' Lina explains. 'They have a different life, one less physically connected with nature, because they are unable to bear the rays of the Great Sun.' A high proportion of albino children are boys, and they are raised very differently from their dark-skinned peers, trained in the ways of Kuna women. Away from sunlight, these yellow-haired, pink-eyed, pale-skinned boys spend their days sitting in the dark cool of the village, sewing *molas* and making handicrafts while the women suck and puff on old wooden pipes.

'Some of our ways seem archaic to outsiders,' Lina admits. 'For example, I wasn't actually given a name until I had my first period. My friends at college can't believe it. Before that, I was known by a nickname. My friends also see it as demeaning that I had to have my hair cut short when I reached puberty. But women don't have a reduced role in Kuna society – far from it. We no longer marry at fifteen years old. I mean, look at me!'

We discuss the Kuna psyche and how the variation in character throughout Kuna Yala reflects exposure to tourism. Around sixty-five per cent of Kuna Yala's island communities welcome visitors – the rest remain closed to outsiders – either to stay overnight in tourist accommodation or as day trippers. A small number are wholly tourist orientated, serving fast food, speaking English, and wearing jeans and baseball shirts. Others accept a limited number of visitors each year. Typically warm, polite and private, some Kuna have been deeply affected by the behaviour of the outsiders they've met. I mention incidences I've witnessed when there has been blatant disrespect for Kuna sensibilities on the part of cruise-ship passengers. She nods. 'It's true, it happens. Skimpy clothes cause offence and present a certain unfavourable image of outsiders to the Kuna, who, in turn, become cynical and disrespectful themselves. This often means that the Kuna people further tighten controls on the tourists they allow to visit.'

Like Ada and her daughter, many Kuna are curious to connect with foreigners and are candid and engaging. They want to know what visitors think of Kuna Yala, and are fascinated by the foods, houses and matrimonial habits of outsiders. Many enquire about world events, such as the global threat of terrorism. Others ask about religion and tradition. Unmarried women, like me, are always a great fascination. Singledom is an unknown concept: they simply cannot take it in.

With skilful ease, the naturally inquisitive Kuna women manage to shift the focus of our informal English-Spanish-Kuna exchanges, so I am hit with a hail of interrogative probes about my private life. No children? They are aghast. They became sexually active at puberty and gave birth soon after. They are grandmothers by the age of thirty-five. Unmarried? Some look alarmed enough to cry. Others are just baffled at my rejection. Surely there must be a man in the world who will take me. They are sad for my lonely future. No family close by? This shocks them. They simply cannot conceive of a life away from parents, siblings, cousins, uncles, aunties and grandparents. My life is unimaginable. It fills them with horror. It is empty, hollow and unfulfilled. To them, I have attained very little in my life: my career, my flat, my social life and the success I've achieved count for nothing. What is good about a life away from everyone who loves me? They shake their heads in disbelief, eyes full of pity.

When I tell Ada's women friends that in Western society women have children well into their forties, I watch the colour drain from their faces. 'Maybe I will ask my uncle to marry you,' one offers, gently rubbing her swollen belly as she stands up to stretch her back in an arc. 'He is a widower, and not a young man, but I am sure he will be sorry enough for you to do it.'

I smile with gratitude, not wanting to cause offence but hoping she will let the idea drop. I have heard of one Kuna union with an outsider, though it involved a French man marrying a female, which has different connotations to the prospect of a non-native woman in a matrilineal culture. As a Western woman, I am happy to leave the destiny of my private life to chance. In Kuna culture, boys are often earmarked as potential husbands before they reach the age of five. The friendship between the boy and the girl is nurtured by the parents, who then encourage a romance. Next, it is time for the much-hoped-for union to ensue – almost by its own accord, but not quite. These consensual agreements strengthen kinship ties by creating larger family units and bolster the strength of the community.

In tribal cultures such as this one, family obligations, often seen as nepotism by other cultures, are a unifying force. Families support one another in every way, providing kinship structures that glue society together. Key decisions are often made in consultation with the entire extended family group, which can be a complex multigenerational network of parents, siblings, grandparents, aunts, uncles and cousins, and include those who are unrelated through blood or marriage. Total and utter loyalty is expected, and freely given.

During the next few days, Lina takes me snorkelling in waters as warm as an Icelandic hot tub. The colours of the brain-patterned coral and parrot fish are so bright and gaudy that they look unreal at first, plastic even. One afternoon, as I'm helping her clean and sharpen her father's machete with a rock – one of the most important household chores – a large wooden boat inches noisily by, spewing dark sooty smoke behind it like a tail. 'More Colombians,' she utters. 'Making us feel we've got a good deal by leaving us a few jars of coffee and canned meat while they chop down half our trees.'

The Kuna aren't the only indigenous people to broadcast their close connection with nature, of course. The Emberá, the Wounaan and almost every other tribal culture I've encountered see themselves as an integral part of nature – not above it, or masters of it, somehow, like the Western world. On the Amazon border between Venezuela and Brazil once, I was heartened to hear a Yanomami boy, no more than eight or nine, talking about how every living thing is important in life's balance, be it an animal, human, body of water, rock, tree or plant. It seemed so mature, so enlightened. Then I remembered that, from birth, these children are taught that Mother Nature sustains them, and are warned that anything taken from nature must be replaced in some way. The belief that every part of the natural world has a spiritual counterpart somehow makes it relevant, real and personal. In contrast with the Western world, where children often lose their affinity with nature during their teenage years, in Kuna culture this is the age when the bond is strengthened. It's the same in Peru, where the importance of the jungle is part of the lifelong narrative that accompanies the Aymara people to the grave, and beyond. Their God of Life manifests itself through the mountains, the water, wind, sun, moon and *wa'qas* (sacred places), and the Aymara give offerings to protect the spirits of the family and community and the divinity of Pachamama (Mother Earth). In Guatemala, Costa Rica, Paraguay, Uruguay and Nicaragua, the biggest celebrations are those that honour the bountiful inheritance bestowed by Mother Earth and her sacred places. Festivals give thanks for the planting and the harvest, and involve rites to ask for rain and protection against extreme weather.

At the same time the imprint of climate change, set against these ancient celebrations of the landscape, is shaping the modern psyches of indigenous communities. The Anchorage Declaration, put together during the Indigenous Peoples' Global Summit on Climate Change in 2009, states: 'Mother Earth is no longer in a period of climate change, but in climate crisis. We therefore insist on an immediate end to the destruction and desecration of the elements of life.' Their reliance on the land – culturally, spiritually and physically – makes indigenous cultures across and beyond Latin America particularly vulnerable to climate change. The difficulties and opportunities it poses differ wildly from region to region. While tribal people in the Colombian Andes are worrying about thinning ice on the glaciers, communities in the Brazilian Amazon are contending with the loss of their rainforests. A Native American commentator phrased it poignantly at least four decades ago: 'Only when the last fish has been caught, only when the last tree has been cut down, only when the last river has been poisoned, only then will you understand you cannot eat your money.'

On the day that Lina is leaving to head back to Panama City, we rise early to watch the sunrise, slipping silently into the canoe to head to a small, crescent-shaped bay on a nearby deserted isle. We furrow through the navy-blue waters, watching the chalky sky above us take on a pearly-pink hue, our oars barely making a ripple. It's too early to natter, so we settle into a rhythmic paddle along a languid stretch dotted with islands. Wading through the bay's bath-warm waters reveals a sparkling broth of undersea riches: hundreds of colourful, needle-thin fish dart around my feet. It is then that the bombshell falls, literally, from the sky, sending plumes of powder-fine sand into the air. We can't be one hundred per cent sure what it is, but it is wrapped in sheets of thick plastic and bound with orange twine. At a guess, it probably weighed at least ten kilos. Before the plane can double back, we jump back into the kayak, deserting the most beautiful islands I have ever seen and leaving an ugly secret behind.

It seems wrong even to mention it. So I don't.

Shapes and Stones

Colombia
2007–2010

As I step inside the shadow cast by a giant stone monolith, I am reminded of life's great final exit. Tombstones, funerary chambers, graves and statues tower over my head. A palpable spiritual energy almost crackles in the hazy heat. Without morbidity or sadness, I am sharing in the passing of others, the final phase of an earthly existence. Death holds no fear here. I am comforted by the essence o f a thousand souls around me. I consider the outcome for my own mortal body and imagine the peace and joy of a departure into the afterlife. This ancient, sacred place celebrates the passing from one world to another. And the living of a life before.

My decision to see the world as an independent traveller suited the loner in me perfectly. It never occurred to me to seek the safety and companionship of a group – something that surprises me now. Wouldn't I have had doubts about my ability to travel alone? Apparently not. Being free of the constraints and distractions of other people felt utterly liberating. For the first time in my life, I didn't have to please anyone other than myself. I didn't need to compromise or accommodate anyone else's personality or priorities.
    My early travels didn't involve wandering far off the main tourist drag. I booked the most ambitious trip I could afford: a

round-the-world ticket taking me to New Zealand, Australia and America's east, west and southern coasts, followed by Japan, Singapore, Paris and Iceland. I'd snapped up the ticket from a bucket shop and had just days to board the plane, stuffing too many things into an oversized case – I had a lot to learn about packing. A melancholy sun was on the rise as the plane took off, its bright optimism matching my own joy and elation.

I soon discovered that I liked to get up bright and early. As an egg-yolk sunshine rose up in the sky, I'd be out and about before the air was too hot, discovering weird and wonderful wildlife that would often have disappeared by 9am. Other guests in the hotels I stayed in would hit the breakfast buffet, having missed all the action. Initially, I was travelling to cover ground, escape, see the new, encounter the bizarre and stick another pin in the map, but this would slowly alter over time.

During my travels around Australia, I stayed at an avocado and garlic farm on the Gold Coast and helped look after rescue horses in return for a few weeks' B&B. By the time I reached hot and sticky Darwin at the northernmost tip of Australia, I'd volunteered at a wildlife reserve that was home to water monitors, freshwater crocodiles, wallabies, cormorants and pelicans. I'd also done a short stint at a Perth-based rehab shelter for injured kangaroos, wallabies, possums and echidnas. In Darwin, I helped out as a tour guide's assistant on hikes around the UNESCO World Heritage-listed Kakadu National Park. I ferried water coolers and picnic supplies to meeting points within its 19,000-square-kilometre expanse, lugging huge backpacks along rainforest trails to boulder-strewn streams and waterfalls.

These early moves away from mainstream travel would change how I journeyed forever. When I arrived in Japan, I secured unpaid work teaching English via a contact in Tokyo's expat community. It opened several doors to me and I enjoyed the kind curiosity and hospitality of a family keen to learn about England. From America, I sent my first written dispatches to travel editors in the UK. By the time I arrived in Paris, my notebook was full of scribbled reminders of my incredible adventures and friends I'd made.

I booked further trips almost immediately I reached home. I chose familiar places – in Europe, mainly – but chose to experience them in a different way. In recognition of the buzz I

Left: This distinctive aqua-green former US military tower, set in spectacular rainforest on the outskirts of Panama City, is hailed 'Bird Central' by visiting birders.

Below: The Bocas del Toro archipelago. This group of scattered islands in the Caribbean Sea in north-west Panama is famous for its button-sized frogs, each isle home to a frog of a distinct colour – my favourite is the strawberry frog on Isla Bastimentos.

Above: A stunning roadside view en route to the Azuelo Peninsula in Panama.

Right: A great companion, inspiration, Central American guiding legend and friend: Hernan Arauz.

Below: I spotted numerous species of monkey in the Darién, from Panamanian night monkeys, Geoffroy's and brown-headed spider monkeys, to the very rare Guatemalan black howler.

Above: With a couple of Emberá children at the helm, we explored the creeper-clad rivers and rustling knots of jungle around Mogue village.

Right: Strong, wiry, fearless, astute, and with a penetrating stare, the Kuna women are formidable.

Below: In Kuna Yala the wooden homes are built close together in family units, neatly divided by broad, well-swept, mud-packed paths that are punctuated by piles of chopped firewood.

Above: When a baby girl is born into Kuna Yala's matriarchal society entire communities gather in unison to celebrate. As she grows this girl will learn that creativity, strength and fastidiousness are highly valued by the womenfolk around her.

Left: Reddish quartz tinges the rocky freshwater creeks in parts of the Darién – a burst of unexpected colour in this otherworldly jungle terrain of a zillion different shades of green.

Above: Waiting for fresh, homemade tamales at a family-run Colombian roadside eatery wher[e] chickens sat on the tables and customers ate from trays on the floor.

Below: Though its name means honey, the coastal settlement of La Miel, close to the Colomb[ia] border, has witnessed its fair share of violence. So all is not sweet.

Above: Misty mountains form a dramatic backdrop to the trail to Alto del Duende in the Colombian Andes.

Bellow: Worldwide there are 40 species of toucan. They are everywhere in the Amazon and seem not to fear humans, often hopping down to noisily say hello. None are louder than those on Panama's Isla Popa.

Above: Bedraggled and soaked to the skin: me with the white-rafting guys on the bird-filled riverbanks of the Panama–Costa Rica border.

Above: Almost everyone on Isla Bastimentos in Panama's Bocas del Toro archipelago relies on the Caribbean Sea for sustenance. The word 'Panamá' means 'an abundance of fish' and this is particularly true in this important National Marine Park.

got from pushing myself to do things that alarmed or scared me, I went bungee jumping and sea kayaking, and undertook gruelling mountain hikes. I'd been a reluctant participant in sports as a child, so I was astounded at my newfound enthusiasm for strenuous challenges. My confidence grew as I filled my passport with stamps. I walked taller, got smarter, felt more humble and had a calmer, clearer mind. I could hold a basic conservation in several languages. I ate foreign food and had a grasp of alien cultures. I felt as light as a feather, unencumbered, vital and alive – and the happiest I had ever been.

Like a red-necked phalarope – a rare European breeding bird that migrates thousands of miles west from the UK to the Pacific Ocean – I would start planning escapes to the warm, sunny tropics as soon as British temperatures began to plummet. My mammoth annual migration took me on a similar route to that of the little phalarope: from the UK, I'd fly across the Atlantic via Europe, head south down the eastern seaboard of the US, journey across the Caribbean and North America, to end up on the jungle-hemmed South American coast. Once I'd overwintered on good food and amazing landscapes, feeling the pulse of salsa music and the golden beams of the sun, I'd wait for my seasonal cue and head back to England, a contented long-distance migrant on the home stretch.

When I first heard of shape-shifting, while in the jungles of Peru, I held a typical westernised view. It brought to mind images of werewolves and cat people from B-movies. I laughed it off, deeming it preposterous, illogical and disturbing. From what I could tell, it wasn't supported by sensible evidence-based science or sound reasoning. While thousands of cultures embrace the idea of shape-shifting, mine isn't one of them. And that was enough to decry it.

However, I was forced to face the possible existence of shape-shifting when my Peruvian wildlife guide – a kind and healthy, fit young father with a loving wife and child – disappeared one evening 'to become an anaconda'. Abimael wasn't a radical given to extremes or theatrics. He was an ultra-conservative man of traditional family values. Yet he simply vanished, leaving everything he owned or cared about behind. Perhaps, I reasoned, it was time to consider the topic properly, without derision, in an attempt to understand what it is and what it does (or doesn't) do.

In my gut, of course, my feeling was that he had simply 'gone away', for reasons unknown – to start a new life with another woman, perhaps. Or just to escape the life that he had. But both those possibilities seemed out of character. And there were other things that didn't add up. For a start, his pretty young wife accepted his account, explaining to me, as best she could in broken Spanish, that her husband was now a snake. Secondly, Abimael took care to place all of his possessions neatly on a chair before he disappeared. I saw them, in an orderly pile: his only clothes, belt, machete, boots, penknife and hat. Thirdly, his wife was heavily pregnant with a second child. His two-year-old firstborn – a cherry-faced son with a halo of downy hair – was crawling around her tiny feet.

At the time that he disappeared, Abimael had been guiding me for several weeks, working reliably and diligently to a daily routine that rarely varied. That is, until he shifted his human form into that of a serpent. I was left with many questions and nobody to answer them. Weeks later, while I was waiting in a mile-long queue on the Peru-Brazil border for the frontier bus, I chewed it all over. By chance, in the same line of people, there was a student of anthropology, archaeology, history and heritage studies. Gareth, an Australian with a strong scholarly interest in aboriginal cultures, chatted easily about his year in South and Central America. When I asked what would cause a grown man with everything to live for to vanish, he gave me some advice.

'Suspend every belief and every assumption Sarah. Your Western sensibilities count for nothing with this one. Accept that stuff just happens that you can't believe and will never understand. The Western world doesn't have all the answers. Some things are outside of our realm.'

For weeks I ruminated on this, see-sawing from one explanation to another. I asked my friend Alejo if he could arrange for me to meet a community for whom shape-shifting was common practice. With a well-connected family, he secured all the right introductions – that's pretty much the way things work in South and Central America – securing me a visit to meet Huitoto hunters in a small, newly established settlement on the outskirts of the cattle-ranching cowboy country of Los Llanos.

Los Llanos – meaning 'the flat plains' – sprawls to the east of the Andes in north-west Colombia and into Venezuela. Seasonally flooded lowlands cover more than fifty per cent of the country's total landmass, and as I drive out of Bogota it's not long before I feel as though I'm heading to a rodeo. Rolling prairies lie dotted with large ranches and horse-stud farms, with undulating grassland that is home to vast droves of cattle. Corralling, roping, ranging and lassoing are all-important skills to the Llaneros (plains-people), who live proud, hard, macho lives dedicated to cattle-rearing from the cradle to the grave.

The German explorer Nicolas Federmann (1505–1542) discovered the great grassy plains in 1536, during his search for the legendary lost city of El Dorado. However, Los Llanos wasn't settled until a small group of formidable horsemen decided to try taming the land in the 1840s. They moved from villages in eastern Bogotá to establish a rural outpost, snapping up pockets of land offered by the government for free to tempt them in. The entire stretch known as Los Llanos forms a gentle, elongated curve that sweeps north-easterly from the foothills of the Andes along the Orinoco river, before dispersing into a river delta of swamp forests and coastal mangroves as it approaches the Atlantic. This single eco region, an area of extensive grassland covered mainly by savanna vegetation, includes dramatic alluvial plains and scenic highlands.

Like folkloric heartlands all over the world, Los Llanos has a romantic charm that stems from the rugged earthiness of its people and its landscape. Unlike the dramatic chequerboard of topographical textures across the rest of Venezuela and Colombia, the region is characterised by a never-ending series of rolling pea-green meadows and mysterious sloping forests interspersed by skinny country roads. The plains are home to more than 100 mammal species and at least 700 species of bird – roughly the same number as found in the entire United States – as well as thousands of insects, fish and reptiles. One is among the most critically endangered reptiles on the planet: the endemic Orinoco crocodile, a whopper that can reach around seven metres long.

There is no better way to explore and watch the wildlife than in the saddle. After negotiating the loan of a couple of chestnut-brown steeds, Alejo and I spend a full day on horseback, journeying the raw beauty of Los Llanos like locals. We both relish the opportunity to roam free in the saddle, enjoying the proud, dependable companionship that only a horse can bring. An age-old equine tradition is evident at every turn, from the farriers who drink in the kerbside bars to the many breeders that own ranches on the plains. Alejo, an experienced rider full of easy confidence, charges ahead in a turf-churning cowboy canter. As a 'Pony Club' rider schooled in the formal style of Britain's Home Counties, I always feel liberated to ride so loose. Without hat or riding crop, I tear across juicy green pasture, hair wild and flowing, before my horse and I pick our way carefully down stone-scattered valley paths steeped in demonic legends. Screeching raptors evoke the cries of the broken hearted, as a heavenly glow bathes the hilltops in a warm, buttery gold.

The highly developed horse culture of Los Llanos is born out of the centuries-old riding culture of Spain. Horseback riders gave the Spanish conquistadors great advantages in warfare over the local tribal people, but once they acquired horses themselves in the late sixteenth century, the indigenous people were harder to overrun. Llaneros rarely gallop unless there's a problem. The style is mellow, with reins held loosely in one hand. Then, ever so slowly – in keeping with the national pace of life – man and horse pass from field to forest at a gentle roll, wading through streams and climbing slopes to reach great herds of cattle. Llaneros measure distances uniquely, in terms of the time it takes to smoke a cigarette. Strangely, it is a pretty exact measurement. Occasionally, the horse will decide upon a five-minute detour to sniff out something lively in longer, grassier patches.

According to local lore, friendships blossom and love grows in the saddle, where language, age and culture form no barrier to a shared physical pursuit. With Alejo and his charge back by my side, I trot out to the chiselled foothills of a perfectly sculpted peak that mirrors the knotty scrawls on our hand-drawn map. In recent decades Llanero ballads have become cherished for their raw emotion by Colombians nationwide – everyone seems to have a favourite. Alejo's voice carries across the grassy terrain as he breaks into song:

I was born in this shore
  of the vibrant Arauca
I am brother of the river foam,
  of the herons, of the roses and of the sun
I was lulled by the lively reveille
  of the breeze in the palm trees
And that is why I have the soul
  like the delicate soul of the crystal
I love, I cry, I sing, I dream
  of carnations of passion
I love, I cry, I sing, I dream
  to ornate the fair mane from the colt of my lover
I was born in this shore
  of the vibrant Arauca
I am brother of the river foam,
  of the herons, of the roses and of the sun.

From a grassy slope, I survey the landscape: it looks a bit like an unmade bed draped with an oversized green duvet full of folds, furrows and undulating mounds. On this textured scenery, every isolated woodland draws the eye, together with the thin strips of jungle that edge the marshes, rivers and streams. We chart a course across a grassy expanse bathed in orange sunlight. I have never seen light like it, but if it were captured in oils or watercolours, I am sure the artist would be chided for an outlandish choice of hue.

The capital of Los Llanos is the town of Villavicencio, where saloon bars, saddle makers and cowboy-boot cobblers rub shoulders with kerbside restaurants grilling man-sized slabs of beef. Though it is not unaccustomed to welcoming migrants, Villavicencio seems a strange place to find a community of Huitoto people. Los Llanos has no surviving indigenous tribes, so it has 'adopted' a small community from one of South America's largest indigenous groups. The Huitoto hail from deep in the Peruvian Amazon, along the snaking green-black Ampiyacu river. Skilled craftsmen, they have a long tradition of making masks and carving rattles and blowguns. Like the other tribes living along tributaries of the Amazon, they fish by day from wooden boats and gather fruits, nuts and seeds, and hunt peccary, monkey and wild pig at night.

When I meet the Huitoto, they are clearly experiencing a culture shock, having moved from the dense, creeper-clad jungles of the Amazon basin to the wide, grassy spaces of Los Llanos, where cows and horses are more important than canoes. 'Everything is new and strange: the music, the language, the food, the culture and the societal values,' says community elder Santiago Kuetgaje. 'There are no cars or roads in the Amazon. Imagine! In Villavicencio there are three rush hours each day.'

Like many of the hundred or so indigenous tribes of the Amazon, the Huitoto have suffered persecution at the hands of government officials, who have made forceful attempts to eradicate their tribal identity and culture. Exhausting battles have been fought, won and lost to protect the Huitoto costume and language. When the Huitoto were systematically bullied out of town by rubber barons, oil companies and drug-trafficking guerrillas, the police and government officials refused to get involved. In a last-ditch plea, Santiago decided to speak out on Peruvian local radio – a high-risk strategy, which was followed by death threats. So he and around twenty Huitoto companions fled in darkness to settle in Los Llanos, securing US$22,000 support from the Corporación Andina de Fomento (Andean Development Corporation) to establish a new home. Today the community incorporates an education facility that anyone can visit to learn more about the Huitoto's patriarchal culture, ethos and traditions, and to better understand what caused the Huitoto population to plummet from 50,000 to 5,000.

The Huitoto believe that they emerged from the Earth with tails, thanks to their god, Jitoma. A bee removed their tails with its sting, and the Huitoto tribe were born. According to legend the Huitoto went to wash in a lake, where they saw an anaconda. Hungry, the Indians killed the snake, cutting it into four. This signifies the birth of the tribe's four dialects.

In a damp wooden hut the size of a bus shelter, Santiago opens with a bit of background. Shape-shifting doesn't appear to rely on a specific pantheon of gods, because it occurs across many disparate cultures. There are few hard-set rules, and several different types of shape-shifting. Westerners can, with the right programming, shape-shift too, he insists. At the heart of the

Huitoto's beliefs is the 'human-nature' connection known as 'El Mambeo', when the men, collectively, ingest a paste made from ground coca. Considered the 'female' energy in the Huitoto version of yin and yang, the coca is counterbalanced by the 'male' energy of tobacco in thick black jelly form, consumed from a small earthenware pot with a small toothpick. This is part of the grounding, the strengthening of the connection with nature, that is a vital part of shape-shifting.

Santiago explains that to shape-shift successfully, people need simply to learn how to interact with the spirit world. Shape-shifting changes our form, partially or completely, when we achieve a higher level of consciousness. To be successful, one must also feel a strong affinity with Mother Nature and all of her creations. Whatever bestial form you choose to shape-shift into, it will manifest in the same way. I confess to being unsure whether I'm capable of a higher level of consciousness, not because I have already reached a lofty height, but because I may be spiritually limited.

'Pah!' It's an idea he won't accept. 'Everyone wants knowledge and spiritual enrichment, even if they don't know it. They form the bedrock of every culture throughout the world since the beginning of time. Your problem is, as a human, you haven't disconnected yourself from the rest of creation. But you are part of it, never forget this. You are an animal, plant, rock, wind, fire or tree.'

So, I venture. We can take on whatever shape we want to: animal and non-animal. What power does it give us?

'It isn't as one-dimensional as you see it,' Santiago counters with some frustration. 'Because you may not need, or want, to shape-shift entirely on a physical level. You may prefer to acquire the wisdom, skills, psyche and acumen, but not take on the form.' This type of 'dream-time' energy level is a sort of 'astral realm', he continues, meaning that a different state of consciousness has been achieved for the purpose of learning, self-development and personal growth. 'This is usually done to help the wider community, and is still shape-shifting, but it involves assuming a form from within.'

I nod. That last bit makes sense.

A man sitting beside Santiago, with straggly jet-black hair and a thin, handsome face, introduces himself as Salvador before interjecting with a question. 'Sara, tell me. Have you ever wondered what it is like to be a puma, a giant oak tree, a morning wind, an ocean, a fire or an eagle?'

My eyes light up.

An eagle? 'Yes, I have.'

Taking both my hands into his, Salvador looks me squarely in the eyes. His pupils search mine.

'In order to free your state of mind, Sara, put aside all you have learned in Western society. Only by doing so, and attaining a real belief and mental control, will you be able to shape-shift spontaneously into an eagle's form. It's a form of self hypnosis, a subliminal power. A higher force.'

Aha. So, my brain is hijacked by negative energy that has control of my instincts and emotions? I am already possessed? I don't have full control over my mind and strength of will? To shape-shift, I need to regain control?

'Yes!' He leaps up as he cries out, his hair flopping over his face like a damp mop.

'Shape-shifters change their energy to match their chosen animal, but often their shape-shifted form is in a parallel world to their own. They can sense them, "feel" them, but normally don't actually "become" them. A bit like a ghost in Western lore.'

Right. So these shifts don't have an effect on the physical body? Meaning that I probably won't encounter Abimael in the mangroves by the Orinoco river as a fifteen-foot anaconda?

Possibly not, he concedes.

'A person may not always entirely shed their human mind for an animal one – especially if they are shifting to a prey, not a predator.'

My head is spinning as I gather my notes, a dull ache spreading across my frontal lobe.

'So,' I ask. 'How do I practise?'

Grounding myself properly first is absolutely crucial, Santiago stresses, as I must gather up every drop of energy to funnel back into myself. I need to feel the energy around me, in me and all over me. It may help to imagine a circle of bright light, he suggests. Once the light is there before me, clearly in my mind, I should draw it in. Then, imagine long, twisting roots reaching deep down into the earth. And breathe. While in a fully relaxed state, I should focus on my chosen animal, he says. First, I should see it. Then, I should concentrate on how it feels. Next, I should centre on its personality, characteristics and the colour of its wings or fur. Then feel the animal taking over me: its instincts, behaviour and thoughts.

'Feel the limbs. Feel the paws. Feel the sharp talons. Shed your human self. Conjure up the smell, sounds of the animal. Become it. Become the animal. Do what the animal wills!'

Wild gestures and animated expressions give Salvador a shaggy-haired intensity. With fresh sweat bobbled on his forehead, he stands to pace the freshly swept clearing.

Over the next hour or so, I learn that shedding your animal to return to the human side simply requires a reverse of the process. One assumes human characteristics and leaves the primal, animalistic energies behind – an adjustment that can take time to perfect. Again, with practice, this metamorphosis and altered state becomes much more fluid and soft.

Santiago advises me to start off slowly, to choose a beautiful woodland or meadow, where I feel safe. Then I should work on becoming part of the trees, the waterfall and the rocks. This would allow me to become accustomed to the new perspective. He doesn't recommend that I jump straight in to incarnate myself into one of the world's most powerful and fearsome birds of prey. So I will need to leave shifting into a harpy eagle for another day.

Human reasoning and logic are no help when attempting to understand shape-shifting as a topic. I keep an open mind about beliefs that centre on us as multidimensional beings, and on the many inexplicable and mysterious things that fall outside our accepted natural laws. Yet something fundamental within me makes me scrutinise every notion. And fear prevents me from altering my 'natural' state. It does, however, occur to me that if more humans shape-shifted there would be a richer, fuller and stronger affinity for the natural world, one that could guarantee its future. Nature would, I assume, no longer be in trouble if it was so valued. Shifting could be a unifying force involving every location, age, language and gender, every religious, philosophical and cultural preference.

I've never considered myself an animist, but the natural world certainly possesses a tangible, spiritual essence. In all the indigenous cultures I've encountered, stories of humans descending from animals are a common thread, woven through the generations and richly entwined in the fabric of modern life. In fact, most, quite sensibly, question whether their human form or the animalistic one is the altered state? The Emberá believe in invisible forces called *jai*, which manifest as animals. Other life-giving energies come from beings that inhabit the water or the forest. According to the Kuna, the world was created by an octopus, while the Huitoto owe a debt of gratitude to a bumblebee. To them, there is no gulf between human and animal kingdoms; they are seen as spiritual companions. Tribes and individuals adopt totems – animals whose power and knowledge could serve as sources of strength, insight and renewal. And in stories, myths and dreams, animals share secrets about the magic and mystery of life.

The idea that there is a separation between the spiritual and physical world and between all souls, both animal and non-animal – plants, rocks, trees, mountains, rivers, thunder, wind and shadows – is unthinkable in many of South and Central America's indigenous tribes. This absolute and total integration with the environment is at the forefront of every philosophy. Even hunters who don't practise shape-shifting as part of their culture routinely engage in behaviour that mirrors and mimics the characteristics of their prey. And I have yet to meet an indigenous person who doesn't believe that all parts of the natural world are deserving of equal levels of respect.

As I leave, the Huitoto men gather to pray that the spirit of the jaguar will allow them a good hunt that night. The indigenous Arikapú in Brazil, Mayans in Guatemala and Mexico, Chango in Chile, Kogi in Colombia, Guaraní in Paraguay, Miskito in Honduras, Hupda in Brazil and Shuar people in Ecuador all use shape-shifting to hone their hunting skills. By taking on the fearless stealth, cunning, agility and predatory urges of a jaguar, for example, they are able to move soundlessly through jungle in order to stalk in leafy shadows before executing a perfect deadly pounce. By the time I leave, the men are wide-eyed, wild-haired and dishevelled – the result, I assume, of overindulgence in El Mambeo and its coca paste. I can see no resemblance, spiritual or physical, to the sleek, killer feline of the group's chosen animalistic form.

I wish Santiago and his men well, as we swap telephone numbers. 'We feel hunted ourselves, Sarita,' he admits, his eyes empty and dark. 'It's good for us here. New, different, but good. Our sad and turbulent history is the past now. Soon all the stories we tell will be happy ones.'

That night, I can't resist the urge to imagine stepping outside my human form into a harpy eagle. Closing my eyes, draining every last bit of energy from around me to ensure that my own reservoir is full to the brim, I allow myself to become aware of the eyes, the wings and the heart of the harpy. As my mind calms and my breathing deepens, my stomach rumbles loudly: a reminder that a harpy eagle is a carnivorous predator with a blade-like, angular bill and a ready appetite for the flesh of opossums, sloths and iguanas. Then the shape-shifting theory propounded by the former BBC sports presenter and conspiracy theorist David Icke – who believes the world is ruled by lizards in human form – fills my head, and I become nervous of my astral levels. For now, the mysteries of shape-shifting will have to remain just that. I never see Abimael again, and neither does his family. And the harpy eagle, in all its spiritual manifestations, remains elusive, for now at least.

Should I ever be asked to choose a piece of ground in which to be laid to rest, I would like to think I would opt for somewhere as a resplendent as San Agustín. To be here, amid lush jungle in vibrant emerald hues, surrounded by birdsong, is to be in heaven on Earth. This ethereal, soul-stirring and prayerful place, the site of South America's largest group of religious monuments and megalithic sculptures, is almost 600 kilometres from Colombia's capital Bogotá, but, spiritually, it is in another dimension. There is great emotional comfort to be found within these serene and consecrated grounds in the imposing Colombian Massif of the south-western Andes mountains. For here, against a backdrop of meadowy carpets and wild horses, lie canyons, funerary chambers, etched boulders and giant standing stones among lush foliage and billow-petalled scarlet blooms. Dating back to an ancient civilisation, this elaborate graveyard holds a million mysteries. To walk around the tombs is to wonder about one's own earthly life. There is no sense of its shortness. Life feels eternal in these archaeological treasure troves: bigger than time. It feels good to reflect on the momentous and to ponder the prelude to the life that lies ahead – for these ancient peoples surely viewed death as a stepping stone; a bridge between the womb and the afterlife.

Recollection, as a writer, is an approximate science. Yet, without even closing my eyes, I can transport myself effortlessly back to San Agustín. The taste of the pure Andean air, spritzed with mist; the musty smell of the old grey stones; the bright blue crowns of the endemic indigo-capped hummingbirds that dance among the fruiting foliage; the teasing frog-like croaks of the blue-beaked wattled guans that perch in the tallest hardwoods. A quick tot-up suggests I've been to San Agustín as many as ten times, yet I never tire of visiting this extraordinary site. Like Britain's Stonehenge, the Sphinx of Egypt and the Nazca Lines in Peru, it is one of the world's great ancient wonders. Each time I put a foot here it bestows rewards. I always depart understanding something new. Sorority. Perspective. Life. Death. And a sense of my own mortality.

Set in about eighty hectares, this collection of more than a hundred sculpted stones and catacombs confounds the experts. Most say that they date from the second century AD, although this is based on hunch, not fact. What is known has been drawn from Olmec sites in Mexico and Hopi sites in North America, where similar elements suggest a possible shared character. Carvings on the stones, or the position or style of the stones themselves, appear to symbolise themes of continuity: of birth and life and eventual departure from Earth. Motifs – both human and beast – range from the grotesque to the eye-pleasing, and are a mix of primitive and more sophisticated designs. Some have been dated to the tenth century AD – tombs, small temples, sculptures and anthropomorphic figures – suggesting that the site has been added to over many thousands of years.

My first visit, in 2002, took place when the park was still officially off limits due to guerrilla violence. Since then considerable work has been done to offer greater protection to this UNESCO World Heritage Site, after a spell of grave robbing during Colombia's worst decades of unrest. Strolling the paths around the monuments, I tune into the wild speculation and scientific guesswork of passers-by. Many visitors attempt to unravel the secrets of San Agustín and the extinct cultures that created the carved stones. The best-selling Swiss author and broadcaster Erik Von Daniken created quite a local stir with his theory. His controversial ideas about intergalactic influences on early human culture and ancient-astronaut hypothesis has led to claims that the stones were positioned by an extraterrestrial force.

After several months in large cities, it feels good to be in a tiny forgotten corner. San Agustín could well become one of the most visited archaeological sites on the planet during my lifetime, so I am determined to enjoy its unspoilt natural beauty, and undisturbed wildlife, while it is still relatively unknown. Two-wheeled carts drawn by horses remain a popular mode of transport here. As I sit on a roadside bench, I count half a dozen such horse-pulled jalopies in various states of disrepair among vendors selling mouthfuls of strong coffee in miniature polystyrene cups. As the plaza clock strikes nine, a van pulls up and a friendly face grins at me through the glass. I grin back, downing the dregs of my coffee. My walk around the archaeological site will be all the better for having Marino with me again. His brain is stuffed with all sorts of local knowledge, and facts and figures about the origins, designs and structures of the stones.

Marino is a leading guide in San Agustín, where he was born and raised. Now in his early fifties (at my rough guess), he is a man whose life took an unexpected twist thanks to the kindness of strangers. As a booking clerk at one of his home town's first hotels twenty years ago, he would greet guests as they arrived at the reception desk and wish that he could speak their tongues. He came from a large family with very little money, and had received the scantest schooling. One day, a couple from America – regulars at the hotel – offered to pay the fees to put him through university in Bogotá. He set off to join the capital's eight million residents, a battered suitcase in his hand. It contained a change of clothes, a couple of books and some pastries – the few comforts that could be spared from home. Struggling to cope with the traffic, noise and crime of the big city, Marino was dreadfully homesick and counted off each day until he'd see his beloved bird-filled slopes again. Four years later, after graduating in languages with honours, he travelled straight home. Now fluent in German, Italian and English, he runs his own tour-guiding business, and absorbs every fact and snippet of news about the

archaeological provenance of his patch. He always has something
new to offer. Today is no exception.

First, he tells me, great news: a scientist is arriving from Europe
to conduct fresh studies on the 'Double Self'. Apparently, this
striking statue of conjoined heads represents a dual soul of male
and female elements, and could have some real significance in
regard to the ancient shamanic powers of this civilisation. Second,
Marino has something to show me, leading me up by my arm to
a raised mound. 'Look!' He points to a vast, etched stone depicting
a large anthropomorphic figure – it looks as if it has a child in its
grasp. 'See, a harpy eagle!'

The short, stubby wings and elaborate double crest lack
intricate detail, of course, but the eagle – albeit in an exaggerated
and macabre etched design – is definitely a harpy. 'Power and the
political hierarchy,' Marino offers by way of interpretation. 'This
ancient civilisation, born thousands of years before you, Sarita,
was as fascinated and humbled by the power of the harpy eagle as
you are today. Incredible, huh?'

As I stand on this sacred land, a place of spiritual pilgrimage
and divine worship, I marvel at the carved towers that soar above
me, some more than four metres high and weighing several
tonnes. Hewn, by hand, from mammoth blocks of tuff and
volcanic rock to protect the tombs, sarcophagi and burial sites,
they are imposing. Crude mocking features; exponents of pain;
warmth; love and rebirth – all are recurring themes.

Among the trees, at an area known as La Fuente de Lavapatas
(the foot-washing fountain), Marino and I lean over the side of a
bamboo bridge to appreciate the sophistication of this beautifully
decorated ceremonial bathing site. Carved intricately into a large
area of stone, the result is quite unlike anything found anywhere
else on Earth. Water flows across a maze of channels and pools in
a representation of the journey of life. The cycle of existence,
glorified in etchings, standing stones and monuments, is magni-
ficently depicted in a sloping, tree-shrouded basin. One thing
flows into another, just like life itself. Splashes, trickles and rivers
of water run down from the source. My spirits drop when I look
onto the rock and see how faint the carvings appear, worn almost
smooth by the watery trickle over many millennia. I can't help

but wonder why sections that have survived for thousands of years are ageing so rapidly now, year on year.

Thankfully the standing stones nearby, set deep into the footings of the stream bed, are faring better. Cleared of moss, these phallic towers still bear their lizard, snake, salamander, iguana, toad, chameleon and turtle motifs with great clarity. We huff and puff our way up to a magnificent statue-guarded crypt to soak up views that stretch forever across velvety slopes, and are rewarded with sightings of a beautiful fasciated antshrike foraging mid-canopy, utterly visible, its blood-red, beady iris staring out from the leaves and its slender body striped with narrow monochrome bars.

Marino has booked me into the best hotel in San Agustín, the Finca el Cielo, located on a winding road about three kilometres from the centre of town. Mesmerising views over the cordilleras of the Andes from this family-run bamboo farmhouse take my breath away. It's prettier than any place I've stayed in locally, with its flower-filled gardens and working farm edged by terraced coffee and sugar-cane fields. After befriending the resident yellow Labrador, noisy rooster, several fussy hens and a handful of ducks, I take a closer look at the birds tucked in the trees, hidden in the hedgerows, soaring in the skies and perched on fenceposts. Nobody can accurately name them, and I am never able to pinpoint the species in the field guide, but these large, mocking birds with nut-brown feathers and an ear-splitting caw laughed like drains all day long.

The owner of the lodge, Luz, is an enthusiastic artisan who treats guests like long-lost friends. When a troupe of travelling musicians stays en route to play the main stage at San Agustín's annual fair, the hotel transforms into a family fiesta. The band members enjoy themselves so much, propping up the hotel bar, that they stay up all night, grabbing their instruments from their rooms to play Colombian classics until the cockerel crows.

San Agustín is surrounded by a contrasting hotchpotch of vege-tation zones on one of the longest mountain ranges on Earth. Stretching more than 7,000 kilometres along the west coast of South America, the rutted spines, velvety folds, scrubby peaks and rounded curves of the Andes pass through seven nations: Argentina, Bolivia, Chile, Colombia, Ecuador, Peru and Venezuela (if you are listing them A to Z). A backbone in both spiritual and topographical terms, they shape the culture, character and psyche of a large segment of South America. The highest mountain range outside Asia, twice the length of the Himalayas, the Andes forms a barrier between the Pacific Ocean to the east and the rest of the continent. It is a major force in controlling the climatic disparities of the entire region, from the hot, steamy lowlands and humid rainforests close to the equator to the frozen plains nearer to the Antarctic.

Most people map the soaring peaks of the Andes into three natural regions: the southern, central and northern. In the northern part (Venezuela, Colombia and Ecuador), the climate is typically rainy and warm. Central Andes is extremely arid and includes Peru and Bolivia, as well as the Atacama Desert in northern Chile; the eastern portion of the central Andes is much wetter. The southern Andes (Chile and Argentina) are rainy and cool. Many thousands of mountain rivers, lakes and streams have their headwaters in the Andes, where glacial meltwater, a result of climate change, contributes to the flow running from the mountains into the ocean. Studies suggest that glaciers above 5,400 metres will lose mass but survive because temperatures will remain relatively cool. But those at lower elevations seem doomed to disappear, having shrunk dramatically over the past two decades. In 2013 scientific surveys confirmed that fifty-seven per cent of the glacier mass of the Colombian Andes has been lost so far. Glaciers are receding so rapidly that the Andean nations are losing between three and five per cent each year. Should this trend continue there will be no snow-capped mountains left in the Colombian Andes by 2045.

One chilly morning Marino and I take a scenic road trip to the remote, cloud-topped Andean village of Tierradentro, where he has arranged for us to climb down into the catacombs to see drawings on the walls. From the fogged-up window of our rattling minivan, we marvel at the plants thriving in this unique place. On some of the vast, open panoramas the slopes look like naive paintings, their lower sections covered by dark, pointy trees and their upper portions clad in sponge-like vegetation and grasses. In the tropical Andes, the treeline occurs at around 3,200 to 3,500 metres. In the dustier, drier, Pacific-facing south the woodlands are small patches. Here, in Colombia, the wetter high-Andean mountain formation (páramo) is characterised by cloud forest (*selva nublada*) and a staggering array of vascular plant species – more than 1,200 at the last count.

The Andean region is a major conservation headache because it faces many problems in each of its seven host nations. The clearing of land – both legally and illicitly – for agricultural pasture, and the wide-scale burning associated with cattle husbandry, are the greatest threats. Coffee, rice, sugar cane and soy grow at elevations below 6,500 feet, but rely on water from higher elevations, areas already under increasing pressure from expanding populations. At higher altitudes, the planting of potato crops and other root vegetables is common. Increasingly cloud forest in the most remote areas is being used to grow marijuana, coca for cocaine and opium poppy for heroin. So far, expensive attempts over several decades to control the drug crops through toxic spraying by light aircraft have had minimal success. The drug supply has been unaffected, but the chemical deluge has killed livestock, made children sick and decimated the natural ecosystems of the Andes.

'You know, the Andean forests are among the most threatened of all tropical forest vegetations,' Marino says, gloomily, as we climb out of the van to stretch our legs. 'In Colombia, for example, less than ten per cent of the Andean forests remain intact.' He adds that although areas of relatively intact forest remain on the eastern slopes of the Andes in Ecuador, Peru and Bolivia, all three countries have active road-building programmes that rely on massive amounts of forest clearance. Shivering, I pull the zip of my coat up to my chin and huddle down into my thick, woolly scarf. It is bitterly cold now, and with a damp, bone-chilling wind, it feels a lot like winter in the Scottish Highlands. No wonder the serious outdoor clothing brands test their gear out here. My chest is being battered by a headwind, rods of rain are pummelling my face sideways, and my toes are numb. Yet nothing can detract from the rich plant life all around: tall grasses, small shrubs, stunted trees and a colourful profusion of wild flowers are set against the pea-green misty canvas of the Andes. Some must be extraordinarily hardy to survive at high elevations. Others, in the driest plains, allow moisture to run down their leaves to form natural reserves at their bases. Many remain small to conserve energy. In harsh winds and severe frosts, only the stiffest leaves survive. Grasses and flowering cacti sprout in every size and shape: Marino points out some that reach six metres tall.

He climbs down into a grassy gully to the crazy-looking plant that Colombians believe resembles a hooded monk: *frailejón*, a triffid-sized groundsel plant named after a friar with a narrow head and unruly sprouting hair. As one of the strangest plants in the Andes, it can grow to three metres tall and has a pompom of soft, furry leaves on top. Strangely, in such a wind-beaten landscape, *frailejón* doesn't have a very extensive root system and is relatively easy to up-end. Equally odd-looking is cojines (meaning 'cushions'), a sponge-like plant that spreads across large stretches of land. It creates sweeps of lumpy ground cover that can be hard enough to jump on or mushy enough to sink into. Weird and wonderful nature at its most peculiar.

Blowing on our hands and rubbing them together, we climb back into the van and flick the heater onto full blast. It squeaks a mournful tune as we wind our way through low marshmallow clouds. 'So many amazing species have a home here,' Marino says. 'Flamingo, Andean flicker, condor, hillstar hummingbird. Oh, and the mountain lion, llamas, giant toad, iguana and spectacled bear. Incredible, Sara, isn't it? In-cred-ee-bal. The Andean iguana is one of just a few lizards in the world that don't need warm weather. All this, plus hundreds of volcanoes and many of South America's most important cities. The Andes is a world all of its own.'

The facts and figures of the Andes mountains are incredibly impressive. More than 700 kilometres across at their widest point, they average a height of around 4,000 metres and contain vast quantities of copper, silver and gold. They are home to 30,000 plant species and 600 known mammal species, more than 1,700 bird species, 600 reptiles and 400 species of fish. With globally significant biodiversity levels, the central and western cordilleras of the Colombian Andes support several species that exist nowhere else. More than half of the amphibian species found in the Colombian Andes are endangered.

A sudden stream of brilliant sunshine makes me blink. I unravel and discard my scarf, pulling my sunglasses out of my backpack.

Smiling at the warmth, I tilt my head, leaning back into my seat and pointing my chin towards the sky. Weather wise, even a minute in the Andes is a long time, with bubbling pewter clouds on a milky sky magically metamorphosing into a sun of marigold hues. It is amazing to feel my body thaw.

So far, after a whole morning's driving, we have yet to see another human soul. We have passed a few domesticated llamas and alpacas, their ears twitching on high alert, startled by the engine noise. Other than that only the rockiest stretches have yielded wildlife, with roadside boulders alive with bouncing viscachas – long-eared, rabbit-like rodents. They scamper around like crazed lunatics, heads bobbing up from the top of rocks or from under cracks and crevices. Some make a mad, last-minute dash across the road in front of us, and Marino curses as he repeatedly tugs at the wheel.

It is then that we spot it, gliding serenely high above, its giant wingspan sending an oversized shadow across the pale rocks. '*¡Dios mio!*' Marino exclaims in a sharp intake of breath, pushing the door open and jumping out of his seat before the van has had time to stop. 'My God, yes!' he whispers, for fear of repelling it with human sound. With its ten-foot wingspread, there is no mistaking the commanding presence of the Andean condor: a majestic species that the whole South American continent holds dear. One of the largest flying birds on the planet, it nests at altitudes of at least 4,000 metres and lives for up to seventy years. Indigenous tribes across the Andes have long considered it a messenger of the gods and harbinger of good fortune. Condors are often depicted on pre-Colombian pottery and in cave drawings, including the thousand-years-old crypts of Tierradentro.

Marino and I crouch down behind buttermilk-coloured rocks and press our scopes to our eyes. We are rewarded with a magnificent swoop, the condor's giant black wings fully extended to reveal grey-white underwing patches. Like me, it is sunning, warming its body through after the cold temperatures of the morning and courting the rays to reshape the wind-bent tips of its feathers. It soars directly above us, held steady by a thermal current, treating us to an unbeatable view of the white ruff around the base of its neck. Its face looks tiny compared with its robust body, and isn't particularly attractive, with mottled deep-pink bare skin and a fleshy caruncle on the top of its head. But the strong, dark grey bill is handsome and imposing, with a whitish hook that runs to ivory at the tip. He is silently watching us; we are silently watching him. It feels amazing to be eyeballing the largest raptor on Earth.

The Andean condor can soar like this, effortlessly, for several hours. The species can cover great distances for food, travelling up to 250 kilometres per day. Pinpointing potential food with a keen eye before landing, it is well adapted for feeding on carrion: its bald head, with very few feathers, is easily stuck into rotting carcasses. Sharp bills and talons help it to tear muscles and viscera through the skin. When it has eaten enough, it cleans its head by scraping it along the ground. Storing energy and fat reserves is important to its survival. Once it has eaten, it can wait several days until the next meal.

'Do they have a call?' I ask, wondering what I should listen for.

'Not really, Sara. Just a strange hissing sound like a sneeze or a wheeze. They are mainly silent, but may become more vocal during the breeding season.'

Unlike the harpy eagle, the Andean condor doesn't build a nest. It lays a single egg on a bare cliff ledge or rocky nook, which offers the egg and chick more safety because it is hard for predators to reach. Numbers of Andean condor have been allowed steadily to decline for decades – an unforgivable situation that initially attracted little Government intervention. At one time it could be found along the entire western coast of South America, from Venezuela to the tip of Patagonia. Today, it is restricted to the higher peaks of the Andes, from western Venezuela to Tierra del Fuego in Chile, and can also be seen sometimes on the coast in Peru and Chile. In the early 1990s more than seventy captive-reared Andean condors were released in the Colombian region to help re-establish populations in protected habitat. Fitted with wing tags and wing-mounted radio transmitters, many are believed to survive, and some have also since raised their own offspring, substantially increasing the wild population.

Colombia's national bird was placed on the Endangered Species list in 1973 and remains in danger of becoming extinct. Makers of folkloric potions have boiled and crushed Condors' beaks and feet to make their traditional brews. The birds fall victim to high-voltage power lines and misguided farmers and peasants, who poison or shoot them because they think they prey on live animals. In fact, condors eat only carrion and aren't predatory, an important message that Fundación ProAves, Colombia's premier bird-conservation organisation, is keen to reinforce. Marino explains that it hires a grassroots conservation army of 'condor guards', whose job it is to teach the local population about condor natural history and conservation. 'There are all sorts of myths, such as condors snatching young children,' he says, despairingly. 'Hopefully, these old wives' tales will die out over time.'

'Wow,' I exclaim with a beaming smile, as we climb back in the van and head to Inza to see the second most important archaeological site in Colombia. 'That was amazing. Now all I need to see is an Andean bear. Is there any way you can arrange that?!'

Tierradentro, in Colombia's north-eastern Cauca region, may just rank as the least-visited UNESCO World Heritage Site in the world. Tucked off the beaten track in an area famous for the niche coffee harvested by a small population of indigenous Paeces people, it is accessible only via crumbling, unmade roads that are under constant threat of floods. Horses still outnumber cars here, so when we pass a broken-down truck on an isolated loose-stone stretch, we stop to lend a hand. Our van is full, but the two young Paeces girls jump up onto the roof rack, giggling each time we hit a bump on the slow slog into Tierradentro. The numerous landslides we pass are fresh and recent, but haven't blocked the road.

Arriving at nightfall, we haul the girls down from the roof and check into the area's most upscale hotel, the family-run Albergue el Refugio. The building is bright and well laid out, but the mood is dark and sombre, as if someone has snuffed every candle and dimmed every lamp. Everyone I encounter looks at me with eyes half closed, as if willing me to evaporate. Dragging my luggage to my room, I hear weeping from an office. By the time I have walked a couple of steps, the tears have become body-wracking sobs. The owners, I learn, are mourning their teenage daughter, who died last week. Now it all makes sense.

Death, like ageing, is unavoidable. The sad passing of this stranger preys on my mind all night. I hear someone outside in the courtyard, offering condolences: 'Nature never repeats herself, and the possibilities of one human soul will never be found in another.' It swirls around in my head before eventually I drift off to the sound of gently thudding rainfall. As I anticipate tomorrow's visit to the dead, I vow to live for the living. For I owe it to those who die so young to live every kind of life I can.

A tiny dot on the slopes of Andean foothills, the village of Tierradentro is extremely easy to overlook. Yet here, amid soaring green peaks and Paeces settlements, are underground chambers dating from the sixth century AD. Monuments, statues and underground tombs spread across several kilometres reveal a complex and elaborate pre-Hispanic culture. Many of the shaft tombs carved out of the volcanic tuff served as burial grounds for elite groups; some have decorated pilasters and columns. They are like nothing I have seen before, daubed expertly with browny-red and black dye in geometric styles across ceilings and walls. Marino draws my attention to the layout: there is a symbolic symmetry between these houses for the dead with the houses of the living above ground. It evokes a powerful image of how closely the living world and the afterlife were aligned. For the first time ever, I realise that I am closer to death than I am to the day I was born.

The artwork on these subterranean chambers must have taken months to complete. If only the British would anticipate death and plan for it in such a magnificent way. Crouching in the gloom, I feel a palpable sense of ancient history among crumbling rock covered in half-moon symbols, lizards and faces. Some of the crypts are topped with vast, rounded stones rising out of the ground, others with totem-like towers or flat, table-top structures. Credible theories emerge each year about how the stones arrived here. Some weigh upwards of five or six tonnes and would have taken considerable force to move. Many were excavated below mountain ridges on rocky plateaus. The sheer magnitude of the construction work involved, and the tools required to carve, build and decorate the chambers, indicates a sophisticated hierarchical society with priestly rituals and burial rites.

We ease ourselves back out of the crypts with great care, musing on why the catacombs face west and sharing wild guesses about the looting of the ethnographic treasures and where the artefacts might be today. While we trek down a waterlogged trail into the valley towards Alto del Duende, an isolated but impressive tomb site, whose name means 'spirit on high', Marino explains that what we have seen is just the tip of the iceberg. 'Hundreds of tombs have been discovered so far,' he says, sweeping his arms out broadly towards the misty Andean peaks. 'But thousands lie undiscovered out there.'

Changing into wet-weather gear for the third time that day, we cast our eyes down to the drizzle-hazed wild flower meadows that form a spongy carpet in the foothills below us. A small child is leading a brown mare and her foal along a leafy trail. He is singing loudly, a sweet song that praises the rich fertility of the volcanic Andes for ensuring that he and his horses will never go hungry. Showers of dandelion-yellow butterflies fill the air as his voice echoes across the valleys. It takes days for his angelic vocals to leave my head.

With my backpack stuffed with ten kilos of ground coffee from a small producer on Tierradentro's tufted slopes, I wave goodbye to Inza. It is time to head to the sultry Caribbean resort town of Santa Marta to meet the Andes once more: this time on the slopes of the Sierra Nevada de Santa Marta.

Minca, where a population of 600 people eke out a living from coffee and birds, is one of South America's best-kept wildlife secrets. I have promised myself a trip here for some time. Another treat is spending a rare few hours in the company of a Kogi tribesman: Minca is one of the few places on Earth where this is possible. As my jeep winds up the steep, rucked road from Santa Marta, the temperature cools by a good ten to fifteen degrees.

Minca's bushy, cool forests are home to hundreds of bird species. More than seventy migrants make the journey to Minca from the US and Canada. Talk is rarely of raptors when I meet birders along the way – although there are red-tailed hawks, common nighthawks and many others in the area's highest reaches. No, it is the charm of the many endemics in Minca's quiet forests that captures birders' hearts: the chattering Santa Marta warbler, Santa Marta sabrewing,

Santa Marta woodstar, Santa Marta antpitta, the stolid Santa Marta bush-tyrant, the screeching Santa Marta parakeet, Santa Marta tapaculo and Santa Marta wren – to name a few. Due to its rugged isolation and towering peaks, Minca has at least nineteen endemic species, as well as more than seventy subspecies. It is a birders' Shangri-La.

On lower ground there's a long list of 'must-sees'. With minimal effort I meet a white-tailed starfrontlet sitting at shoulder height in the leafy elbow of a branch, resplendent in glittering turquoise and emerald-green hues. I've been told there are good numbers of cinnamon flycatcher, black-hooded thrush, blue-capped tanager and emerald toucanet – just running this list through my brain makes me giggle. Despite my best efforts to remain resolutely un-twitchy, I appear to be growing more 'birdy' with each trip. My mind flashes back to the Canopy Tower in Panama, where I'd roll my eyes in sheer frustration at the squawks of disagreement from overwrought hardcore birders. While they were ruffling their feathers about which tree to shin up, where to place a strategic ladder and what sort of binoculars would work best, I was actually watching the birds.

Guides from the indigenous Kogi tribes have a great affinity with the birdlife of the Sierra Nevada de Santa Marta. They live in splendid isolation high up in the mountains, where huge boulders, gushing rivers and sparkling freshwater whirlpools are found in lands that were once used for ceremonial rituals. Today, the Kogi's consecrated ground is further up the slopes, so scenic spots such as the Arimaka waterfall have become accessible to visitors keen to swim. As I'm readying myself for a dip, I spot a beautiful rufous-breasted hermit hummingbird in bushes delicately scattered with mint-green butterflies. From the water, I watch a legion of leafcutter ants marching determinedly along the rocks carrying bright green leaves.

My guide, a small, crinkle-faced man with kind eyes and a tatty blue baseball cap pulled down over shoulder-length hair, cups his hands and scoops up some of the gloop gathered in small reservoirs beside the deep, cool pools. He smears it on his wrist, slathering it on and massaging it in plentiful dollops. Puzzled, I shoot him a questioning look and he tells me to try it. 'It's an elixir for health, wealth, youth and longevity,' he laughs, cackling like a rooster.

According to local legend, this nutrient-laden clay is a deeply penetrating therapeutic cure for all manner of ills. It's rich in living organisms. I know this because I can feel the wriggle of live invertebrates as I smother it onto my face. The Kogi use it to heal, purify and deep cleanse, mixing it with the purest spring water. Infections are treated with it, too, and a generous coating can help drain a congested lymphatic system. After ten minutes or so I scrape off the gunge and splash my cheeks with river water: my skin feels soft and silky. 'Ha! Marilyn Monroe!' my guide exclaims mischievously. He says to call him Hermano (brother).

The Kogi people, whose name means 'jaguar' in the indigenous Chibchan language, believe they are guardians of life on Earth. Through mind power and meditation, they keep the world in balance. The landscape will provide them with everything they need, as long as they ensure it thrives and survives. They rely on Andean plants for every part of their lives: food (they consume thirty-two plant species); health (they use eighty-one for medicine); houses (they use forty-four in construction); clothing (they use twelve for dyes); and culture (they use thirty-six mythologically). Curative traditions are staunchly upheld, yet the Kogi don't hold onto the past for the sake of it. New discoveries are incorporated into an extensive healing repertoire, and old remedies are continually updated to ensure relevance to modern health conditions.

Their lives are led according to a simple, nature-led rulebook. Achieving and maintaining peace with nature is the nexus of everything they believe. At the heart of this is the 'Great Mother', the ancient Kogi creator figure. The Kogi civilisation (the Elder Brother) distinguishes itself from the modern world (Younger Brother). Wearing white robes to symbolise the purity of nature and the Earth, the Kogi consider that in every respect the health, life and well-being of the Earth should be paramount. By them, it is considered a living, breathing being. From birth, they are taught to support the balance of harmony in the natural world, because anything else would be detrimental to the Great Mother's health, weakening her, leaving her vulnerable and sick. These deeply spiritual people worship a holy mountain they call Gonawindua (topographically Pico Cristóbal Colón) a sacred land that they consider the 'heart of the world'.

When Hermano realises we share Spanish as a language, the conversation flows. He is typically curious about my life. First, he asks about snowmen and snowballs. He hasn't touched any, he says, but he can see the distant white frosting on the upper peaks of the Sierra Nevada most months of the year. Is it as cold and wet as they say it is? Does it taste sweet? He then asks me about the Spanish and if I have been to Spain. As a proud Kogi, he is keen to remind me that his ancestors suffered no brutal persecution at the hands of the Spaniards. Today, he says, the Kogi are growing in reputation for their outspoken views on conservation. Collectively, they have issued strong warnings about the dangers of money making at a cost to nature, allowed a BBC film crew to broadcast their ecological message – despite their deep mistrust of cameras – and predicted catastrophes unless the Great Mother's children help change the world for the better. It frustrates them that their voice has no resonance with the world.

'We're foolish if we trash our own beautiful back yard,' he says with sadness, his eyelids drooping, face clouding and lips tightening. From an overhanging bough the iridescent flash of a vivid green kingfisher colours the air before my eyes, diving into the river in a torpedo swoop. Further along the trail I spot seven keel-billed toucans in a single tree. Then we hit the jackpot. A black solitary eagle circles above us, scouring the forest floor for prey from the skies. Hermano points to a clump of tall trees in the distance, where there's a makeshift platform of sticks and leaves. A nest! I can just about hear the eaglet's thin, sorrowful cries. It is almost certainly just one chick. The male black solitary eagle's distinctive white central band and tail-tip help us train our eyes on his sleek, charcoal silhouette. From a distance he looks like a great black hawk, but as he loops towards us the flinty-grey of his plumage catches the light. Hermano and I nod at each other knowingly. What we've seen is a perfect reminder of how lucky we are and how wonderful nature is.

Fish Man and the Floods

The Amazon (Colombia, Brazil and Peru) and Costa Rica 2006–2010

With tears stinging my cheeks, I ran distraught to my parents as fast as my five-year-old legs would allow. In my chubby hand was the sweet-smelling posy of wild flowers I'd gathered that morning for my mother. I'd plucked them from the roadside, where, against all odds, they had sprouted up between the broken slabs. I'd shrieked at the sight of each burst of brilliant colour. But now, the sunny, upturned face of the daisy was wilted and forlorn, splayed into a soggy jumble of slackened stems. The dandelion and buttercup, once both proudly erect, sagged limply. In a few short hours, I had witnessed the swift passage from life to death. My father, ever the pragmatist, provided the perfect solution. I learnt how to press flowers, carefully wrapping them in folded newspapers and wedging them under the hall carpet. Unwrapping them a fortnight later — dry, paper-thin and delicately lace-like — was always a revelation. My eyes would widen in wonderment as I studied each petal, bud and leaf. My little mouth would gape and I'd feel as if I could burst with joy. This Sarah was full of innocent, heartfelt glee.

And it is this Sarah that I rediscover three long decades later: a beautiful and poignant reconnection with a part of myself that I thought I'd lost forever.

'He's coming, he's coming!' The children scream as loud as their lungs will allow them. 'Fish Man is coming!' There are hundreds of us at the riverside, all waiting patiently where the rainforest offers up shade. Some of the onlookers have walked for several hours through the Amazon jungle, braving heat, bugs, wild animals and thorny trails to reach the river in time. They are sitting on their haunches, eyes fixed upstream in anticipation, swatting away persistent flies with leafy twigs. At the shrieks of the children we all shoot upright, stretching and loosening the parts of our bodies that are complaining the most. Noise ripples through the crowds, like a Mexican wave. The expectation is immense.

Then I catch sight of Fish Man – the guy who has battled piranhas, crocodiles and exhaustion to become the first person to swim the entire length of the Amazon. He is a curious sight, submerged in the murky depths of the world's largest river wearing a ladies' wide-brimmed straw sun hat. To help guard against sunburn, he has wrapped a white pillowcase round his face, with holes cut out for eyes, nose and mouth. A young girl starts to cry, frightened by the panting 'phantom'. Obligingly he pulls the mask away. The girl looks unconvinced.

As a hard-drinking Slovenian, Fish Man (real name Martin Strel) can't claim to have the well-honed physique of a world-class athlete. He is in his fifties, overweight and has a stomach that sags over his swimming briefs. Yet, here we all are, shouting encouragement in a cacophony of different languages and dialects to rally behind the man who is on target to complete a perilous 5,265-kilometre marathon swim in just sixty-six days. When we hear that he is passing along a stretch near Tabitinga in Brazil, we are told that he is suffering from dizziness, nausea, diarrhoea and sunstroke. Having seen bull sharks in the waters recently – not to mention the poachers, fugitives and drug runners that roam throughout this secluded jungle – I am in complete awe of Strel. Especially because, in a swirling soup of razor-toothed fish and anacondas, he is averaging more than fifty miles a day.

'C'mon Martin, you can do it!' I holler, adding a cheery *'srečno!'* – 'good luck' in Slovenian – for which I am rewarded with a weary wave from a thick-set, hairy arm. Strel is no stranger to such challenges, having set three previous long-distance swimming records: the 3,004-kilometre Danube in 2000, the 3,797-kilometre Mississippi in 2001 and the 4,003-kilometre Yangtze in 2004. For a while I walk alongside him as he front crawls relentlessly on, hitting tidal swirls that are strong enough to push him backwards at times. 'The hero in a Speedo', as the press in South America have dubbed Strel, has trained hard for a year for this epic challenge. After bouts of debilitating diarrhoea and threats from terrified machete-wielding native tribes, his major fear remains the candiru fish: a needle-thin parasite that enters the body by swimming up the penis. His bizarre pillowcase attire is a final attempt to protect his pale skin from the blistering heat – he has developed second-degree burns on his face that doctors fear may become infected, and sores that have scabbed are visible on his nose and upper cheeks when he passes.

His escort boat, skippered by a captain and a team of guards, is constantly on the lookout for floating debris and predators. As he slowly swims out of view, I watch as he shakes his head violently to remove a spider from his hair. Not far from where he is heading, a giant catfish the length of a pick-up truck recently attacked a dog, gobbling it up – whole.

Strel will finish his swim in the small jungle town of Urucu-rituba on 17 March 2007 – one of the wettest years in the Amazon on record. The aim of his swimming odyssey is to increase awareness of the effects of rainforest loss on global warming. Often referred to as the lungs of our planet, the Amazon rainforest plays a crucial role in recycling carbon dioxide into oxygen. Its deforestation is a contributing factor to rising temperatures across the world.

Like Strel, I have trained to be in the Amazon after taking the advice of others who have spent extended periods of time here. A stern ex-army major put me through my paces, tutting and sucking his teeth. His constant reassurances that he could 'get me jungle ready' made me worry needlessly. In truth, surviving the Amazon is as much about mental strength as physical fitness.

Creeping shadows can play cruel tricks on your mind. Strange, blood-curdling cries chill the bone to the marrow. And the darkness of night sometimes has no end. There is a submission required to survive this, a resistance that harvests inner reserves. You accept the fear but fight it. Mainly, I use a silent dialogue with myself to overcome the looming spectre of imagined harm. So far, at least, I have made the grade.

Few places in the world are as untamed as the Amazon Basin, the vast jungled watershed, roughly the size of Germany, which blankets almost half of South America. The river itself starts life as a tiny trickle atop the snow-capped Andes mountains, then flows steadily across the continent until it surges into the Atlantic Ocean at Belém in Brazil. I was not prepared for the girth of the Amazon, or the 'Great Sea', as many indigenous cultures know it. Parts span forty kilometres – roughly the distance between England and France – becoming so bloated during the rains that they can flood up to 350,000 square kilometres of land, an area that guidebooks tell me is more than twenty-one times the size of Belize.

Stretches of the Amazon are deep enough to accommodate ocean liners. More than fifteen of its 1,100 tributaries are greater than a thousand miles long. The entire watershed contains more than two-thirds of the Earth's fresh water, flowing for 6,400 kilometres from the Peruvian headwaters of the Ucayali-Apurímac river system to Brazil via Colombia – a distance slightly shorter than the Nile. According to the latest tally, the region is home to at least 7,500 species of butterfly, 1,800 birds, 800 insect species and almost 2,000 species of reptile and amphibian. It contains 3,200 species of fish and, so far, botanists have recorded 51,220 species of plant – although they doubt it'll be possible to catalogue everything during the lifetime of our planet. A staggering ten per cent of all the species on Earth call the Amazon Basin home.

Antonio is waiting for me in the lobby of the Hotel Anaconda in Leticia, mobile phones attached to both ears. Something of a rarity in this frontier town on the Colombian side of the tri-border region, where Colombia meets Peru and Brazil, Antonio is an Amazon-born worldly traveller who lived in California for a while but is happy to be back home. I reach to shake his hand, but he opts to back-slap me, American style, before assuring me that

I will find him a plain-talking, easy-listening guy. I warm to him over a coffee, but I feel less sure about his companion: a middle-aged man with menacing looks who picks at his nails with a large, silver-bladed knife. When he glares at me, I avert my gaze and my stomach feels uneasy. 'Mr Menacing' will be our boatman.

Fluent in English, Italian, Spanish, Portuguese and some indigenous dialects, Antonio claps his hands together with relish when I point to a route from Leticia out along the Río Yavarí, the natural border between Brazil and Peru. Colombia's stretch of Amazon rainforest is low-lying, he explains, with as many as a hundred arboreal species in a single acre. Where we are heading is especially scenic, so I'll be blessed by extraordinary views of jungle and wildlife, he says.

My arrival coincides with sunshine after a string of rainy days. Torrents of mud have seeped through the marshy, forested plains and into the river and tributaries. The choppier waters around rapids and waterfalls give the river the look of gravy made from a rich beef stock. In the Amazon, the rising waters are part of life's natural rhythm. Entire communities take down, then reassemble, their villages according to a cyclical season. Rising waters can cause the river level to increase by up to fifteen metres. It engulfs entire wood-and-thatch villages, immerses huge tracts of jungle and allows only the highest ceiba trees to peek out above the surface. Rivers break their banks between the end of December and the end of June, with levels reaching their highest between March and late May. Ebb tides begin in July and last until the beginning of December, reaching their lowest levels during July and November. At this time, sandbanks are formed at the river borders, turtles nest and lay their eggs, and rice is planted on exposed mudflats. Decomposing plant matter adds nutrients to the land from the river. In the Amazon, land and river are one.

The entire Amazon Basin generates up to 121 million litres of water per second, depositing three million tonnes of sediment near its mouth each day. More than twenty per cent of all the fresh water that drains into the entire world's oceans comes from the Amazon's annual outflow. If I seem overwhelmed by the magnitude of these watery statistics, it's with good reason. Flooding accounts for around forty per cent of all natural disasters, with drowning the third leading cause of all unintentional deaths – ninety-five per cent of which are in the undeveloped world. In fact, South America tops the table for most flood deaths per million people per year.

The force and brutality of water flow is something that continues to astound me. At ankle deep it can be powerful enough to knock a grown man off his feet. When two feet of fast-moving water swept away my jeep in Guatemala, I couldn't believe my eyes. Naively, I'd assumed its weight was enough to anchor it down, but it bobbed about in the water like a polystyrene cup. In Nicaragua, while I popped into a grocery store, a surge of water from a burst riverbank carried my waiting taxi away. The driver jumped out, but I never saw my brand-new pair of HD binoculars again.

Caught in a downpour on a busy thoroughfare once in Panama City, I learned first-hand that rainwater rolling down a sloping street at walking pace can exert pressure at more than three hundred kilograms per square metre. One minute I was strolling along a crowded street lined with cafes, department stores and hotels. The next, the street was deserted and I was caught in a massive body of water, clinging to a street light like a koala bear wrapped round a eucalyptus tree. My shoulder bag and shoes were ripped from my body. After a hellishly long ten or fifteen minutes, the downpour slowed and the water level dropped. Within less than half an hour, every bit of moisture had evaporated and the street scene had returned to normal, my sodden clothes, wet hair and shoeless feet the only evidence that it had rained at all.

In another instance, at the end of a flight from Caracas to Panama City, a flash flood at the airport deluged the runways with water, causing the pilot to divert our plane to a nearby military airstrip. The rain was relentless, pounding the plane with such force that it wobbled on the strip. When the passengers on the claustrophobic little aircraft demanded to alight, fights started on board and an armed response unit was called for. In rising floodwaters, with the army surrounding the plane in full riot gear, the lights went out. The siege went on for four terrifying hours. In Los Llanos, Colombia, it rained so heavily one night that the room I was staying in filled with rats. One by one, to escape the torrents, they entered through a ventilation gap, then raced around my bed in a blind panic. As their claws click–clacked on the floor tiles, I gathered up my sheets and hid underneath until the downpour ceased. After several hours the rains relented and the rats felt safe enough to venture out. But not before at least two dozen had run across my bed.

Though our journey will take us through stretches of the Peruvian, Brazilian and Colombian Amazon, Antonio and I plan to overnight in the village of Puerto Nariño, South America's only citizen-led eco jungle settlement about two hours upriver. At Leticia's flooded jetty, muddy furrows show where heavy crates of yam and yuca have been dragged up from boats. I feel the menacing presence of our boatman, who is now picking his teeth with the tip of his blade. With exaggerated suggestion, he starts undressing me with his eyes. My cheeks burn as I shoot him a look that says: 'Back off, sonny.' As he unloops the mooring on the boat, he utters the worst possible insult from beneath his thick black moustache.

The river is just as brooding: an oily, petrol–green stew of fallen branches. We inch out of the clutter, and 'Mr Menacing' pumps the throttle so that we barrel into clearer water. Vine-tangled boughs entwined around one another form a bridge above us, lined with crimson parrots. A chattering troop of fast-moving howler monkeys races around us through the highest trees. Above the growl of the outboard motor, our ears fill with the stereophonics of whining insects. Conversation is pointless, so we point and grin instead. A handsome Amazon kingfisher catches my eye. It is poised, waiting, on a hanging branch as a giant catfish in the waters below casts an enormous shadow. Hot, sticky clouds of hungry mosquitoes hang in the air. A slick of red mud pours into the river's inky–green shallows from the riverbank.

Carbon dioxide is absorbed at a phenomenal rate by this enormous, resplendent biomass, which is a vital ecological component of the planet. I wonder, gloomily, why humankind seems hell-bent on dominating the region's natural resources and lift my spirits by reminding myself that, unlike the Brazilian section, the Colombian stretch of the Amazon is still relatively undisturbed.

Here, communities seem to fell single trees for their own small-scale needs; there is very little evidence of logging. Smaller clearings re-establish themselves quickly, unlike the gaps left by commercial felling.

Even conservative estimates suggest that rainforest deforestation will destroy almost half of the world's species of plant, animal and microorganism, or see them severely under threat, within the next twenty years. Some 137 plant and animal species are lost every single day – a staggering 50,000 species each year. The Amazon is one of the planet's most complex chemical storehouses. Rainforests across the globe already provide sources for twenty-five per cent of all modern medicines, but a massive amount of untapped potential remains. Scientists are confident that some seventy per cent of rainforest plants have some anti-cancer properties. However, at the current rate of deforestation, many of these plants will be extinct before studies can be carried out. The National Institute for Space Research (INPE) showed that more than 30,000 square kilometres of forest were cleared in 1995 in Brazil alone. Alarming, when you consider that just a hundred hectares of Amazon rainforest can contain up to 1,500 plant species – as many as the whole of the UK.

The impact of the coca-cultivation trade is another strain on the Amazon's ecosystem. In some of Colombia's key biodiversity hotspots, vast quantities of glyphosate have been sprayed as part of a government initiative. Although figures suggest drug production has been slowed, serious concerns about the effects of the sprays fuel protests from local indigenous peoples, who claim that surfactant chemicals and herbicides have penetrated the foliage of plants vital to their traditional medicines and diet. There are several hundred tribes and more than a hundred languages and dialects in the Amazon. Though some indigenous communities welcome visitors, many care little for interaction with outsiders. They simply want to be left in peace.

In Nazareth, a small tribal settlement about three hours from Leticia, reached via a muddy channel that leads off the Amazon river, the villagers once opened up to outsiders but changed their minds a few years ago, warning local tour operators – and curious travellers – to stay well away. This ban followed growing concerns about the number of people who openly appeared to disrespect the heritage and hospitality of the Nazareth people. Most complaints related to what outsiders chose to wear when they entered the village, followed closely by how much rubbish they left behind. As always, the sensitive issue of taking photographs has led to communities warning that enough is enough. On the approach to Nazareth, wooden signs in Spanish caution the uninvited not to proceed any closer where once there were banners of welcome. Even in Leticia, I spotted a mural painted on a wall that read: 'Don't enter if you don't respect'. I felt gloomy until I saw another offering the Amazon version of the Latino 'mi casa es su casa' sentiment: 'The drum is my home, the cradle my canoe, the river my road, the jungle my science, the land my base, the sun my reach, the air my lungs and the blood my sap – and, as a visitor here, it is yours, too.'

Above the chugging of the engine, Antonio bangs the side of the boat as a signal to stop. He has promised me some astonishing bird sights, but jokes that this takes no skill at all when one in five of all the birds in the world are found in the Amazon rainforests. We wade through thick mud as sticky as glue and slide into deep puddles. Dense vegetation sheds sticky seeds into my hair. The Amazon is home to 2.5 million insect species, and it feels as though most of them are crawling inside my shirt.

Back in the boat 'Mr Menacing' quietens the engine again when Antonio raises his hand and points towards the entrance of a large, arching curve in the river. 'We know that this region dates back to the Palaeozoic period, somewhere between 500 million and 200 million years ago,' he says. 'It probably once formed part of the proto-Congo river system from the interior of present-day Africa, when the continents were joined as part of the Gondwana supercontinent. When the South American and Nazca tectonic plates collided fifty million years ago, the resulting Andes mountains blocked the river and created this vast inland sea.'

'So the wildlife here today, in the rivers, marshes and freshwater lakes, would originally have come from the sea?' I venture. 'Sí, Sarita,' Antonio nods. 'Marine life adapted, mammals migrated, plants flourished and species spawned subspecies to create this unique area of nature. During the last ice age the levels of the great Amazon lake dropped to become a river.'

Antonio shows me what birdwatchers all over the world rave about: a staggering array of Amazonian species. These include the white-vented euphoria, purple-throated fruit crow, grey antbird, spot-winged antbird, ochre-bellied flycatcher, black-spotted barbet, cinereous antshrike, reddish hermit, black-throated hermit, violaceous trogon, ocellated woodcreeper and brownish twistwing on Yahuarcaca lake, a serene setting of breathtaking beauty. A succession of large, inky-green pools in the drier months, merging into one giant floodplain after heavy rains, the lake is cloaked in pea-green algae and surrounded by a curtain of leafy vines and trailing branches. Still and silent – apart from a symphony of wild bird calls, crickets and croaking frogs – the lake is shielded from direct sunlight by huge trees with rope-like roots, which form mysterious islets under dappled rays. Victoria water-lilies float on top of the lake, their giant, white, bowl-shaped flowers tinged with palest pink. The world's largest water-lily is named after Queen Victoria; it was taken to England in the 1830s and became a symbol of the British Empire during her reign. Today, many communities in the Amazon tell the tale of a girl who wanted to touch the moon and the stars, but found them out of reach, however far she travelled. The spirits took pity on the girl, transforming her instead into a moon-like shining flower of incredible beauty – the Vitória-Régia.

It was clear from his body language in the hotel that Antonio wasn't wholly convinced about travelling to meet the Amazon's Tikuna people. But a South American usually finds it impossible to say 'no' outright. Direct questioning is counterproductive in such situations. So I settled back in my chair, poured myself another coffee and watched the Amazonian sky awaken with a rising sun the colours of saffron and pimento. I played the long game, gently probing with several lines of subtle questioning that approached the subject from umpteen angles. Later, once Antonio seemed certain I was no longer interested, he opened up, grabbing a stick from the ground and drawing indecipherable squiggles in the dirt. For hundreds of years, he told me, the Tikuna people have suffered persecution in one form or another. Recent years have been no exception. In the late 1980s, fourteen Tikuna living on the river Solimões in the Brazilian Amazon were murdered while trying to defend their land. Six of them were small children. And while the logger who ordered the killings was sentenced for genocide in 2001, the length of the sentence was reduced on appeal in 2004, causing considerable anguish in Tikuna communities Amazon-wide.

Of all the people living in the Amazon, around eighty per cent are of Tikuna heritage. Almost all feel bullied by the Brazilian, Peruvian and Colombian governments, and the powerful barons that run the rubber industry. Most have been displaced by wars, logging or development. Many feel resentment and a complete lack of trust. The majority are, understandably, cynical of authority. In the past decade or so the Tikuna have been persuaded to venture into tourism, but have been largely unimpressed. The indigenous people don't benefit from encouraging visitors to the Amazon, they have observed. It is only the travel agencies and government who make money, while their lives are ridiculed by outsiders and disrupted. Another source of despair is the use of Tikuna land by drug traffickers, especially around the Solimões river area on the Brazilian border with Colombia and Peru. To the Tikuna, this is sacred land. They believe their god, Yoi, fished them from a tributary of the waters of the Solimões in the scenic upper stretches of the Brazilian Amazon, close to the confluence with the Rio Negro.

With Antonio and our boatman, 'Mr Menacing', I am keen to visit the Tikuna who live in Puerto Nariño in the Colombian Amazon, a community of around 5,500 on the border with Brazil and Peru. This community has some contact with the outside world, with the occasional boat bringing in marine biologists, backpackers and conservationists, together with grain, pigs and other provisions. Puerto Nariño, around eighty kilometres upriver from Leticia, is unlike any other jungle community I have heard of. It demonstrates that, even in such challenging times for the environment, man and nature can coexist harmoniously. This experimental ecological settlement, tucked amid the Colombia-Peru-Brazil triangle west of Leticia, is known locally as *el Pesebre del Amazonas* (Cradle of the Amazon). It is part of the Ticoya indigenous reserve, a flat, narrow plain that stretches from the waterfront before rising like a many-tiered cake.

Antonio seems satisfied with my intentions. If we go, he advises, we should visit it as a centre of ecotourism and shy away from anything vaguely political. I assure him that my intention is to observe a triumph of 1960s' 'green vision' in this most unlikely setting, where solar-powered electricity runs for four hours a day and drinking water is recycled from the rains. 'Tensions are running a little high at the moment, Sarita; we will need to tread carefully,' he continues. As one of the first major tribes of the Amazon to be contacted by the early conquistadors, he explains, the Tikuna have struggled to preserve their personal identity through their native language, traditional religions, rituals and cultural art forms. All the pain and hurt of four hundred years or more came pouring out at a meeting there last week, he tells me. 'The anger turned into rage, but it is calmer now. However, we need to be mindful that we are invited guests and should not talk about things we don't understand.'

I nod, and recall reading a news story about how trauma-suffering Tikunas have succumbed to drug and alcohol abuse. Self-harming, too, has become a problem in some communities, where more than thirty adolescent suicides have occurred during recent years. High unemployment and low morale have impacted upon some Tikuna villages. Until the 1940s the Tikuna were largely isolated, but today they play a growing role in politics to fight their corner. They are still finding ways to cope with new social problems and the swirling new influences of outsiders, whose consumerism and materialistic values many believe to be threatening traditional Tikuna culture. Basically, they are walking between two very different worlds.

Our boat brushes the shaggy grass at the edge of the river and Antonio, upright and ready to jump, leaps onto a flattened stretch of bank. He will meet village elders, to pave the way for our visit. I am alone with the our heavily moustached boatman and his silver blade. Things are fine for five minutes or so, but as we enter a wide expanse of water, he cuts the engine and allows the vessel to drift, staring at me without blinking. Slowly, the boat moves silently and uncontrolled into the flow of the river. My heart races. What is he doing and why is he doing it? I panic, chest tightening. Then a wave of calm resignation floods my nervous system and I feel, well, like I am ready for death. First, he will slit my bag open and steal my cash, credit cards, camera and laptop. Then he will cut me from ear to ear, although I am unsure if it will be before, during or after the rape. My body, and my luggage, will be discarded into the murky depths of the fast-swirling Amazon. I doubt there'll be any distinguishing marks, features or dental records by the time my carcass washes up thousands of miles to the east.

Under the peak of my cap, I look up at him. His eyes are still boring right through me without a flinch. I glance around the boat and consider my options. Land is no longer in sight. Jumping is a possibility, although I won't last long in the soupy waters among the crocodiles, stingrays, sharks, piranhas and snakes. My world goes silent other than the sound of my pulse and the water on the wooden hull. The knife, now clasped between his hairy hands as if part of a prayer ritual, is glinting in a yellow light. There is no point screaming. There is nobody to hear me. I draw a long, deep breath and close my eyes to steal myself a final moment alive.

'Yeeeeeeeeeeeeeek!'

The long, high-pitched shrillness of the scream shakes me to the core. Only it isn't my voice. It is the psycho boatman. 'Mr Menacing' is jigging up and down, bobbing the boat alarmingly. He's pointing. At the water. Shrieking like a girl who's seen a fluffy bunny. Only, this big lump hasn't spotted a rabbit. He's seen a beautiful pair of frolicking pink dolphins. The strange gurgling in the pit of my stomach isn't seasickness: it is high excitement, and sheer, utter relief. Our four eager eyes scrutinise the water. Unlike dolphin-spotting out at sea, there is no jettisoning spray, just still waters. This means the experience is a calm spectacle in a tranquil setting: one that starts with wide-eyed, quiet expectation and ends with a truly magnificent encounter. The boatman stands up and scours the horizon, climbing over my backpack with deft athleticism for a better view. I notice that, at long last, he has reacquainted his deadly looking machete with its sheath. Sinister stares have given way to childish glee, and I feel stupid for succumbing to intimidation.

The wind-weathered ropes and flapping tarpaulin are the only distraction as we pray for a reappearance of the pinky cetaceans. 'There!' I cry, jubilantly, as a trio of dolphins appears, moving towards us in sleek synchronisation, their rosy-grey bodies cutting through the water in perfectly choreographed leaps and dives. The boat begins to bob with a hypnotic creak as they splash and swim around us, and I dig around for my binoculars. The largest one ventures closest, forming a pinky shadow under the surface of the water beside me, then revealing itself, pounding the water with a mighty swish. A glistening arched back and dorsal fin rise high above the surface, and a peaked snout turns cheekily towards me. Then, a graceful dive into the deep in a spume of water. Our broad smiles are all that's left in the wake.

In Puerto Nariño, life revolves around fishing in and around the Amazon river. No cars or motorbikes wend the streets here. Well, in truth, there are no streets, just a neat grid of well-maintained, tidy paths and gardens for pedestrians and the occasional pedal cycle. Waste bins – a rare sight in rural South America, especially in the wilderness regions – mark each corner of this small rainforest outpost, a model for environmentally friendly living. Every scrap of rogue litter is seized upon within seconds. Even when the rainy season arrives, the residents pride themselves on keeping the place neat as murky knee-deep water seeps over the riverbanks. As the 'capital' of twenty smaller indigenous communities strung along the river Loretoyaco, an Amazon tributary, Puerto Nariño is developing its eco-ethno-tourism. The only motors allowed are those of the engine-powered boats that serve the residents with transport and trade between communities.

At the other side of the cafe we haul Antonio aboard the boat from a soggy riverbank. With a thumb and forefinger he forms an OK sign. He has sealed the deal.

When we arrive at the settlement, a skeletal man as old as Methuselah is waiting on the port side in several inches of mud. Antonio introduces us and he greets us warmly, insisting that he will personally carry our luggage to our lodge. His sinuous arms are as thin as spaghetti, yet he picks up my bag as if it were weightless.

Antonio asks him about the Amazon river dolphins – boto – on my behalf, and I marvel at the sounds, clicks and rolls of the local tongue. For centuries, the man explains, Tikunas have looked upon these beautiful pink-and-grey river mammals with awe and still hold beliefs about their magical powers. They believe that the dolphins were once human. And whether rivals, friends or enemies, the boto are regarded as equals who must be respected.

Dolphins, like man, can be good and evil. Many Tikunas tell of relatives or friends who have been lured by the charms of dolphins, although boto have been largely protected by the superstitions of the Amazon because to harm them will bring bad luck. Most cultures have never been tempted to eat them because of the widespread belief that dolphins were once humans. Babies born with spina bifida, a birth defect that prevents the baby's skull from growing properly, leaving an opening that resembles a dolphin's blow hole, are said to have been fathered by a boto. According to local lore in the Colombian Amazon, women who go swimming during menstruation will become impregnated by the boto. Daughters approaching puberty should also be closely guarded by their parents, lest a river dolphin disguised as a handsome suitor carry her off to live in the water with them.

Boto can bring good luck, too. For example, if a fisherman finds a dolphin's tooth it means good fortune. But if the tooth is stolen, it can cause great harm to the thief. The role of the boto in ancient folklore – some communities consider it a sacred, semi-divine animal – has helped to conserve it, even though, in parts of the Brazilian Amazon, dolphins are killed for their genitals and eyes, which are used in aphrodisiacal seduction spells and amulets. Overfishing is also a threat to freshwater dolphins in some areas of the Amazon, because they rely on a diet of more than fifty types of fish, as well as crustaceans found on the river bed. Fishermen can sometimes harm boto in the churn of their boats, or by the careless use of nylon nets.

I can remember reading an article in a well-thumbed old copy of a *Reader's Digest* about an encounter between Jacques Cousteau and a rose-hued river dolphin during a voyage on the Amazon in the 1970s. The magical image that it evoked was utterly captivating, and I have longed to see boto in the wild ever since. Around 200 live in and around the waters of the Amazon's tri-border region, where the waters are rich in fish. One of the largest established populations is found in Tarapoto Lake, a large, magical expanse of water edged by ficus trees, about nine kilometres west of Puerto Nariño. Steeped in legends relating to a strange green light that glows beneath the night sky, the lake is approached with caution by local fishermen, who talk of decapitated colleagues found floating in the lake after falling foul of night-time demons. Some say pirates ascend from the water's depths, killing unsuspecting fishermen. Others insist that the body parts of fishermen are harvested for research purposes by scientists, who fly here from laboratories in the United States.

It wasn't until the late 1980s that marine biologists from Bogotá's Jorge Tadeo Lozano University began an official study of the dolphins to promote understanding of the conservation threats they face. Today, surveys by a foundation called Omacha (meaning dolphin in the Tikuna language) combine conservation programmes with educational campaigns that encourage positive myths about the dolphins. Children, especially, are taught to draw boto and form a special bond with them through songs and games. By promoting the importance of freshwater dolphins, Omacha has also encouraged the Tikuna, generally shy about sharing their beliefs with outsiders, to become avid supporters. Many communities now see that the preservation of the boto is inexorably bound with their own survival as riverbank dwellers. In the last thirty years or so, many of the negative myths about boto that permeated Tikuna communities have lost strength, as the dolphins have become a focal point of interest throughout the Amazon region.

The boto has an extremely distinctive shape, with a long, plump body, paddle-shaped fins and a ridge along its back rather than a dorsal fin. A bulging melon characterises its forehead, while the face has small eyes, chubby cheeks and an extremely long beak. Most striking is the colour, which varies from bluish-grey to white and a rose-like pink. Like other river dolphins, botos are usually observed either singly or in pairs in the early morning and late evening. They are playful, curious and interactive. Adept swimmers, they can navigate shallow areas and weave in and out of trees in floodwater conditions. Boto feed on a variety of fish and crabs in slow-moving rivers and streams, using clicks and whistles to 'see' their prey.

We wind along the mighty, winding Yavari into dense reaches of unbroken rainforest. A consummate diplomat, Antonio has paved the way for us to enjoy a trouble-free meander along the river, which flows from the border between Brazil and Peru's

Loreto department north east for 870 kilometres, joining the Amazon River near the Brazilian outpost of Benjamin Constant. The rest of the day is spent admiring many more of the Amazon's pink river dolphins, together with common squirrel monkeys, black-mantled tamarins, black agouti, Amazon dwarf squirrels, pygmy marmosets, night monkeys, brush-tailed rats and red howlers. The riverbank foliage is breathtaking, running an entire spectrum of green, from garish paintbox-bright ferns and black-green mangroves to olive-coloured reeds, yellowy palms and a tangle of lush emerald creepers. The colour of the river alters dramatically from a creamy swirl of thick vanilla to a deep brick-red.

Ichthyologically speaking, the Amazon and its tributaries are some of the most exciting waters on the planet. Now seeming considerably less menacing, our boatman tells me that he has caught the cardinal tetras, with its bright panels of scarlet, azure and silver, as well as the peculiar thin-nosed tube-snout knifefish, in rivers full of electric eels and river stingrays. Since 1960, more than fifty species of fish have been discovered, named and catalogued in the Amazon each year. The number of identified fish species currently stands at 3,200, but experts agree that the true figure is likely to exceed 4,000 – at least.

Further along, the 293-hectare rainforest expanse of the Parque Nacional Natural Amacayacu contains two very different landscapes: rolling and relatively dry scrubland, and the swampy marshes of the floodlands. Rising waters make it impossible for us to disembark, so we explore the flooded forests by boat. The trees can reach forty metres high, with mammoth ceiba trees as wide as cars. Red and white cedars, mahogany, rubber, balsam and caoba thrive in forests that support 150 mammal species and dozens of reptiles and snakes. Of the more than 500 species of bird found here, we see large flocks of brightly coloured parrots, scarlet macaws, chestnut-fronted macaws and Amazonian umbrellabirds. What a day!

We climb to the top of the Mirador Nai Pata – a purpose-built wooden lookout platform – back in the western part of Puerto Nariño, to gaze out over rivers and lakes. I play Antonio at cards for an hour in a shoestring bar overlooking a basketball court. Then, having lost several hands, I call it a day. I'm ready to

hit the sack. In the Amazon, light after dark is a mixed blessing –
even the weakest glow attracts every bug and critter from miles
around. Once the sun goes down it makes sense to sleep. That
night, in my simple room at Casa Selva, I use the monastic
silence of my surroundings to attempt to understand the fear I
felt today. I can't. So I think about the reasons for such antisocial
traits. He is probably a man with a military background, who
sees little need for niceties. His crude language stems from the
camaraderie of the mess room. His knife obsession is a result of
a life spent handling weaponry. The unnerving propensity to
stare is most likely shyness. His weird laughter an idiosyncrasy.
It's all presumptive psychoanalysis and almost certainly
untrue – but it helps me to sleep believing I will live to see
another day.

Over a breakfast of mixed fresh fruit and squeezed mango
juice, Antonio confides in me that his biggest bugbear is international tourists who think that the Amazon jungle is a theme
park: open at 9am, closed at 5pm, with a twenty-dollar entrance
fee, toilets and cafe. I laugh at the joke, then see from his face that
what he says is based on first-hand experience. The other
annoyance, he says, is the people who arrive with toxic bug spray.
I mean, he says, would they spray weedkiller all over Kew Gardens?
He simply cannot imagine why some travellers are offended
when they are discouraged from squirting deadly chemicals in
one of the most biodiverse places on the planet.

Herbal insect repellents that contain no chemicals and are fully
biodegradable include citrus essential oils, which can be liberally
applied to clothes, hair and skin. In recent years Amazon peoples
have also developed their own ecological repellent for the use of
whey-skinned, bug-bitten tourists. I buy this in generous
drenching quantities to cope with the prevalence of mosquitoes
that like to hitch a ride on me.

Back on the water I scan the sky, dreaming of a random
sighting of a harpy eagle. They are incredibly rare here now,
because the rainforest is so disturbed. An entire breast of land
floats by the boat like a mini island. It dwarfs us with its shadows.
Two trees, a palm, a fern and some bushes soar out of an enormous
squash-coloured rootball bobbing up and down through the
water like a cork. A wide-eyed opossum is hitching a ride on top.

'Look at this amazing place,' Antonio says theatrically. 'You couldn't make this up, nobody would ever believe you!'

Back in Leticia Antonio is double-booked, so I graciously bow out for a few days. Jumping on the back of a moto-taxi courtesy of one of dozens of scooter owners who offer illegal rides in return for a dollar, we criss-cross Leticia to Tabatinga, weaving through lines of trucks carrying plantain and manioc. An absence of border formalities here means that a wave or a toot of the horn will do. Brazil's Tabatinga is similar to its immediate Colombian neighbour, but has a grittier edge. We head down to the port, pushing through market stalls, street-selling artisans and pedlars. Journeying the river is as much a pastime here as intrepidly exploring the jungle. So when I am offered a ticket on one of the biggest vessels that plough the stretch between Tabatinga and Iquitos, I grab it willingly. The cruiser – battleship-grey and covered in dents, gouges and scrapes – is clearly a bruiser of the sea. She is almost ready to set sail; the last few crates of day-glow fizzy drinks, sacks of maize and boxes of coconuts are being squeezed into the remaining empty corner of her hold. It'll be good to see the Amazon at a slower, less strenuous pace, from the comfort of my hammock. I hook it up in an area of the deck that feels like a refugee camp – there are about forty other people on board – although a Spanish backpacker called Juan Pablo assures me that this is luxury compared with the leaky, rodent-infested vessel he arrived in last week. True, the creaking old battleship is clean and seaworthy. It also has an alcohol ban, which is no problem for me in my teetotal state, but some of the other passengers are twitchy before we've even set sail. The prospect of seven days in a hammock with literally nothing to do but watch the world go by pleases me no end. Wildlife is untroubled by this monster of the waterways. The loud, low rumble of the engine barely registers on its radar, and as we pass overhanging branches we are so close that I can peer inside tree holes and nests. For the Spaniard in the hammock next to me, this beautiful journey of low-hanging, flowered trailing plants and exotic trees filled with red and green parakeets is a prison sentence. He is losing the will to live after a few short hours.

Due to the lie of the river the boat, at times, hugs the shore so tightly that leafy branches snag my hammock ties. I pluck a flower or two, and on one occasion a couple of howler monkeys join us, temporarily, on deck. No TV; no Wi-Fi; no phone signal. This is all the entertainment I need in my simple routine. Rising to watch the sun emerge from behind the jungle gives me a chance to mingle with the crew. I write notes, snap away with my camera, catch up on books I've meant to read until it's time to watch the sunset. At night I listen to a much-replayed conversation between the Spaniard and the others regarding his expired visa. Each discussion seems to conclude with wildly differing sets of advice. Other chats revolve around the mind-expanding merits of ayahuasca, a potent hallucinogenic tea that is fast becoming to the Amazon what marijuana is to Amsterdam.

I resist the urge to chip in here, because I have first-hand experience of ayahuasca. In the Peruvian Amazon, I met a shaman who enquired whether I had ever embraced it as a spirit cure. We discussed it at length. Then I spent several months mulling it over, until I decided to try it for the purpose of an article. The shaman mentioned that he was being approached by a growing number of Westerners who felt they'd 'lost their way'. Ayahuasca (known as *yage* in the Colombian Amazon, *caapi* in Brazil and at least forty-two indigenous names) is believed to open minds, unlock potential and expand spiritual horizons. Used by more than seventy of the Amazon's several hundred tribes, it is also touted to Westerners as a cure for alcoholism and depression, which may help to point a person's spiritual compass, setting them straight. The key ingredient is dimethyltryptamine (DMT), a natural compound found throughout the plant kingdom. It doesn't work if swallowed alone, because an enzyme in the human digestive system breaks it down. However, Amazonian shamans worked out centuries ago that boiling a DMT-rich shrub and ayahuasca vine together produces a tea that the human gut accepts, allowing the DMT to slip into the bloodstream.

The prospect of taking ayahuasca concerned me, for I feared I would lose control – a strange worry when you consider that I once glugged away at enough wine to stupefy myself. The horror stories about vomiting didn't alarm me, because I have always found a purge strangely blissful. I was, of course, curious about how I would feel after the trip was over. I vowed to keep notes during the whole experience, and wondered what, if any, long-term therapeutic benefits there would be.

I arrived with a guide, Carlos, a trusted friend of a colleague in Bogotá. Because the ceremony can render participants immobile for several hours, it is important to have trust in the people around you and be in a safe place. For me, this meant a lone experience – I didn't want the worry of being around total strangers, although the jungle lodge also ran 'healing groups' for up to ten people most weekends. My room was large, wooden and empty, apart from a jug of water, a blood-red woven throw and a rolled-up mattress. Carlos sat outside on a chair. After listening to a lot of chanting that referenced sacred power and divination, I took a swig of the ayahuasca. It carried the rank acidity of fruit juice long past its sell-by date, and my natural physical response was a gagging convulsion. Retching, I ploughed on to finish the cup as directed. For thousands of years, Amazonian shamans have used ayahuasca as a window into the soul, I reminded myself, as I jotted down a few observations about the early stages of this ancient ritual. Somehow, knowing that the practice of imbibing ayahuasca had been endorsed by the Peruvian government since 2008 eased all fears. In Peru, it is considered 'one of the basic pillars of the identity of the Amazon peoples', although the Pope, apparently, had something to say about this during a visit in 2013.

Though nauseous, I felt peaceful, calm and floaty. Everything around me took on a bright and beautiful colour more vivid than a giant morpho butterfly or the feathers of the scarlet macaw. From a swirling of fiery, crimson glow, I saw an amazing yellow light in the distance and felt enlightened, clear and pure. At this point I was unsure what was hallucinatory and what was real; was it inside my head or outside my body? It was a stronger sensation than I'd imagined. It was as if I had shed my ego, my attachments and every shred of fear. In the light a figure came in and out of focus for what seemed like hours, and I found myself smiling into the shadow. Then I saw her fully: a child, a beautiful brown-eyed girl with smooth, round cheeks and rose-coloured lips. It was me, aged no more than six, maybe seven. It felt wonderfully reassuring to be face to face with myself, and I reached out, arms outstretched.

Slowly my ayahuasca vision faded and I felt different, complete. I didn't feel alone in the universe; I felt part of something amazing and rich. Far from being ambushed, my senses felt massaged. As I sat up on the throw-covered mattress, my reflection stared back at me from a water bucket. I was smiling broadly. I looked younger. Refreshed. Calm.

Ayahuasca is named for the Quechua word meaning 'vine of the soul', and I can vouch for its soul-soothing powers. I was surprised to find that my thoughts began to circulate freely within a head that wasn't cluttered. The practitioner who administered my tea had learned from an elder shaman almost fifty years earlier. Part of his education was to understand the plants, the harvesting and the concoction – and also the workings of the mind, body and spirit.

After my experience my body felt somehow mood-regulated, although it was difficult to explain it away as some kind of profound psycho-spiritual epiphany. But I did feel better for it and suffered no emotional trauma, self-destructive urges or harmful demons. Not everyone is so lucky. Ayahuasca is believed to be responsible for a number of deaths, some among young backpackers keen to 'feel the buzz', who have bought cups of it on the street with no way of knowing who concocted it. Although scientific evidence of the clinical benefits of ayahuasca is scant, it is known to provoke potential bad reactions with other medicines, such as antidepressants. For me, the biggest issue was putting my soul into the hands of another person – it felt uncomfortable and scary.

I also hated being in the dark for so long; never have I been so pleased to feel daylight on my face. As a child, I was fearful of anywhere without bright light: cupboards, night-time or the coal shed. To be unable to see clearly filled me with panic. I didn't have a specific fear of monsters, I just hated to be scared and vulnerable. It turned out to be a passing phobia that disappeared in my late teens, although it still pays occasional visits. When it does, I return to being a terrified child again, stumbling about in the dark: blind, scared and feeble.

The next day, with strict instructions to avoid alcohol, sugar, salt, spicy foods, milk, cheese, red meat and pork, I spent the day relaxing in a hammock. I tried to reflect on everything, but the whole experience no longer seemed real. It felt supernatural. Dreamy. Only my stomach, which felt as though it had been put through a wringer, was proof that it had happened at all. That, and a peaceful, happy feeling.

A few days later, as the sun faded, I sat in a park, flooded by the sounds and colours of several thousand screeching *pericos* (small parrots), which treated me to a choreographed aerial display. Suddenly, I felt a flood of childhood memories and I sensed that the six-year-old was with me again. Today, across the Amazon jungle, ayahuasca is being sold to psychedelic pilgrims from around the world seeking a cathartic and life-changing power. They throw up. They wail. They suffer excruciating stomach cramps and lose control of their bowels. They roll around. They scream. They cry.

Me, I feel a warm rush of glorious colour. Then I see the younger me.

Jailbirds and Whales

Panama
2003

The gentle rhythm of my loose-thread hammock is disrupted by the clumsy arrival of a toucan, which attempts to ride the syncopated sway with an awkward dance. With its large bill and long tail feathers, it forms a cartoon-like silhouette against the egg-yolk sun of Isla Popa, where a cooling breeze crackles the palms above me. With a sweeping forearm, I push beads of sweat from my eyes. The heat is fierce on this remote rainforest island in the Caribbean Sea. Isla Popa is an ornithological dreamland. Today, I am one of just a handful of *Homo sapiens* among hundreds of custard-coloured beaks, big glossy eyes and black crests.

Panama offers plenty of quick wins for first-time visitors. This skinny stretch of land harbours exotic contrasts on every section of its gentle reverse curve. You could, in theory, swim the gin-clear waters of the Caribbean Sea in the early morning; eat lunch on dusty plains of cattle-rearing country; take a stroll along the silver sands of the Pacific coast in the afternoon; track pumas in an unmapped jungle after dark. Hundreds of rivers rise in its cool, leafy highlands and flow down through beautiful bird-filled forests before forming large deltas and emptying into the Pacific. A thousand palm-topped islands scatter both coastlines, some no larger than cars. Boats are the default mode of transport in coastal regions that asphalt has yet to conquer. Dozens of hollowed-out tree trunks skate the waters round the shoreline and steal silently along jungled inlets.

Flying from Panama City to Isla Colón, the main island of the Bocas del Toro archipelago wedged between Panama and Costa Rica, the plane bellies low over dense emerald forests. As it skirts the Caribbean shoreline, I glimpse a sparse scattering of wood-and-thatch farms set on the banks of orange serpentine rivers. The small plane is full, and there is a fist fight for available taxis, so I start walking into town. The road shimmers in a dust-cloud haze as I trudge slowly past a line of hammock-strung craft stalls and bracelet makers, a heavy rucksack on my back. Eventually, an open-backed truck pulls up alongside me, beeping a horn. 'I got a spare seat, senorita,' the driver says, nodding to a gap between two oil drums on the flatbed. I accept it gladly, for rides are hit and miss on this long, hot stretch. I wedge myself and my pack tightly in the back beside a crate of yams and the wired eyes of a live cockerel.

Horses once ruled the dust-track roads on Isla Colón, the capital of Bocas del Toro and one of the six main islands that dominate this archipelago of tiny islets and sandy squiggles. I've been a regular here since the late 1990s, when I penned a series of articles for the British and American travel press. As a result I secured a commission to write the Bradt guide to Panama, the first Panama travel guidebook written by a British author. It was named the British Guild of Travel Writers' Travel Guidebook of the Year in 2005, which led to more extended visits. These allowed me to get under the skin of the isthmus and witness a mind-blowing pace of change. Some has been much needed and beneficial to all, such as the modernisation of the infrastructure and transport in Panama City. But in Bocas del Toro the change has been baffling, like somebody deliberately taking ink to a blotter. As testament to how palm-scattered isles can become tainted by the uglier side of paradise, this enchanting Caribbean coast has encountered the grubbier side of progress, in which greed, envy and deceit play a part.

This visit to Bocas del Toro coincides with a period of drought. In a region that is usually well nourished by long overnight showers, it is hot, dry and brittle. The air feels too harsh for the arrival of early migrant species, yet numbers of swallow-tailed and plumbeous kites are already forming whirling spirals over Panama's western sky. Barn swallows and lesser nighthawks have also been spotted in the skies and forests, together with a few visiting warblers. More will soon follow. Everywhere I go, the locals are praying for a decent period of rain to give the tropics a soaking. Most of the hotels are without water, or on restricted rations. As the land is mangrove swamp, it has no groundwater reserves. On a sweaty Sunday morning, the pastor at Isla Colón's evangelical church delivers an upbeat sermon to reassure the congregation. The early arrival of the island's feathered visitors, he says, means that plenty of 'wet stuff' is on its way. Hallelujah, the parishioners shout from their pews.

Central America is a region prone to weather extremes. A complex mishmash of climatic zones makes it difficult to manage – one part is bone dry and parched to the core as another is being devastated by sweeping rivers of mud and rising flood waters. In Bocas del Toro, people are calling on the government to send aircraft to drop water bombs into the drought zones. In my B&B only one room has water. The occupant of room 12 obligingly leaves his door unlocked each morning so that the other fifteen guests can brush their teeth. Among them are several European birders with their sights set on unseen Neotropical species. While queuing in the backyard for a cup of water in which to take their first shave in more than a week, they jump, literally, for joy when a squadron of brown pelicans treat them to a spectacular fly-past. With their distinctive bills resting on the sinuous folds of their necks, the pelicans dive bill-first like kingfishers. After a deep plunge they rise up out of the sea and, opening their extended fish-filled throat pouches, they eject more than two gallons each of scooped-up water.

When I first meet the birders at breakfast, they are full of questions, few of which I can fully answer. Most pressing is why the smooth-billed ani – not found in Bocas del Toro, according to distribution records – has been a surprise sighting that day. And could they really have seen a northern parula, also not expected so far south? I tell them that, from personal experience, it is always best to expect the unexpected in an archipelago like Bocas del Toro. Scan the trees, plants and rivers for anything and everything, because rarities are common in these most eccentric of isles. Odd-bods, cranks, freaks, wackos, nuts and unconventional barefoot champions of leisure are all found here – in human form as well as avian. Every new tide, new sunrise and fresh coastal breeze seems to bring another new and inherently transient life to the archipelago. And with it, a change in dynamic. For centuries, communities and populations of Bocas del Toro have ebbed and flowed around the islands in a natural rhythm of rejuvenation. On one bright morning the islands are readying themselves to mourn an old life lost. The funeral closes every bar, shop and business on Isla Colón, bringing huge crowds of men, women and children onto the streets with heads bowed. Some are in smart suits; others are fishermen, housewives, school kids and slick-haired teens. Old men with brown, crinkled faces lean on crudely carved wooden sticks at the roadside. Alongside them are wide-hipped Afro-Panamanian women in full make-up and oversized false nails in garish shades. Elderly women shuffle along the street, searching for gaps in the throng, sticky-nosed toddlers tugging on their aprons. This act of unified respect from the masses represents every portion of Bocas del Toro's diverse multicultural community. Few cities can claim the mixed ethnicity of this cluster of pinprick isles, which tallies fifty nationalities at least.

Death, like new life, is celebrated here, and the islands are braced for the explosion of joy that will follow the protocols of grief. Unlike in the West, where solemnity amplifies the sorrow of loss, Boca's Afro-descendant population – one of two dominant ethnic groups, alongside the indigenous Ngöbe-Buglé people – honours death with music, song, processions and dance. It's their catharsis. Men typically sit aside, drink and play cards or dominoes to show the deceased that they are happy. For only then can the soul depart the mortal world. Where Western mourners favour black funeral attire, women in Bocas del Toro put on their brightest clothes and lipstick. The locals believe that the souls of the dead watch the ritual and are displeased by displays of grief and distress.

In this archipelago of less than 10,000 people, where life expectancy is above average at almost eighty years of age, death was once a long time coming. So when Bocas became home to a psychopathic serial killer in 2008, the impact on the local population was devastating. William Dathan Holbert was a white-supremacist former landscape gardener dodging bankruptcy and unpaid alimony charges in the US. When he arrived in Bocas after spending some time in Costa Rica, he realised that, in this remote location, away from prying eyes, he could get away with murder. He ingratiated himself into the expatriate community, posing as the son of a Mexican diplomat. Planning to amass a serious stash of gringo dollars, he exploited the slow-paced character of a place where crimes often go unreported. His murder spree lasted thirty-six months, during which he shot five American expatriates, stole their houses, pilfered their assets and carried on as if nothing had happened.

Holbert snared his fourth victim while I was in Isla Colón, staying with friends. As I was traipsing along the main drag, updating my Panama guidebook, Holbert was luring his target over breakfast in Lily's Cafe – one of my favourite places to eat. I'd had breakfast there myself that day, buying a bottle of its stupidly hot sauce to take home to the UK. I met his fifth victim, Cher Hughes, too, a friend of a friend who was warm, funny and well liked. It was her out-of-character disappearance that finally led the police to the bodies.

In the tight-knit local community of a decade or more ago, crimes like these would have been the stuff of fiction. But today, on reflection, it is not that surprising that Bocas del Toro has made headlines in such a way. The islands have attracted a steady procession of conmen, hustlers, disgraced bankers and underworld figures. When I first visited, twenty years ago, the archipelago was relatively new to international tourism. Slowly, it has transformed into a destination that people flock to from all over the world. The effect has been destructive, both environmentally and spiritually. While the locals struggle for water and sanitation, expatriates demand villas with swimming pools. Traditional wooden architecture is being replaced by concrete blocks. Wealth making lies at the heart of every community, where there was once a simple love for nature. 'It won't be long before the wildlife is outnumbered by the lowlife seeking the high life,' a birding guide remarked to me one day. 'Beautiful tracts of land are being acquired by dubious means by dubious people.'

In a cafe in Isla Colón, I watched a group of large-framed guys in long shorts and polo shirts swigging from dripping bottles of ice-cold Corona. Laughing loudly, they waved a bulging designer-brand calf-leather wallet packed with hundred-dollar bills in the face of a Ngöbe-Buglé elder dressed in torn clothes. The elder stared at them impassively as the wallet brushed his cheekbone, wide eyed but silent in the face of such blatant disrespect. Some rogue notes fluttered to the floor and scattered at the old man's feet, drawing my eyes to the non-matching shoes on his feet. 'Hey, look!' said the pug-head ringleader, pointing like a child at a circus. 'The guy's got no goddamm shoes!' His sidekicks bellowed with laughter and I felt anger boiling up inside me. Feigning a muteness that the prospectors were all too ready to accept, the elder said nothing. With swirl of his hand, he scribbled a signature on a piece of printed paper. He scooped up the wallet with a skeletal palm, and I watched him striding purposefully away on his laceless red sneaker and velcro-fastened blue tennis shoe. Later, I learned that the revolting men lost $25,000 that day. The old man was being pushed to sell a piece of family land. Under pressure, he had agreed. But their attitude changed his mind. When he signed the papers, he wrote 'John Wayne' – a name he knew from American Western movies. He split the pocketed cash among his community, then vanished deep into the jungle.

I realise that Isla Colón is starting to lose its charm for me. So when I am offered the chance to climb trees with a bona fide nature nut, I seize the chance. Few things promise to cleanse the soul and reconnect the spirit like monkeying up a tall tree, and the Palo Seco Forest Reserve on the mainland side of Bocas de Toro Province is a temple of tree worship. It has a thirty-three metre balsa tree that attracts pilgrim climbers from all over the world. Locals swear that these mammoth specimens, with trunks as wide as I am tall, are nourished by 'special rains' that help them grow to triple-XL size. I've never tried climbing on this scale, but I have arranged to go with a friend of a tour guide I know, Lorenzo. Apparently he is Panama's answer to Tarzan.

Palo Seco shares most of its avifauna with the adjacent La Amistad International Park, a 407,000-hectare UNESCO-listed nature reserve – the largest in Central America – shared between Panama and Costa Rica. It was at La Amistad, on a previous visit, that I saw my first and only Baird's tapir, a shy and rarely seen mammal characterised by a preposterous-looking long, fleshy snout. Baird's tapir was General Noriega's favourite animal – he established a breeding programme for it, flying the creatures to his mountain hideaway to spare them long, bumpy journeys by road, and lavishing them with food and attention. Although the former military dictator famously turned a blind eye to deforestation during his six-year stint as Panama's de facto ruler, he did champion some environmental causes. The wilds of the Darién were awarded UNESCO status during that period, and the proposal to create the Metropolitan Natural Park in Panama City was drawn up. When I learned this from the coverage of his retrial in 2010, it made me think that he wasn't totally rotten to the core.

Palo Seco is an important site for several globally threatened bird species, including the hell-raising three-wattled bellbird, with its abrasive foghorn call, and the grandiose red-fronted parrotlet, whose magnificent forecrown melds in among the fruiting boughs. Lorenzo tells me there have been unconfirmed sightings of harpy eagle here, so I sharpen my eyes.

Lorenzo is a seasoned pro. He guides recreational climbers of every level and also teaches tree workers how to climb properly to scale incredible heights. Using the principals of Tree Climbers International – whose mantra is 'today's mighty oak is just yesterday's nut that held its ground' – he promises utmost care for the trees he climbs. After showing me the rope-and-harness equipment that we'll be using, he guarantees I'll be seeing the world differently within the hour.

The tree he has earmarked for me is around twenty-seven metres tall. After draping a thick rope over a branch, he loops it together and ties both ends into a series of climbing knots on which we'll ascend and descend. The main knot serves as a 'holding knot' that will keep me in place. Lorenzo stresses that I shouldn't feel compelled to keep climbing without taking the time to pause for breath, enjoy the scenery and relish the views.

He picks a route that will mean I won't need to prune back any branches: 'Every twig we snap, every branch we take down, means one less for wildlife,' he reasons. I've developed a fear of heights, but it isn't as bad when I feel safe and harnessed. I can't recall the exact moment that my acrophobia started, although I have vivid memories of the dreams that accompanied it: falling from on high, stomach lurching and palms sweating as my body plummeted to the ground. My technique for dealing with the fear is to strip my feet bare and push them into the earth. Only this 'grounding' stops the palpitating terror and prevents me from falling to my knees. If only it would halt the dreams.

It takes me about twenty minutes to get accustomed to dangling from a rope above the ground. My arms aren't that strong either, so my forearms feel the strain as soon as I've thrown the bag and line. Once I've slung the rope up and over, prepared the knots, put on the harness and helmet, and attached myself, I slowly start to settle, using a foot to help when I need to give my arms a rest. Hauling myself up takes plenty of effort in the heat; my hands feel hot, clammy and bark rubbed. To motivate me to the top, Lorenzo calls up to me to assure that the descent is easy. Apparently, I just let go.

On the way up I get acquainted with a vermilion-spotted bright green tree frog and a sleeping Talamancan yellow-shouldered bat and bump into – literally – a slaty mouse opossum hot-handling a wriggling silver grub. Peering between the leaves affords some truly jaw-dropping views. Gazing out over treetops, calm and serene, I breathe in the scent of bark, tree sap, leaves and moss, so delicious that I want to gulp it down. My body is engulfed by nature: the leaves are all around me, tickling my face, brushing my hair, fanned around my waist like a hula skirt. Not all are from the tree I'm clinging to. Trailing plants with heart-shaped leaves choke the trunk's knobbly lower levels, tangled with smaller, long-leaved vines midway up. Spiny vines from neighbouring trees reach out to entwine with the budding shoots of new growth. My favourite are the palm-sized olive-green leaves, soft as velour, that gently caress my bare neck and chin. Up here, in my treetop heaven, the stressful disconnect I felt in Isla Colón seems a million miles away. It occurs to me that this must be what harpy eagles see from their own particular viewpoint, up here where sunlight finds the tip of each tree. I narrow my eyes and attempt to tune myself into the foliage, but other than some teeny-weeny scratches on the bark that I hope have been made by a silky anteater – the world's smallest, at around the size of a tea cup – I'm unable to spot anything other than the wildlife that presents itself to me. The leafy camouflage is too effective.

In this diverse forest with up to 350 tree species per hectare, I'm told the serious climbers head for the big nutmeg and ceiba trees, choosing between drier primary forests and soggy swamps in which to find these giant species. The ultimate challenge is a ceiba nicknamed The Tree of Pain, legendary among the tree-climbing fraternity. Earning its name from the short, hard spines that grow on the tops of each limb, its sixty-metre trunk is home to hand-sized tarantulas and twenty-inch eyelash vipers.

When it's time to descend I resist the temptation to look down, focusing on what's at my eye level. With a gentle tug on the hitch knot, I pull down slowly: Lorenzo has tied a slip knot to prevent a too-rapid return to the ground. I travel down to the bushy middle layers of canopy, then through the lower leaves and branches. Back on solid ground, I feel rehabilitated and revived. Everything feels good again.

When folk ask me if I have travelled the Panama Canal, I take great delight in replying 'Which one?' Panama City may be the home of one of the world's most important man-made waterways, but it was a dusty old banana outpost on the Caribbean Coast that was chosen for Panama's first canal project. More than a century ago the Snyder Banana Company (now Chiquita Brands International) ploughed huge amounts of capital into developing the Bocas del Toro mainland into a trading hub. Labourers shipped over from the West Indies dug the twelve-mile Snyder Canal out of the jungle on Isla Colón for the purpose of ferrying harvested fruit on slow-moving barges to Almirante Bay, where they'd be loaded onto ships for distribution to countries all over the world. The system worked like a dream for six short years, then a railroad was built. The barges became redundant, and within just a few months Bocas del Toro's role in the precious *oro verde* (green gold) rush was over. The abandoned Snyder Canal became derelict and fell into disrepair. For years it lay forgotten by all save a few local fishermen, who would hack their way through great, tangled webs of vines and mangroves to reach the Changuinola River, Boca del Drago and nearby beaches.

Today, travellers keen to experience a wild, untamed stretch of jungle river are drawn to this magical stretch. It has the feel of an epic wilderness adventure, just a hundred metres from the coast. A simple wooden canoe does the journey justice. Apart from ripples of water, dripping leaves and bird calls, the trip is one of silent tranquillity. A lack of human presence promises space and time to breathe it all in.

My guide is a local fisherman, nicknamed Tongo because of his resemblance to a TV cop (although with his receding hair, caramel skin and heavy-lidded eyes, he could be Panama's answer to Kojak). He assures me that a boat trip with him will blow my mind. It more than lives up to the hype. I lie back, almost flat, to stare up through a funnel of ancient trees to a small chink of sky. Eerie shapes and resonating echoes bring an extraterrestrial feel to an otherwise serene waterway. High banks of water-gnarled mangrove roots and giant palms could be straight out of the film *Jurassic Park*.

We are barely inside the 15,000-hectare San-San Pond Sak Wetlands Reserve when an Antillean manatee comes into view. Tongo seems to know it by name, whispering '*gordito*' (little fat one) to it across the silent, droplet-dappled waters. Around eighty manatees graze in the shallows of the San-San river basin. Tongo tells me that the water was once contaminated by a toxic spill – probably by a farmer – which killed a number of these shy, peaceful giants. Today, Panama's manatees are protected by law but are still often pursued by rifle- and harpoon-toting poachers. Local indigenous tribes believe that the manatee is a form of mermaid, with the Ngöbe-Buglé now a part of a sea-cow conservation drive.

Gordito is a young male, Tongo tells me, and may grow up to four metres in length at full size. The biggest he's ever seen weighed roughly the same as a family-sized caravan. After dipping back into the shadows, the creature gracefully somersaults underwater, as if in slow motion, before slipping quietly away into the mangroves. These reclusive animals can, I'm told, reach a top speed of more than sixty kilometres per hour, but Gordito is clearly not in a high-velocity mood. He will eat for at least eight hours each day, chewing his way through around fifty kilos of sea grasses, leaves, shoots, palms and nuts. I hope I'll get to see his strange, flabby face again, that he will surface for air once more. Sadly, Gordito doesn't oblige.

Tongo pushes the boat off the mud bank and we continue our journey through this dank Ramsar wetland. I am scouring the bank for a Neotropical river otter when an American crocodile the size of a sofa plunges into the depths. Once our dugout has stopped rocking in its wake, Tongo asks me if I want to stick around to see if the crocodile plans to eat us for dinner. 'He'll eat you first,' I observe. 'You have less hair than me.' Wincing in faux offence, he grins and wags a finger. 'Ouch, Sarita, be careful. Otherwise I'll have to feed you to the anaconda!'

Tongo's uncle is a banana farmer, and a late-night call from the fisherman one night enlists me as hired help for harvesting. It's an early start, before first light, to grab the fruit when its firm, and by the time I arrive at the finca high up on a hill, the harvest is already in full swing. Apart from the barely audible crackle of a paint-splattered portable radio, the only sound is the thud of feet on soil. Palms rustle with the nimble fingers of at least twenty people. The air is warm, but still fresh underneath the soft pink glow of an early sun. The bananas, a young lime-green colour, are being handled like delicate crystal. Baskets are lined with thick blankets and soft sacking. We're all handed gloves. Any bruising or damage at this stage will mean a tear-jerking drop in price.

While commercial plantations in Latin America require huge investment in infrastructure and technology for transport, irrigation, drainage and packing, smallholders such as Tongo's uncle rely almost entirely on hard graft. Friends, neighbours and relatives gather to lend a hand at this time-critical, labour-intensive time in the season. Tongo's enterprising seven-year-old son, Pedrito, is selling coconuts from a battered crate, lopping off each crown with a man-sized machete so the milk can be drunk first, then hacking open the shell to reveal the flesh. From his scrawny shoulder, part-covered by a faded LA Lakers vest top, a Hercules beetle the size of a grown man's fist is surveying the scene. There are thirteen known species of Hercules beetle in the jungles of South and Central America, and this one is a whopper. Pedrito's caramel skin provides the perfect camouflage for the beetle's copper-mottled shell, but there are no hiding places for its enormous, horn-like pincers. Protruding like TV aerials, they jut out from its forehead, vibrating constantly with a hypnotic twitch.

I can hear the repetitive, low-pitched '*pzzt, pzzt-weet*' of a pair of Passerini's tanagers: the male is perched on a drooping bough, its black, velvety coat, silvery bill and vivid scarlet rump clearly visible against the green of glossy palms. A tropical kingbird, no doubt eyeing up the beetle, sits motionless on a wooden shed close by. At least half a dozen rufous-tailed hummingbirds flirt openly with a fruiting mango, flashes of iridescent rust-brown and green-tinged gold among the amber-orange orbs. From May to June mangoes fill trees in every corner of Panama, from the rainforests that fringe the beaches and mountain slopes of the Darién, to the moist, thick soils of Bocas del Toro. In the early eighteenth century the Spanish introduced several mango types from the Philippines to Central America, through the Pacific trading ports of Mexico and Panama. It's my favourite fruit, and I feel blessed every time I pluck a plump mango for my breakfast – it's like a slice of sunshine on a plate.

Today, I leave the mangoes to the hummingbirds and turn my attention to the field of stubby yellow fruit. More than 130 million tonnes of bananas are eaten all over the world, and almost all bananas grown for export are harvested in well-drained land within thirty degrees on either side of the equator. Latin America is, quite literally, 'top banana' (although India is the largest producer). Nothing compares to the sweet, pale flesh of a fruit grown here. Regional varieties tend towards firm, with a fluffy texture that softens in the mouth. Some are sweeter than others; some are slightly rubbery, becoming creamy and velvety when chewed, with a hint of apple tanginess. Many have an underlying tartness. Some are vegetal, crisp and clean, better eaten overripe.

In rural Central and South America, where there is limited access to healthcare, banana-rich diets help to keep illness at bay. Islanders use them to combat depression, cure hangovers and relieve morning sickness. While medical evidence suggests they help protect against kidney cancer, diabetes and osteoporosis, they can also stop a mosquito bite from itching. They contain high levels of tryptophan, a natural chemical that converts into serotonin – the happy-mood brain neurotransmitter – and can help sustain blood–sugar levels and protect against muscle cramps. High levels of vitamin B6 help reduce swelling, aid weight loss, strengthen the nervous system and boost white-blood-cell production, while potassium lowers blood pressure and protects against heart attack and stroke. They also aid digestion and act as a probiotic, stimulating the growth of friendly bacteria in the bowel.

'Bananas are good for putting a shine on your shoes, too,' Tongo adds. I laugh, suggesting: 'And bald heads?'

Back on the bar-fringed main drag of Isla Colón, I grab a table in a casual over-the-water joint and unfurl my map. The candy-coloured fairy lights strung overhead cast enough of a glow for me to route-plan, so I study my options and scribble notes on a paper napkin. A stranger pulls up a chair beside me when I am midway through a plate of fried fish, rice and plantain. 'Hey, I'm Tito, a cousin of Tongo,' he says by way of introduction. 'You wanna go to Popa, *chica*?'

I've been trying to plan a trip to the archipelago's remote Isla Popa ever since someone warned me not to visit: nothing makes a place seem more beguiling. Deadly snakes writhe in mulchy pits in Popa's elevated jungle tracts, I'm told. At night the air fills with a spine-chilling spitting hiss that spooks souls and brings on madness. I put down my knife and fork, shake Tito's hand and agree a deal. By midnight I have packed my overnight bag ready to jump aboard his early-morning skit out of town.

The sea, as smooth as glass, reflects the morning's golden rays like a mirror. Even with sunglasses on, the dazzling brightness is intense. Tito's fibreglass boat cuts effortlessly through the water. With a vague wave of the hand, he asks if I've ever been to Isla Parajos (Bird Island, also known as Swan Key). I tell him it's the only place in Panama where the distinctive red-billed tropicbird nests. The ten-metre-long ragged-rock island off the most northern edge of Isla Colón – much photographed because of its strange quarter-moon shape, punctured by two chasms – is home to around twenty-five pairs of breeding red-billed tropicbirds, offering incredible views of this ribbon-tailed seabird in flight.

Tito knows these waters intimately, as only a native can, inching his way through the translucent shallows and greeting familiar dolphins by name. His ears prick up each time the boat picks up the echo of new, deeper water, and innately he understands the shifting sands of the coastal bed. I notice that his eyes often half close, as if he is sensing the many unmarked reefs by smell, not sight.

We skirt the choppier waters around the kite-shaped Isla Bastimentos, a roadless Afro-Caribbean enclave of less than one thousand inhabitants hemmed by sandy beaches. It's an island I know inside and out – literally. Like many of the limestone outcroppings along the Caribbean coast, it is gouged with sea caves and mysterious ragged fissures, and before I began to struggle with confined spaces just a few years ago, I enjoyed submerging myself in their weird, cavernous depths. The cave on Isla Bastimentos is reached by boat along a mangrove inlet, where twisted branches have entwined to create a magical tunnel of vine-knotted boughs draped in trailing bromeliad creepers. When I arrived with my guide, Javi, he led me on a half-hour hike through pineapple trees, cacao and banana palms to the rocky mouth of the cave, where we donned industrial-strength headlamps. It took some courage to start wading through the water beneath dozens of hanging bats. Many others were swooping around us, together with hundreds of leaping crickets. Generally, the water is around chest height, but it isn't uncommon to need to duck down below the surface when water levels are high. After squeezing into some of the slippery crevices, belly down, to reach dark water, I floated backwards through rocky channels, my forehead scraping against the stone-dimpled ceiling.

A second cave on Isla Bastimentos was reached via a boat trip to the Ngöbe-Buglé community at pretty Quebrada de Sal (Salt Creek). Once we'd snaked past Coral Key and continued north towards the eco lodge at Punta Vieja (Old Point), a full-on jungle hike took us along an energy-sapping wet, hot and airless trail, brightened by the presence of monkeys, sloths, numerous butterflies and brightly coloured parrots. Home to a mammoth colony of bats, the cave contained less water than the first, but was a more gruelling underground slog. Impossibly skinny crevices necessitated face-to-face encounters with bats, spiders, cockroaches, small rats and scorpions. Sharp rocks were treacherously slippery and layered with piles of bat excrement and smelly green slime.

From a series of dry, angular boulders at the mouth, the rocks inside become tilted, as if propped against one another. Some are knife-edge serrated, others flat as altars or rounded by the flow of the stream. Breathless, I hoisted up my body using my knees to propel me, inching sideways in slow motion to search out a foothold. A just-wide-enough ledge offered a handhold that kept me from falling into the murky water below. I crawled, scrambled and belly-squirmed until my thighs, ankles and knees ached. Every bony part of my arms was blooming into bruises. Javi's boots in front were dark smudges in the gloom: I reached out for the heel of one of them, and when his knee moved forward, mine did too. Same with the left. We were like a pantomime horse, ratcheting ourselves forward in awkward unison. By folding my limbs, origami-like, I managed to ease my sixty-kilo frame through some last awkward gaps and wondered how bigger folk coped without a tub of grease and a winch. Something squelchy splatted down on my head. It looked like mushy, dark brown grains of rice, fairly uniform in size. Bat faeces. I gagged with revulsion, praying that its stinking microorganisms hadn't infiltrated my lips, eyes and nasal cavities – the droppings can be a nasty source of disease. Scratching my chin on a slitted incline that also ripped a button from my shirt, I pulled upwards and spotted a chink of daylight. Leaving the shadows behind, I sloshed through waist-high water with muffled steps on sodden limestone. Fresh air. Amazing. I couldn't wait to decontaminate.

Of the thousand species of bat that populate the planet – they make up a quarter of the world's mammal population – Bocas del Toro is home to several dozen, from the fish-eating bats that swoop over the bay in moonlight on Isla Colón to the nectar bats that flap high above subterranean lakes. The most prevalent is the greater spear-nosed bat, which forms large harems within the cave systems. Bat behaviour is eerily unfathomable. Some species 'play dead'; others charge around in high-velocity blindness; some just crawl along slowly. In full flight they can reach speeds of sixty miles per hour, locating food in utter darkness using echolocation. Their high-pitched sounds, inaudible to the human ear, are emitted at a rate of ten to twenty beeps per second. They have a voracious appetite, eating their way through up to 1,200 mosquitoes an hour to consume their own body weight each day. A super-efficient metabolism ensures they can digest bananas, mangoes and berries in about twenty minutes – it takes a human three hours.

Several species of fruit-eating bat serve as seed dispensers and pollinators to a huge array of forest plants. According to Javi, light pollution – a relatively new phenomenon in Bocas del Toro because around ninety per cent of the archipelago is off grid – is now threatening the regeneration of rainforests because it disrupts the behaviour of seed-dispersing bats. Under naturally dark conditions bats produce a copious seed rain, but many avoid foraging near artificial light. Even a single street lamp can compromise seed dispersal.

Though just a fifteen-minute boat trip from Isla Colón, Bastimentos is markedly different, rich in the language and culture of the nineteenth-century banana plantations. This Afro-Caribbean predominance gives the island an air of old Jamaica: an English patois is spoken and calypso, soca and reggae music pulsate all day long. Packed with colour and characters, Bastimentos is an alluring place of bright, painted bridges in Rasta shades, rainbow-coloured street signs and mural-painted walls. Its two small Ngöbe-Buglé settlements supplement their income from fishing with guided walks through jungle habitats that are home to sloths, monkeys, crocodiles and a unique minuscule species of strawberry-coloured frog.

Strawberry poison-dart frogs are one of the most common poison-dart frogs in Latin America. But throughout the archipelago of Bocas del Toro, they are a little quirkier than the norm. Each island offers an extreme variation in colour, a phenomenon that lures the greatest frog experts in the world to this far-flung corner of Panama. Some are pinky-red and many have black speckles. Some have white arms. Others are more orange, a few are reddish-yellow and some are tinged with green or coloured midnight blue. On Isla Bastimentos, they are bright red.

There are more than 160 frog species in Panama, of which thirty aren't found anywhere else in the world. But, like frog populations all over the world, Latin American frog numbers are in freefall, largely because of chytrid fungus – the worst infectious disease ever recorded among vertebrates. As a major contributor to the decline of amphibian numbers around the world, the fungus can affect large populations of frogs very rapidly, disproportionately eliminating species that are rare and endemic.

On my last trip to Bastimentos, I was confronted by another threat facing its strawberry-coloured frogs, one that is arguably just as destructive as chytridiomycosis. Greed. The construction site was smack bang at the end of one of my favourite walks, along a breezy upland trail. I'd wound my way through soaring native ferns and trees of breadfruit, guava, sweet plum and avocado. On lower ground banana and pineapple plants dotted the path, and all around me insects, birds, frogs and other wildlife squawked, fluttered, chirped and croaked. Bright red blooms spouted from lush-leaved bushes to match, quite nicely, the crimson-coloured frogs hidden in the trees. Here, just a few years earlier, I had machete-cut a skinny trail to explore parts of the forest that sunlight could barely reach. After laboriously fighting through a riddle of vines and hardwoods for several hours, I'd come to a lake topped with oversized lily pads. I'd put my backpack down, removed my heavy boots and tentatively stepped onto one of the pads, centring myself gradually to let it take the strain. I remembered wriggling my toes against its rubbery surface and looking down into the inky-green depths, locking eyes with submerged caiman. I'd pushed all fears from my mind, stepping from one pad to another and another until I had circumnavigated the lake. I'd been elated, my heart pumping and my cheeks flushed in that mysterious setting, where teeny-weeny pinpricks of sunlight forced their way through the rainforest to dapple the water like fairy dust. But those beautiful memories were to remain just that: a wonder-filled episode never to be repeated. Not long after, the construction workers had moved in, drained the lake, sawed thousands of hectares of rainforest to the ground and ploughed the land for a golf course.

The deep scar left on the landscape made me grimace in pain. To see such damage was deeply distressing: it was impossible to fathom how it could take place on an island designated a National Marine Park. Mangroves and protected bird-rich jungles had been ripped apart, leaving mounds of bare mud littered with upturned trees and severed branches. Monkeys, snakes, caimans, sloths and a host of tropical birds had fled in droves from the diggers, cranes and dredgers. Sapped of all life, the scene was one of annihilation. My emotions brimmed over into a trickle of salty tears. The view before my eyes became blurred as I grieved for the death of the forest. Once I started sobbing, I just couldn't stop. 'How could they?'

Conservationists in Central America hope that Red Frog Beach Resort marked an environmental turning point as an ill-conceived development that ignored the Ngöbe-Buglé population, which fought to stop it. The original developers disappeared in a cloud of brick dust, leaving the new owners to contend with the stigma of a resort 'that wiped out the wildlife'. Today, it is doing its best to repair some of the damage, marketing its rooms to birdwatchers and other nature lovers, urging them to discover the wildlife – there is some left, just. Me, I'm grateful that I once had the chance to delve into the enchanting forest before the frogs, lily pads and peacefulness were lost forever.

Blinking back the pain of the memory, I am brought back to the boat by a massive swell that covers my face with spray. To avoid a floating tangle of mangroves, Tito guns the motor. I can barely hear his nasal tones over the roaring throb and rattle. Gesturing over his shoulder at Isla Bastimentos, he tells me about the rhythmic reggae beats and the island's famous local musicians. It is, he says, home to two bands, both called the Bastimentos Beach Boys. Confusing, eh? The same name! He cackles, head shaking. And admits that with virtually the same repertoire, it is difficult to tell which band is which. Music forms the heart of every celebration on the island. Both bands, he says, boast incredible stamina, jamming non-stop for fifteen hours to thrill crowds with their high-energy dance rhythms. Scandalous lyrics ensure that they are hero-worshipped across the archipelago. Tito tells me that one of his friends is a roadie – well, 'boatie' actually, because all the amps, percussion, microphones and guitars are lugged around by canoe.

The jutting tip of land on Isla Solarte (Nancy Key), where the United Fruit Company hospital once stood, is now widely known locally as Hospital Point, although only the footings remain. Built in 1899, the sixteen-building complex set a new standard in employee care, being well equipped to treat the numerous health problems and tropical diseases that affected workers in the UFC banana plantations. However, after an outbreak of wilt fungus in the early twentieth century, the banana plantations of Bocas del Toro collapsed, forcing the company to shift its operation to the mainland.

Today, anyone who talks of Hospital Point usually has snorkelling in mind. This is where brightly coloured tourist boats flock to tip crowds onto a shallow reef. With a narrow dusting of sand, this small horseshoe bay below the former medical camp isn't the best dive site, but it is the most accessible. On a busy day, a swarm of outboard motors churns the blue waters into a silty froth. I am lucky. I once arrived here early, before the tour boats had left the dock, and caught the low-lying reef at its clearest and most spectacular. For about an hour it was just me and the lobsters, eels and squid peering out from the rocky underwater peaks. Then, the tour boats arrived and about a hundred people splashed into the water. I took my leave, hopped back into Tongo's boat and powered off to nearby Coral Key to get a head start there, swimming away from the anchor-pounded coral near the jetty to venture just beyond the reef, where I was nudged around by a vast shoal of rainbow fish. Coral Key, a rustic cluster of thatched-roofed cabins strung together by wooden boardwalks, has a laid-back vibe. That is, until it becomes the next stop on the boat-tour itinerary.

As a travel guidebook author, I am fully aware of the role I play in bringing a destination to a wider audience, and the responsibility can sometimes weigh heavy – particularly when a place is relatively unknown. Tourism can often destroy the USP of a place that is remarkable for its untouched, extraordinary beauty. Yet tourism may also offer a lifeline to communities that have suffered long-term hardship in the harsh economic and societal realities that can go hand in hand with being undiscovered. Tourism requires thoughtful planning as it so often results in large-scale development that changes a landscape forever. Investment in infrastructure and hotel accommodation means the arrival of trucks of asphalt, cement mixers and block paving. Swimming pools sap every bit of available water at the expense, perhaps, of local residential supplies. The changes may be slow, creeping in over time so that scenic views and rustic landmarks are adjusted, almost unnoticed. Or they can be announced in a heartbeat by efficient, motivated – and well-meaning – administrations that attack the terrain with dynamite blasts, earth movers and drainage pumps. Languages change, behaviours alter and foods adapt to tourism needs. And, within a lifetime, an unknown place of hidden charm and unique character can become a homogenised mishmash of every other place on Earth. I've stared at pages of text and tried to risk assess simple recommendations and it is impossible not to feel anxious about what they may lead to. Will the quaint little honey-stone cove with empty sands and hundreds of nesting seabirds hold the same lure once a guidebook has shared its secrets with millions of travellers around the world?

Tito curves the boat into a leaning tilt and signals Isla Cristóbal to our right. It was named after Christopher Columbus, who, after sailing along the coast of Honduras, arrived in Bocas del Toro in 1502. According to the locals, when Columbus dropped anchor here he was so overcome with the archipelago's beauty that he began to put his name to its islands and beaches: Bahía Almirante (Admiral's Bay), Isla Cristóbal (Christopher Island) and Isla Colón (Genoan-born Columbus called himself Christopher Colón after settling in Spain). Columbus sought no argument with its people, giving strict orders that his men should not harm them on this, his last voyage into the New World. Today, the people of the archipelago consider him a hero, not only as the man who first introduced Europeans and the peoples of the Americas to one another, but also as a first-class navigator who placed Bocas del Toro on the map.

A salty splash of spray across my face takes me by surprise and tells me we're nearing the choppier waters around the tiny rocky islets and dive site dubbed Shark Hole. In the hope of seeing some telltale black fins, I swing my shoulders to the right, but there's just a ruffle of waves. Tito points vaguely to the west and tells me the horrific story of a dolphin killed by a tour boat earlier in the year. Apparently, the boat was loaded with fee-paying passengers determined to see dolphins, but Mother Nature wasn't playing ball. Once they started groaning and asking for refunds, the boat driver bowed to pressure. Keen to redeem his credentials, he churned up the water and a pair of dolphins came into view. Determined not to infuriate his passengers, he began to encircle the dolphins, inching closer and closer to encourage them to leap. As the passengers whooped and hollered, the dolphins panicked and the boat got too close. Tito shudders. 'It didn't stand a chance,' he says, shaking his head. The young dolphin sustained propeller injuries that penetrated to the bone. When the waters turned red with blood, the tourists' yelps of delight became horrified screams.

In reflective silence, we pass Cayo de Agua (Water Key), where the over-the-Caribbean thatched-roof houses are unlike others in the archipelago because they've been covered in red and sky-blue paint. Tito pulls out a clear plastic soda bottle from a rucksack, takes several swigs and offers it to me. Out of politeness, I press the bottle to my lips; it is filled with neat Seco, the potent liquor made from distilled sugar-cane juice that is Panama's national drink. With an alcohol volume of thirty-five per cent and a price tag of less than five US dollars per litre, a bottle of Seco is a cheap way to get hammered. In the UK, it would be sold in a brown paper bag.

The engine splutters in deep water and I'm thrown forward in a clumsy lurch. Isla Popa is, at last, on the horizon. My legs have seized up, my spine has curled and my bottom half is rigid from bouncing around on a wooden seat for well over an hour. Tito grins at me, mimicking my slumped and crumpled posture. His speech is slurred, my heart sinks and I turn to look out to sea. Whistling, like you would to a pet, he tries to attract my attention. When I eventually look round, he winks at me and asks if I'd like to party. I roll my eyes. He is clearly planning to make a night of it on Isla Popa, but my steely stare makes it clear it won't be with me. Gulping at the bottle, he drains its contents and tosses the empty plastic at my feet with sulky petulance. Frostiness replaces flirtatiousness. His eyes are like ice.

Characterised by steep hills, dense forest and beaches hemmed by thick mangroves, Isla Popa is home to two Ngöbe-Buglé communities. Popa Uno is the oldest, a settlement of more than three hundred people by a creek on the south-west side of the island, while Popa Dos comprises migrants from nearby islands, enticed by cheap land in a Government bid to boost the population. The islanders fish the waters and live without electricity and phone connection, their fresh water supplied via a primitive aqueduct system.

As our boat nears the shore, the sky fills with terns, frigatebirds, shearwaters and gulls that herald our arrival noisily. Tito cuts the engine and allows the boat to drift slowly into a soft bank of sand. Crystalline waters sparkle tantalisingly, so I swing my legs over the side to give my bare feet a dip. Wriggling my toes in water is one of life's simple pleasures. Today they are nibbled, gently, by a shoal of finger-sized fish. Raising my face towards the sky I shake my head to loosen the tie in my hair and encourage the warm breeze to blow it behind me. Then, lifting my backpack high above my head, I jump down, thigh high, into the Caribbean Sea.

Tito, the tenth child of a fisherman father, disappears immediately onto the island, moving seamlessly between sea and land as if carried by an invisible, slow-moving wave. I wade ashore behind him, noticing that the sands bear no sign of his footsteps. Beyond the mangroves, a perfect beach unfolds. Apart from three-toed sloths and toucans – the only ones in Bocas del Toro – I've read that there are millions of stick insects on Isla Popa. These are not the inch-long variety found in many British schoolchildren's bedrooms – in my house, where we had a very liberated approach to pet ownership, our stick insects lived as comfortably as we did, breeding in large numbers and living in the airing cupboard and cooker vent, and on the back of the sofa. No. The Caribbean stick insect is up to sixty centimetres long, a formidable beast the size of a forearm. With an exoskeleton armed with sharp, spiky-edged barbs, it is one of many South and Central American insects that seem to belong to an alien world.

'*Bienvenido*. Welcome!' A wide-eyed teenage girl with a lilting voice appears from the bushes. Valentina is no more than sixteen, her dark hair plaited into a knot at the nape of her neck. Big eyes shine brightly on a youthful face that glows with a light spritz of perspiration. Resting against a hard-bristled broom with her hip, spray-tight jeans clinging to a willowy frame, she tells me that her job is to sweep the sand spotless 'like a carpet'. She smiles broadly, tucking a small pink flower behind her ear like a Tahitian beauty, as I offer my congratulations, for there isn't a single unsightly fleck on the entire beach. She laughs, sweetly, joking that she can spot rubble or driftwood forty miles out at sea. 'Dirt beware,' she says, wagging her finger at the sands.

The island is preparing for the opening of a new beach resort operated in partnership with a private rainforest sanctuary. Large swathes of jungle will be protected under the resort's stewardship scheme, with trails cut for guests to explore from a cluster of cottages set high atop a hill. Each will be equipped with cable television, a DVD player, air conditioning and a hot-water shower. The ambition of the project astounds me. Where there were once only hammock hooks, there will be a VIP suite and penthouse apartment – complete with butler service. Will it provide good job prospects for local villagers? Valentina is hopeful, but there is nobody around to ask. At the water's edge I burrow my toes into the cool, damp sand and admire the sweeping idyll. The holidaying jet set will adore it, I'm certain of that. But looking around me, I find it impossible to imagine starch-collared waiters shouldering platters of Martini cocktails and sashimi. It is the raw simplicity of this place that has put me at ease. That, and the constant squawks of toucans.

The keel-billed toucan is distinctive for its bill, which is mostly green but often daubed with red, yellow and orange, too. Like other species of toucan, its bill makes up around a third of its size. On Isla Popa it nests in holes in trees, often with several other toucans, which sleep with their beaks and tails tucked under their bodies to make room for one another. The bountiful quantities of different fruits and berries in the forests here sustain them, although they may supplement their diets with insects, small lizards, eggs and frogs.

Extremely sociable birds, toucans prefer to travel in small flocks of up to fifteen. They're not proficient fliers, preferring to hop between branches, which they do with deft precision, despite appearing clumsy and awkward. Snakes and rodents prey on their eggs, but the main threats to toucans come from humans, who gather the eggs to eat and disturb birds during nesting. Despite this, they rarely remain hidden, showing themselves readily and being characteristically vocal. On Isla Popa, you hear them at every turn: grunting, snoring, snuffling or emitting a distinctive '*kkreekk*'.

The beach is delicately pocked with the minuscule sand holes of a zillion fiddler crabs. With their comedic oversized claws, these five-centimetre-wide creatures look as if they are waving crustacean versions of the giant foam hands given to spectators at basketball games. Found around brackish tidal marshes, sandy beaches and fertile mudflats, fiddler crabs dig their cylindrical burrows to escape harsh sun, high tides and predators. They live in large colonies; find one fiddler crab and you're not far from several hundred. The friendly wave from the male's enormous claw is actually a courtship ritual. In Peru the motion is compared to sewing, and the crab is named after a master tailor (*maestro-sastres*); in Brazil their name denotes someone beckoning the tide to return (*chama marés*).

Valentina taps me gently on the shoulder, and once I've wriggled my toes free of the sand, she shows me where I can sling my hammock. A looping trail takes me across a grassy slope interspersed with a mixture of giant mature hardwood trees and sprouting palms: a shady, cool spot in which to soak up the view in a breeze straight off the sea. Even when the path dips down into a valley, I can hear the waves and seabirds on the beach. Though some sections of its dense rainforest have been cleared for pasture, Isla Popa remains rich in birdlife. Endemic birds include the handsome purplish-backed quail-dove, with its dignified, regal stance, and the well built sulphur-rumped tanager – an easy one to spot with accuracy on account of its large yellow rear end. The rare and endangered black-and-white owl has made a few appearances here. There are also giant, blue morpho butterflies and large numbers of sloths, and the local tribal people swear that ocelets live here.

After resting by a stream, I follow a narrow trail that leads me to herons and egrets in a tangle of butterfly-scattered mangroves. Deep ravines cut with freshwater sedge marsh lead to extensive thickets and small crops of banana and plantain. Tongo had speculated that North American birds would outnumber Panamanian species on Isla Popa, and it looks as if he may be right. Frequent sightings of pale-billed woodpeckers, chestnut-coloured woodpeckers and a pair of brown-capped tyrannulets delight me, and within twenty-four hours I've seen at least half a dozen pairs of olive-crowned yellowthroats. Golden-collared manakins are also abundant, although less easy to spot. Olive-throated parakeets and yellow-bellied elaenia also hide well in the bushes. Valentina says she's seen white-throated crakes in the marsh and adjacent grassy slopes, but there are none to see when I stop by, even though I can hear the distant sound of their sharp, explosive metallic trills. Then, just as I am about to leave, a semi-plumbeous hawk swoops down from nowhere. It plucks a mouse from the swamp in a lightening snatch, a stunning display of primal predation that makes my skin tingle.

After watching a lone ruby-throated hummingbird darting back and forth in a clearing, I double back under a giant spider's web strung with glistening droplets and small red flies to head towards the sea. It feels good to let the water swirl around my skin. Lying down in the wet sand, I suck the air in deeply as the waves lap across my legs and waist up to my arms, chest and head and into my hair. I'm sunning, with face turned up towards the yellow-gold rays. The water is so calm that it is almost noiseless, and I bury myself deeper into the wet. A delicate white flower drifts towards me, landing by my cheek. Taking a leaf out of Valentina's book, I scoop it up and place it in my hair.

Only once the sun starts to dip do I pull myself out of the water to follow the riddle of trails back to squawks and rustles. Pausing momentarily at a dog-leg turn, I listen to see if toucans are the cause of the commotion. They are. By pure chance, my hammock is perfectly positioned for observing their eccentric behaviour. An hour or so passes before my stomach insists on dinner. My nose tells me which way to walk, and I soon arrive at a rack of skewered meat sizzling over a smoky fire. Tito and I are the only guests, and our hosts are a nimble Ngöbe-Buglé elder and a woman I assume to be his wife. While we wait for the meat to cook – it's a type of island rat, from what I can gather – the elder, who stands less than five feet tall, walks me around the lip of the forest. In laboured Spanish, he extols the health-giving powers of his surroundings, plucking, pulling and picking at an array of berries, fruits and herbs. The woman, wearing the traditional bright-coloured smock dress of the Ngöbe-Buglé, calls us over to eat, wiping her hands self-consciously over the triangle design that seems common to every dress.

The pattern symbolises a snake skin, based on an ancient Ngöbe-Buglé legend about an ill-fated love affair between a serpent and a girl. On finding the pair together, the girl's brother lashed out at the snake in a violent rage, an act that forever broke the pact of peace between humans and serpents. This in part explains why Ngöbe-Buglé communities, which are unafraid of almost every other creature, fear snakes. But there's a practical reason, too. Snakebite is a very real worry in the Americas, especially in Latin America, where the number of incidents is estimated at around 129,000 each year and deaths may be up to 3,000 – although this could be a serious underestimation given that so few forest communities fill out reports. Of Panama's 130 snake species – many of which are harmless tree-dwellers – the venomous fer-de-lance, known as 'ekees' by the Ngöbe-Buglé people (for the letter X), is the most feared. After a Panamanian government minister was killed by a fer-de-lance bite in 2005, the National Snakebite Programme led by the University of Panama called for a fourteen-million dollar investment into the research and development of antivenom serums.

I became a snakebite statistic myself when I stepped off a muddy trail in the rural lowlands of Costa Rica to seek out a drier path. As I straddled a small creek, I felt a sharp bite just above my boot top. Then I realised that what I'd stepped onto wasn't a small, round boulder, but a coiled snake. Ignacio, my driver, grabbed his phone and snapped a photo. He then ushered me, at speed, into our jeep nearby. Nothing hurt. I felt fine and there wasn't any swelling. So I spent the entire ten-minute journey to the clinic assuming it was all a mistake. At the medical centre, despite my embarrassment, Ignacio slung me over his shoulder like a sack of plantain and sprinted to the door. By now I felt nauseous, but it could have been carsickness. Ignacio had been screaming round the hairpin bends like Starsky and Hutch.

There weren't any qualified doctors on duty, so a young trainee vet was holding the fort. On glimpsing the photo he leapt into action, pulling on a pair of disposable gloves and switching off a blaring TV set. A local policeman turned up to witness proceedings. To lighten the mood, he introduced himself as Spongebob Squarepants. I laughed weakly as tubes were stuck in my arms and a massive syringe was pumped with gloop. My fists were clenched tight; the pain now was intense. It took seconds to administer the antivenom. The relief I felt was overwhelming; I knew that a river of poison was no longer threatening my vital organs.

As I share the story with my Ngöbe-Buglé host, I run a forefinger over my leg, tracing the ragged scar that still tattoos me today. Earlier this season, while trekking in the Brazilian Amazon, I suffered an allergic reaction to multiple mosquito bites that made my face swell up like a beach ball. My throat was slowly being squeezed tight shut as my eyes sank deep into my forehead. Soon, my skin looked like pink blancmange and my lips like tractor tyres. A racing pulse told me time was of the essence. I reached for my EpiPen, now a constant companion after five or six similar episodes – on one occasion, in Venezuela's capital Caracas, the swelling was so rapid that I fed a plastic drinking straw down into my throat to keep the airway open. The adrenalin brought instant relief from the stinging and a euphoric floating feeling as the swelling receded. The 'trout pout' took a few hours to calm, but was the only remaining sign of potential anaphylactic shock.

Mother Nature can scare me. She's entitled to do that. Floods, rainfall, droughts, deserts, wild creatures, bee swarms and flesh-eating bugs have all made me fearful or humble. But when it comes to other issues of safety in Central and South America, I have never felt seriously threatened. I haven't been stolen from, other than when someone nicked my only bra from an empty beach on Isla Providencia, Colombia – an audacious act of theft that would only have been more remarkable if I'd been wearing it at the time. Other than a case of crossed wires in a boat on the Colombian Amazon, I have never felt that another human had plans to harm me.

I take care, of course. Always. There is never any substitute for that. I stuff money, inventively, into hard-to-reach places. I always dress down. Being sensible about whom I buddy up with, whom I trust, is imperative – as is doing my best to attract zero attention. It helps that I am a dark-haired woman with olive skin and dark features, who blends in relatively easily. Where possible, I pick accommodation that is safe and secure. I never forget that I'm a single woman.

I'm often asked if I worry about being a target for abduction in Latin America. But criminal gangs have little appetite for kidnappings tourists these days, preferring to snatch domestic members of the wealthy elite. Though I have sometimes been scolded by the locals for refusing to carry a gun, I try to resist the temptation. Most people I meet seem to carry one: a twitching hand in an inside pocket or the subconscious twiddle of a trigger is a giveaway. Guns are part of life in Central and South America, so I no longer flinch with every shot. In San José, Costa Rica one day, in daylight, a guy pressed a gun barrel to the side of my temple – the cold, hard metal left an imprint on my skin. He had a crazed look in his eyes. Fear, resentment and anger clouded his face. I did nothing, just met his stare. He ran away.

I have received training on how to use a firearm. It was on a course designed to give 'stopping power' to women in case of assault. I learned how to handle a revolver, sending several dozen shots down range at a target until it no longer felt totally horrifying to shoot someone in the head. Once I could hit five out of five in the chest, and could control the power, weight, kick and accuracy of the shooter, I knew I had shed my nerves. I can use a gun. Have held a gun. But I have never needed to fire a weapon again.

In the absence of a revolver, a Swiss army blade is my constant companion. Like the comfort a mobile phone can bring, it makes me feel happier when it is there. Unlike a gun, a knife is useful in every setting. Running the tip of the blade around a coffee jar; sliding it through the seal of an envelope; weakening tight knots; removing rotting branches – a knife can do it all. Tongo advised me once always to assume that the people I meet are carrying blades.

An impromptu knife-stance masterclass on an early trip to Peru was useful. How you stand, it stressed, is crucial in combat, defence and hunting, because it dictates how quickly you can react, manoeuvre and engage. A forward stance, resting on the balls of the feet, requires even weight distribution. The front knee should be slightly bent, elbows at the sides. Holding the knife with the lead hand trains the second hand to check, steady and deflect. The chin should be tucked in to ensure that the throat is protected. When moving silently through the jungle, this stance ensures that you can defend yourself, fight or escape. When in the company of indigenous hunters, I am always aware of their posture. Stealth, astuteness, fearlessness and strength combine with the flat-footed steadfastness and surety of a squat, short body. Clear evidence, should we need it, that we only develop the qualities that we need.

Should I ever feel threatened, a quick mental checklist helps to put me into this position: stooping slightly with rock-solid legs that are bent a little to aid speed of flight. But, essentially, I have always travelled in the belief that there is more good in the world than bad. Cynical views about the human race are often borne out of fear. To travel scared is, for me, to move from one point on the map to another. Travelling without fear – but always with an open mind and heart – is the only way to truly encounter. There are such things as happy endings, when you accept a drink, a meal or a helping hand, or share a kind word with someone new. For me, the only way to get under the skin of a new culture is to walk down ordinary streets, eat in ordinary cafes and strike up conversations with ordinary people. To travel without fear enables you to seek out quiet backstreets where people go about their daily lives. It allows you to let go of preconceived notions and embrace new experiences by taking a leap of faith.

Otters, Flamingos and Jackboots

Colombia, Venezuela and Panama
2007–2010

I have always travelled light. If my trip is less than ten days and I'm carrying more than ten kilos, I've packed too much. But I travel with different things now than I did a decade ago. Today, I rarely skimp on home comforts, often opting for a single change of clothes in order to make room for chocolate biscuits, some decent face creams, a pack of good coffee and some British teabags. The other essential item is my radio. I grew up listening to the BBC World Service, tuning into crackly broadcasts from distant locations. The images it created left a lasting impression and fuelled my interest in far-flung places. I love twiddling the dial to discover new music and eavesdrop on daily programmes, even if the language is one I don't understand. I let the unfamiliar words wash over me as I drink in the textures of each new sound.

Asked by a newspaper editor to list some of the things I have seen and done, I realise that I have had an incredible few years. I've visited several hundred of the Panamanian islands in both Pacific and Caribbean waters and have spent extended periods with four of Panama's indigenous tribes. I've hiked solo up Panama's highest peak, Barú volcano, and pitched a tent on its frosty summit. I've fished for my supper; shared waters with dolphins; startled massive capybara and been tracked by a prowling puma. I've jumped onto huge lily pads and was once so close to a giant sea turtle that I could have leaned out of the boat and touched its back. I've seen more hummingbirds than I could ever have imagined and encountered some formidable raptors.

On every trip I have sought out local wildlife experts and drained them with endless questions. I have eaten it up, gulped it down, hungered for more and begun to get involved, in a quiet way, in aspects of habitat conservation. My writing – already colour-rich in style – has become even more vivid as the wildlife I meet adds bold daubs of wonder and wow to my travel adventures. My binoculars now journey everywhere with me – although, unlike Ted from Wisconsin, I do draw the line at the toilet or shower. I also continue to resist the logic of wearing khaki.

I realise how full of wonderment I am again. Bonded once more with the world. It feels good to travel for encounters, not miles on a map, and for a better understanding of life on Earth. I'm a woman who knows and loves her planet. Who feels it breathe and pulse. Not by poring over books, but by sleeping under the stars, walking on the soil, wading through sands, jumping streams, washing in cold rivers, diving into crystalline lakes, hiding in caves, climbing trees, lying flat on my back in a meadow to gaze up at the clouds and experiencing the natural rhythm of each sunrise and sunset. I suspect I'm still a useless birder, for I am still unable to identify a species in a matter of seconds, like the pros. But I can sense that my wild guesses are becoming less left of centre. What I lack in accuracy, I more than make up for in enthusiasm – much of it roused by the infectious enthusiasm of others.

Sure, I still wrestle with birds that are virtually indistinguishable by sight, and I'm pretty rubbish at deciphering vocalisation. But I've never felt like having a meltdown because I don't know what type of antshrike I'm looking at. Like gambling and other compulsions, I can see how birding can become addictive – especially if you're ticking boxes on a list and counting numbers. But, even now, I simply cannot imagine experiencing wildlife in that way.

For me, it is about the thrill of the incredible encounter. I don't want to start thumbing through a bird guide at the first sound of a cackle or chirp: I'd miss the main event. I figure it is better to spend time shinning over fences and waiting, stomach-down, in a bog-filled ditch for a species I don't recognise, than to know what it is but miss it because my head is stuck in a book. I see more, know more, but also accept that however much I learn it will never seem enough. Part of me envies the more knowledgeable folk I met at Canopy Tower, although I accept that my quest is different from theirs. For them, spotting wildlife offered the thrill of a hunt, without the bloodshed. For me, it is all about revelling in the simple joys of a complex planet, the pleasures bestowed by Mother Nature.

Today my guide is Alvaro. I meet him in Boquete, in Panama's green and misty Chiriqui highlands, where I have plans to walk a section of the Talamanca Mountain Range in the hope of spotting one of Central America's most delightful birds: the resplendent quetzal. Revered by the Aztecs and the Mayans, it is still considered the most beautiful bird in the Americas, held dear in the hearts and minds of ordinary people. Gorgeously plumed in baronial hues, the quetzal is a dazzling mix of ruby, sapphire and emerald daubed with copious iridescent gold. I am one of many quetzal admirers to have arrived here on a pilgrimage of adoration. Though royalty and priests no longer wear its feathers during ceremonies, it is honoured on coins, flags and stamps, and, as the cover model for the first edition of my Bradt travel guide to Panama, it will always be *la guinda* – Panama's version of 'the icing on the cake' – to me.

It's a wet day; the tenth day in a row that the heavens have opened. The trails are treacherous in places, so we slip and slide through muddy forests of oak, cedar, magnolia and laurel – known locally as *aguacatillo* – the main food of the quetzal. Thick tufts of soaring ferns and lush mosses provide habitat for a great number of birds, such as buffy tuftedcheek, ruddy treerunner, spotted barbital and spectacled foliage-gleaner. Hummingbirds of every colour flit around rain-soaked heliconias: I spot fiery-throated hummingbird, volcano hummingbird, white-throated mountain-gem, magnificent hummingbird and violet sabrewing prancing around a single flower. The choreography of this feathery dance troupe is every bit as beguiling as its collection of evocative names.

Alvaro, one of several children born to a large local Chiriqui family, is quietly spoken and erudite. A talented painter, he also plays guitar and is recently returned from living in Paris with his German girlfriend, where he studied art. He is great company: thoughtful, sensitive and warm. As if personally responsible, he apologises repeatedly for the lack of quetzals on the Quetzal Trail, until I tell him to stop. When I ask for help with the Spanish names of birds in the region, he tells me to assume that most of names are onomatopoeic, because most imitate the bird's call. I just need to remember to pronounce the 'I' as an 'ee' to get the name right. A loud, chirped echo makes us squeal with delight, as an iridescent shimmer of green pokes out from the hedgerow. The unmistakable jewel-toned plumage and oversized tail belongs to the resplendent quetzal. It looks every inch the sacred species. I am almost moved to tears.

Alvaro mimics the song of the resplendent quetzal in a series of deep, smooth, slurred but melodious notes: '*keow kowee keow k'loo keow k'loo keeloo*'. The quetzal, showing off its golden-green upperparts and bluish tinge, acknowledges him with a slurring response from its bright yellow bill. Even under the moody skies, I can see its pitch-coloured iris, glittering like freshly cut coal. I can't claim this as a skilled sighting. As quetzal-spotting goes, this is a total fluke. It makes it no less thrilling.

Before long, with the rain still relentless, the paths have deteriorated into a river of sludge. We start to slip more than we step. In fact, we are sliding backwards more now than moving forwards. Alvaro and I dissolve into fits of giggles and admit defeat. It is time to turn back. By this time I am soaked to the skin, despite wearing a full set of waterproof clothing. The cool, misty rains of the highland region are deceptively piercing. Both our faces are pasted with swipes of sticky mud. We link hands on the descent to stop either of us sliding feet first: it doesn't work. While covering our slow couple of miles, there's been a landslide. Our path is blocked by a pile of freshly fallen soil topped with a large, rain-sodden rootball. Alvaro shins up the mud pile, sinking to his calves before turning to haul me up. We struggle across, somehow. We are covered in mud of various shades of brown, grey and red. It is even in my ears.

On the drive back we take an elongated route to make the most of the curtailed morning. We pass the Rio Caldera, a rock-strewn stretch of loud, babbling water hemmed by brightly coloured windflowers and lush foliage. After changing our clothes we share lunch at Boquete's Hotel Ladera, a bowl of lemony ceviche accompanied by the pitter-patter of rain. I drop Alvaro off and take the slow scenic drive to David, Panama's third-biggest city and the capital of Chiriquí Province, leaving the verdant green highlands. With every mile, the rain thins and the air becomes more tacky. In sharp contrast to the uplands, it is hot, steamy, sunny and low. After a swim in the pool at my hotel, I flick on the local news channel. I can hardly believe my eyes. Filling my TV is the Rio Caldera. Terrible images of devastation. Crying families. Everything swept away. A record eighteen inches of rain in just four hours has burst the river's banks. The road that was once in front of the Hotel Ladera has been carried away by an angry torrent. I am rooted to the spot, staring at the footage, open-mouthed. The brown river is tearing at the hotel's entrance, spewing debris against its perfectly painted sugar-white walls. It is ripping apart houses, sending hundreds of families running for refuge on higher ground. I scoop up my keys and jump in the jeep to speed back towards Boquete. After checking that Alvaro and his family are safe and well, I stop off at a roadside store to pick up blankets and bedding, which I hand to a policeman at a roadblock. The river is a roaring mass of branches so strong that it is tossing boulders into the sky and demolishing bridges. Miraculously, there is no loss of life that day. The mayor, government workers and teams of volunteers work tirelessly to repair all the damage, consigning it to history within a few short weeks. Yet Boquete pledges never to forget its river's dangerous past.

Before driving up to meet Arturo, I made a mental note to pick up some extra matches because I knew I'd need to build a fire. Often I am so freezing cold in Cerro Punta that even when I do add extra blankets to the bed I still sleep in all my clothes. Nights are bitterly cold in this higher-altitude mountain town less than ten miles from Boquete. Rain is constant – and it's icy rain at that. On the plus side, the region is renowned for cups of thick, creamy hot chocolate topped with fluffy whipped cream – and after a wet walk, there is nothing more tasty or warming. The landscape of Panama's Chiriquí highlands is adorable, with its fruit farms, fields of black-and-white dairy cattle and colour-rich, flower-filled market gardens trimmed by roadside stalls selling jams and fruit wine. Arturo has called ahead to book accommodation at Los Quetzales, a fine wooden lodge with amazing views and some remote hillside cabins tucked among the forest.

The sheer abundance of wildlife, especially the dozens of hummingbirds right outside my window, makes up for the upset of getting my notes wet in the rain. Each of my notepads is completely sodden, so I place their streaky pages close to the fire. My clothes are drenched, too, and my fingers so cold and blue that I struggle to unzip my bag to pull out the box of matches. Thankfully they are in a watertight purse. I opt to sleep in my dry hammock because the blankets on the bed feel damp to the touch. There's a tight knot in it that has worsened over the weeks, and I try again to untie it. Then I become so frustrated that I saw at the ropes like a loony, attacking it with my serrated knife, swearing loudly until it frays and splits. A short, wet, muddy walk improves my mood. I manage to scope study, briefly, a long-tailed silky-flycatcher, a slate-throated redstart and some very lively yellow-thighed finches.

I am hungry, again, despite having eaten just an hour ago. However much I eat these days, my stomach grumbles constantly, like an echoing, empty cave. Because I burn off 2,000 calories in a single morning's wet-weather trek my usual snacks of nuts, berries, fruit and cereal bars don't touch the sides. At night, I dream of doorstep slices of granary toast slathered in Irish butter. A big, steaming mug of strong English tea would be perfect right now – the dark, strong, inexpensive stuff that hairy-arsed British builders drink. I settle for a swig of bright green Gatoraid and try not to think about food.

Also on my mind is the toenail on my right foot. I was too tired to cut it down before this morning's trek and I'm paying for it now. The nail on the big toe doesn't need to be very long to cause problems; even half a millimetre can cut into the flesh. It then bruises, splits the skin and can get infected. This afternoon, I am hobbling and feel livid with myself. Under the nail I can see the mushy pink flesh riddled with vessels; a large bubble of blood has already formed and the toe is bruised. The tissue I've wrapped round it is wet with a pink fluid that looks like a mix of blood and pus. Excess shards of nail that have already lifted, I carefully trim away, but it is as sore as hell.

The annoyance I feel at myself clouds my mood. A simple sixty-second trim would have prevented all this. If an infection is left untreated, it can spread into the bones – I met a Norwegian hiker once who required an amputation. If it doesn't improve in the next few days, I'll have no alternative but to pull the nail off to allow the toe to drain. Ouch. Ouch. Ouch.

The next day, after sleeping fitfully with my foot raised on three pillows, my toe is no longer hot to the touch, but I wonder if that is because my entire body is so cold it is rigid, as if it is covered in a frosty glaze. I pass on a morning shower – the water is cold enough to form ice pellets – and try, unsuccessfully, to revive last night's fire. I am wearing every piece of clothing from my rucksack, rotund like an Eskimo. Outside, in the woods, the magnificent treescape looks like a scene from the movie *Avatar*: a stunning, dreamlike panorama of bountiful foilage in rich colours. I draw it in, slowly. Then hobble away.

After wrapping my foot in wads of tissue, I pull on an extra two pairs of socks and squeeze it snug into my boot. It's an early start to reach the Panama–Costa Rica border and the Chiriquí Viejo river, a stretch of water renowned among thrill seekers for its froth of white-water rapids. In the final throes of the rainy season, after a succession of night-long showers, the rapids are at their wildest; water levels are scarily high and the currents have a will of their own.

The Chiriquí Viejo river snakes for almost 130 kilometres from the slopes of Cerro Picacho, on the north-west side of the mighty Volcán Barú, before trickling through the mountain village of Cerro Punta. From the highlands, nourished by alpine torrents, it crashes down craggy slopes to emerge as a gushing, rock-strewn river at the Volcán plains. Wide, choppy and prone to powerful surges, with spectacular waterfalls and canyons, this turbulent, frothing stretch offers long and continuous rapids and steep gradients – a strenuous day at the paddle requiring precision, strength and nerves of steel. There are five sections to choose from, however, and Arturo assures me we'll being doing the easiest stretch. Hector, Eusebio and Humberto from Chiriqui River Rafting are waiting for Arturo and me on a grassy bank. For them, the river holds no fear. Despite their wicked laughs at the crazy state of the water, I know I am in safe hands. All the men are advanced native paddlers, who have ridden this river hundreds of times and know its quirks and traits. The only female, as usual, I am the focus of a lot of ribbing and teasing. I take it in good humour and try to give as much as I get.

When I climb into the dinghy, I am most concerned at the many fearsome boulders. The two near to our launch point are each the size of a single-storey house. The rain is soft and doesn't trouble us at first, until we hit the first of a massive string of rapids. Within seconds, our top halves are wet and the raft is spinning round and round. We bash into a rock and get sucked into a pool, then spat out again. We are propelled backwards before hitting the force of the water; it is so powerful it folds our raft in two, and I am squashed in a crease down the middle like a slither of pastrami in a bagel. As the lightest on board, I am vulnerable when the raft bounces high then pounds the surface of the water; I cling on desperately as I am thrown into the air. When we hit an epic eddy, Arturo's bulky frame hits the deck, causing the raft to fling me off like a demonic bouncy castle. After soaring far and wide, I drop back down in an awkward tumble into the water. I feel as if I am churning around in a washing machine. The raft has left me far behind, so when eventually I surface I cling to a slippery rock. Drenched and gasping, I am alone in a wide stretch of river with only a trio of curious cormorants for company.

After a while, probably ten minutes or so, I try pulling myself up onto the rock, but my waterlogged clothes weigh me down. A kingfisher flashes across the river, landing on a fallen log to plunge for fish deep below. Thundering torrents warn me that there's a waterfall nearby. To distract myself from my predicament, I scan the trees for spider monkeys on the riverbank. Then, I spot the speed-paddling scout who is kayaking our trip. He grins, teasingly. 'Your eyes, Sarita, they were like this!' he says, mimicking me, wide-eyed. I can't help but laugh, for I know that he is right. He pulls me, like a heavy weight, into the kayak.

The rest of the trip is uneventful, a tame, slow-paced paddle through some utterly beautiful scenery. Arturo and I take the opportunity to admire the wonders of the dense vegetation and listen to the hoots, chuckles, trills, caws and clucks of the ducks, egrets, kingfishers, quails, woodpeckers, pigeons, flycatchers and woodcreepers tucked amid the sponge-like green foliage. Sections evoke the foothills of the Andes, with giant ledges forming stepped gardens of grasses, moss and ferns.

On this gentler section, such a marked contrast to the initial stretch, we see large hawks and vultures overhead. Jaguars have been spotted here – a young male likes to stretch out coolly along a wide ledge and pat its paw at passing butterflies and river spray. Arturo tells me that the communities living alongside the Sixaola, another river running along the Panama–Costa Rica border, have noticed that it has been gradually changing course in recent years, causing huge problems for the farmers and villagers eking out livelihoods along its banks. Mudslides and watery meanderings have altered boundaries and borders, with farms belonging to Costa Ricans ending up on Panamanian soil, and vice versa.

Shivering, I take a team photo on the riverbank. Behind a particularly bushy hedge, I strip off and towel myself down before hypothermia sets in. Having removed every piece of clothing, I survey the clump of soggy tissue around my poorly toe and search in my bag for something dry. Two faces pop round the bush. It's Hank and Tom from Chicago – our fellow rafters. Could they have my email address, they ask, proffering a pen and a piece of paper. Why, of course, I reply, scribbling it down, trying not to drip or sneeze. Not one of us mentions my naked state.

Something equally embarrassing happened to me once in Cartagena, Colombia, at a beautiful UNESCO World Heritage Site. I was ill, having picked up a bug on the flight out from London. Under a fiercely hot sun, I'd agreed to film something for tourist television. Shadows and glare made filming tricky in the midday heat, but we persevered. Orbs of perspiration formed on my brow and upper lip. Sweat ran down my back and I felt nausea rising. Then, tiny stars fizzed in front of my eyes before someone flicked out the lights. Momentarily, I fainted. I didn't fall, because the thick stone walls of the ancient fort propped me up. Strangely, nobody seemed to notice: the camera was still pointed at me and the crew was still milling around. Then I realised that when I'd passed out, I'd lost control of my bodily functions. A noxious brown slick was seeping down my legs. The smell was dreadful. In the midst of all this, someone tapped my shoulder. It was a smiley man with his young son, holding a copy of the travel guide to Colombia I'd written. 'Could we have a photograph taken with you, please?' I replied: 'Of course.' We linked arms in a huddle and smiled for the camera. The father shook me by the hand and bid me farewell. The recollection still horrifies me. Back in David, a doctor jabs my toe with antibiotics. Advised to rest, I stretch out on the sofa in my hotel room and try to convince myself that I'm happy doing nothing. Large floor-to-ceiling windows frame the city. For a while, I watch women walk by, slowly, weighed down with shopping bags and children. Large flocks of small dark birds darting across the cityscape provide a recollection of starling murmurations that takes me, mentally, from David to the UK. Winter starling murmurations are one of the UK's finest wildlife spectacles on the calendar. In the evening, just before dusk, swirling, whirling flocks of starlings gather in large groups to perform aerial dances of sublime synchronicity, a jaw-dropping vision that echoes the intensity of the gradual deepening of the skies from yellow to orange to inky-red. Each bird strives to fly as close to its neighbour as possible, instantly copying any change in speed or direction to create a ripple effect. Murmurating clouds can be up to a million birds strong, rolling across the sky in mesmerising waves.

As a confirmed nomad, I am happiest when living in hotels. Yet I like to assume some sense of being settled, so I try to look for a long-term deal so I can put down roots. Settling into a hotel's rhythm of meal services, menu changes, laundry, shift patterns, tips and evening turn-down is part of the fun of travel to me. In a major city I like to be in the thick of it. In remote towns or small villages, there may only be one choice of hotel. I've encountered every level of comfort, from the most basic to the deluxe. Once, I took a room in a small, family-owned lodge with a concrete-screed floor, no plug sockets, no light bulb, no furniture at all – apart from a bed – and no door. There were hinges where a door had been, but they were just hanging, impotent. I slept in my clothes, spooning my heavy backpack, having stuffed my cash, passport, driving licence and USB stick into my boots. My mobile phone tucked into the pillow, I lay with my cheek on my knife. When I woke early, aware that some of the dozen or so other guests were stirring, I couldn't just hear them, I could feel them. As they passed by my gaping doorway, my body lay just a few feet from each swish of clothing and toss of hair.

On another trip I stayed in a thatched beachfront cabin in Peru that was occupied by several giant crabs. One was particularly aggressive, objecting violently to my presence. At nearly a metre wide, he was a monster, rushing at me as I jumped to safety on the bed. When I tried to sleep the crab shifted my rucksack noisily across the bare dirt floor. The hotel owner admitted he was powerless against this tough-nut gang of crustaceans, which hurtled at him during the night when he got up to pee, sending him flying. As I showered in the morning, they pressed their bodies against the screen and rattled it with their pincers.

I have time for one last odyssey before I fly back to the British Isles: a visit to the magnificent Isla Coiba. Comprising primeval forests, sparkling rivers, sandy coves and the second-largest coral reef in the central and eastern Pacific Ocean, Coiba is one of the largest marine parks in the world. Until a few years ago the island was used as a remote penal colony for about 3,000 of Panama's most notorious and dangerous criminals. A more breathtaking setting for incarceration is difficult to imagine.

From June to November, when they migrate to the Pacific coast of Panama to mate, humpback and sperm whales can be seen swimming and leaping out of the water. As we hop aboard the boat from the Azuero Peninsula to Isla Coiba, every one of the six passengers on board is scouring the waters for a black body and blue pectoral fin. There's a gurgling feeling in the pit of my stomach as the boat rolls with the swell, and it's not seasickness. We gather together to make the most of six pairs of whale-watching eyes. After creeping out of waters off the southern tip of Vereguas Province, we start chugging towards Isla Coiba and open waters, where the boat gathers real momentum. Soon the boatman has cranked up a gear or two to bounce atop the chop. Spray is jettisoning out in a fantail, drenching every wide-eyed passenger and inciting whoops and hollers. Our captain emits his party piece, roaring 'Thar she blows,' Captain Ahab-style, to excited claps of approval. He informs us that a whale's moan is louder than a 747 jumbo jet upon take-off. They also sing the longest and most complex songs of the animal kingdom.

Though I have a keen nose for the sea, my sea legs are decidedly wobbly. But the promising shadow that lurks not far from the boat transfixes me. Wow! Just three or four feet away the waters part to allow a hull-shaped black beast to break through the surface of the water. Whoosh! It is so near I can almost touch the glistening hefty tail twitching alongside us. We stare, astonished, as the humpback whale arches and raises its tail skyward. A powerful surge of seawater is sent spurting to the heavens, then the beady-eyed king of the ocean is gone in a towering spume of mist.

Before prison gangs, rapists and serial killers arrived on Coiba, it was home to a peaceful nomadic tribe – well, until the Spanish disembarked in 1560, bearing arms. After that, it lay deserted for centuries, until the Panamanian government acquired the island in 1918 to make it a 'prison from which there is no escape'. For more than thirty years, from the 1970s, it was referred to as Panama's Alcatraz: a place where political prisoners who angered dictators were sent, never to be seen again. Yet, during the last decade or so, this palm-topped island has been anything *but* a highly fortified military jail. When a decision was taken to close the facility in the late 1990s, prisoner numbers were allowed to dwindle. Yes, Panama's most dangerous criminals were kept here, far away from home, but only a few were housed in a central cell block. The rest stayed in rooms overlooking soft, sugary sands, able to fish, dive and pick coconuts. When we arrive, the few remaining jailbirds are helping to welcome, cook for and guide visitors to the biological station and rangers' cabin. They are tanned, lean and fit, as if they have been on a luxury resort. A decade or more in 'detention' has clearly done them no harm. For these guys, Devil's Island has been devilishly good.

Designated a national park in 1991, the island and its surrounds cover a 270,125 hectare site now part-funded by the Spanish Agency for International Cooperation (AECI) and the Smithsonian Tropical Research Institute (STRI). The park, managed by ANAM (the Panama government's environment agency), attracts conservation and scientific organisations from all over the world to study its marine fauna, which includes hundreds of fish species and twenty-three whale and dolphin species that inhabit its waters year round. Half a dozen shark species have been sighted, including white-tipped, bull and tiger sharks, as well as large numbers of migratory humpback whales.

Coiba is the largest island in Panama and was part of the mainland until 12,000 to 18,000 years ago, when a land split cast the island adrift, isolating its endemic species in remote segregation. Today, Coiba is much as it was then. Of the 147 species of bird found on the island, twenty-one are endemic, and the agouti, howler monkey, possum and white-tailed deer on Coiba are wholly unique to the island. Conservative estimates by botanists suggest that 1,450 plant species grow here, of which fewer than 800 have been identified. There are also freshwater and saltwater crocodiles, six species of iguana (including green and black), umpteen frogs, salamanders, caimans, four species of turtle (leatherback, hawksbill, olive and loggerhead), and twenty species of snake (including fer-de-lance and coral snakes).

To be honest, I felt a niggle of apprehension at being 'off the grid' among the few last jailbirds on a remote island (although the provenance of the place was part of the initial lure). I needn't have worried. The prisoners are every bit as hospitable as Coiba's large population of nesting scarlet macaws: posing for photos, swapping jokes and harvesting fruits and berries from the trees. One, a badass gang leader in a former life, spends his days rehabilitating injured wildlife. None wear leg irons or shackles around their ankles; they seem like ordinary folk.

Our guide, a heavy-set man sentenced to twenty years for the murder of his brother, has only a few more weeks in paradise, but clearly doesn't want to vacate. I feel the same, and share his obvious passion for this Garden of Eden. Only streams and marshland break an island almost entirely covered by thick tangles of virgin rainforest. Jagged rocks, palm-fringed silver sands, flower-filled coves and mangrove forests are filled with butterflies, and just a short walk through the jungle reveals many white-faced monkeys all intent on a human encounter. Two separate water trails allow exploration by kayak through thick mangrove forests in the north and the south of the island. Three forested hiking trails cross the island and pass wetland, caves, waterfalls and thermal pools up to observation points high on the headlands.

The island is a refuge for crested eagles, which are fast disappearing from the rest of Panama. Among its endemic bird species are Coiba spinetails, easy to see foraging among the creepers, even though this smallish bird, with its long rufous tail and olive-brown underparts, rarely comes out into the open. We see thousands of crabs, several eight-foot crocodiles (the largest is nicknamed 'Tito') and the rare brown-backed dove, once thought to be extinct. White-tailed deer, large green iguanas, caimans and red macaws all congregate on a soft breast of grass-fringed sand, living in harmony with one another. The prison officers describe it as a 'Noah's Ark of an island', with the inmates themselves admitting they are guests on 'Little Galapagos'. Both descriptions aren't far wrong. Honestly, it's a crime to leave.

I've returned to the UK for a while to get my fix of Wimbledon tennis, Sunday pub roasts and cricket on the village green. After a few weeks downtime, I am nicely rested after long lunches, afternoon naps and walks along the Greensand Ridge – the region's prime long-distance walk, passing though Bedfordshire, Buckinghamshire and Cambridgeshire. Crossing the dry, sandy soil of Bedfordshire under dishwater skies, delving off route to scenic Old Warden – famous for its chocolate-box thatched country cottages – it feels natural once more to be among mature hawthorn and blackthorn bushes, large ash and oak trees rather than soaring palms. A crunchy trail crawls along the top of an old railway tunnel through which steam-belching trains once passed. From dark woodland, the path emerges to magnificent views of sweeping countryside, with a steep cutting covered with grassland and scrub falling rapidly away to chalky trails. I explore grassy flower meadows and bogs bisected by wet woodland and shallow rivers. Among pyramidal orchids and dwarf thistles, I become adept at spotting the song posts for summer warblers – although it took several weeks for me to stop scouring the treetops for giant branch-built harpy nests.

The RSPB's heathland reserve at The Lodge in Sandy is also just a few miles down the road. This 180-hectare woodland, heath and acid grassland reserve stretches along the Greensand Ridge. With its giant oaks and spellbinding views, there are few nicer ways to spend an afternoon than strolling five miles of bird-filled trails, rich in flycatchers and hobbies hunting dragonflies round the ponds and heath. There are many newly fledged blue and great tits in the woods, and green woodpeckers on the heathland, and I am lucky enough to spot a grass snake wriggling through ragged tufts while I watch butterflies and bumblebees darting and buzzing round the edges of bloom-filled gardens. It is wonderful to see family and friends again. Catching up with pals from school, whose babies are almost fully grown now, makes me realise how often I've been away. Roads have been built, buildings demolished. There have been umpteen births, deaths, marriages and divorces. I have missed milestone birthdays, weight loss, weight gains, good times and bad, graduations, new haircuts, first steps, marathon challenges, cancer scares, TV debuts and driving-test triumphs. When I am home, I hear about them all in a jumble. Attempting to shuffle them into a proper chronology is a never-ending puzzle. Then it is time to reacquaint myself with salad cream, brown sauce, English Cheddar and proper bacon – an absolute joy. Technology has made the world a smaller place; email and mobile phones have made us all neighbours. Yet there will always be tastes of home. Decent television is another highlight. Even the weakest BBC show easily eclipses the slew of Spanish-dubbed American teen dramas and homespun soap operas (*telenovelas*) that fill Panamanian TV channels night after night. But the truth is, I can feel my feet beginning to itch. I start planning my departure almost as soon as I arrive back on British turf. And while I enjoy reconnecting, an urgent exigency soon rises from within. It's a compulsion to leave; to make tracks.

Though I am busy writing articles for British and Panamanian newspapers – as well as researching another guidebook – it is travel itself that fires me up. Once I hit 35,000 feet and settle back into seat 7a on an Iberia Airlines Boeing 747, the unseen tension eases. I'm me again. With liberation comes the clarity I need to restore order to a cluttered brain. I am content. On a mission. Journeying to do, see or experience something extraordinary. To be something extraordinary.

Enjoying wildlife is supposed to be a relaxing hobby, not a maniacal mission. I often regret that I'm not the type of traveller who can settle for easily attained goals. But years ago I set myself the challenge of seeing a harpy eagle in the wild, and recently this unfulfilled yearning has become a borderline obsession. During the past few months I've trekked wilderness trails in Brazil, Peru, Venezuela and Colombia to follow up on sightings – to no avail. Avid birders have warned me that South and Central America, with their rich profusion of wildlife species, can turn sensible pursuits into serious neuroses. And with this in mind, I am keen to ensure that my quest remains one of travel, not addictive compulsion, because the joy, for me, is to be among wildlife in the most compelling landscapes on Earth. For let's be clear; I'm a professional traveller and an amateur birder, devoted to seeing the world and the wildlife that calls it home. Time is suspended when I watch a mother feed her chick, a birthing seal deliver her pup, a coral spawn or a hawk fledge in South and Central America's glossy, green jungles. It calms me, quietens me, soothes my restless spirit and drives me on in my quest to voyage, explore and discover.

The harpy eagle is all the evidence I need that birds evolved from a small, two-legged dinosaur, which grew feathers and eventually used its wings to fly. Today, it still resembles a prehistoric winged creature – it inspired animation designers working on the Harry Potter films in their creation of Fawkes, the gold-beaked phoenix that is Albus Dumbledore's companion and defender. The word 'harpy' comes from the Greek *harpazein*, which means 'to snatch', and these eagles are named after the harpies of ancient mythology: part-raptors with human faces that symbolised the destructive nature of wind. Eagles play an important role in the beliefs of the ancient peoples of the Americas. In the pre-Colombian civilisations of the land that is now Colombia, ancient

standing stones and funerary chambers are carved with
magnificent, fearsome eagles as protection from evil forces. Their
feathers have long been used by Central and South American
society's elite. Tail feathers were traditionally sought to make
ceremonial headdresses in Neotropical tribal rituals. Some
indigenous peoples across Central and South America once kept
cages containing harpies, whose long flight feathers would be cut
periodically. Such birds were often considered the personification
of the chief, and when that individual died, his harpy was also
killed. In Brazil, Honduras, Paraguay, Argentina and Costa Rica,
hunters would keep the talons of harpy eagles as amulets. Today,
thousands of years on, the enigmatic harpy has a powerful hold
over me, too.

For several weeks I've been trying to enter Venezuela from
Colombia, to survey sites where sketchy reports suggest that a
harpy has been seen. But bureaucracy, storms and political unrest
have combined to conspire against me. Even the most detailed
preparation can't prevent messed-up travel plans. Unforeseen,
unexplained, unavoidable circumstances often cause perfectly
planned trips to be canned. I try to take it in my stride – after all,
there isn't much I can do about red tape. Each trip requires a
guide, a cooperative national park system and a whole host of
obliging weather and infrastructural conditions. Everything bar
my own time and willingness is outside my control. In recent
years volcanic ash, military coups, terrorist threats and deadly
epidemics have all red-lined travel plans in my diary. For a jobbing
travel writer, such cancelled trips bring financial hardship – one
of the reasons I'm 'on the road' for more than 200 days of the
year. But, as I've grown older, I have ceased to view disruptions as
a teeth-grinding annoyance. I accept that some cancellations
deliver an important message. An overbooked plane once left me
stranded, but then ended up smashing into the side of the Cumbal
volcano, killing all eighty passengers on board. On another trip a
long delay en route resulted in my arrival after a devastating bomb
blast. Sometimes – however much you want something – things
just aren't meant to be.

As a consolation prize I treat myself to a road trip to Camerones
at Los Flamencos National Park. It may not be home to harpy
eagles, but close-up encounters with vast colonies of flamingos

are out-and-out guaranteed. It lies next to the Colombia-Venezuela border running along La Guajira, a narrow, palm-lined peninsula fringed by the Caribbean Sea on one side and the Gulf of Venezuela on the other. Crossing the frontier here requires a drive to the lawless cowboy town of Maicao, where you can jump into an old 1980s American station wagon displaying more rust than original paintwork – known locally as a *por puesto* (meaning 'by the seat') – to rattle across to Maracaibo in Venezuela. Or risk being carjacked and drive over in your own vehicle. Or catch a bus. The driver of the *por puesto* won't even start the engine unless he has a minimum of four passengers, so it pays to stump up cash for the whole car if time is tight.

En route to Maicao, a visit to the palm-trimmed salt pans of Camarones (the Spanish for shrimp) is unmissable. For where there are bountiful amounts of shrimp, there are flamingos, and at Camarones there are literally thousands of these impossibly pink waders. Every inch of the 7,000-hectare coastal lagoon at Los Flamencos Flora and Fauna Sanctuary is home to vast flocks of these iconic tall, slender birds. Hot, boggy, sweaty and airless, just five metres above sea level, this silvery marshland plateau is backdropped by spectacular twists of mangrove forest. For three dollars, I share a small wooden canoe with a shrimp fisherman who has a high-pitched nasal laugh.

Over two hours, in temperatures that climb to well over thirty-five degrees, we shed a reservoir's worth of sweat while being wowed by this salty lagoon. If there are any more days as hot as this, the entire lagoon will surely evaporate into a salt-encrusted plain topped by a deep layer of sparkling crystals that crunch underfoot – like a pocket-sized version of Chile's mineral-rich Atacama Desert, Peru's unearthly Salinas de Maras and the sun-bleached Salar de Uyuni in the brackish plains of Bolivia. Algae-rich brine puddles and pools emit a pastel glow as the flamingos study their reflections in the moisture – an almost hallucinogenic vision. There are thousands of pink birds all over these low-lying saline wetlands swirled with dozens of mudflat isles: three thousand, four thousand maybe? We watch as the birds tend to their exotic, tower-shaped mud nests on the raised flats. Drawn here by the lure of a rich bounty of wriggling shrimps and invertebrates, some cluster together around the shallow, reedy pools. Others stand alone and visible, perching on the raised mud in the main body of the lagoon. Drifts of pink feathers float like cherry blossom in the shallows.

Flamingos are fluid swimmers, despite their apparent gawky awkwardness. Their one-legged stance is believed to help regulate their body temperature, although numerous theories about the reasons for this odd-looking posture abound – from resting fatigued limbs to balancing in strong winds. In Camerones, the rose-pink species is American flamingo, a smaller variety than the greater flamingo, with a long, lean, curved neck and a black-tipped bill with a downward bend. We watch as the birds use their long legs and webbed feet to stir up mud at the bottom of the lagoon before burying their bills in the shrimpy muck. With a strange slurping noise, my fisherman friend mimics the flamingos' filter mechanism for sifting out the shrimp and other nutrients, such as algae, tiny fish, larvae and insects.

The surrounding forests and bushy marshland scrub are home to numerous shorebirds, which play second fiddle to the main attraction. When the boatman inadvertently knocks a heavy oar with a splash, a nearby flock of flamingos emits an ear-splitting call. It has been likened to a 'crazy-sounding duck', a bizarre vocalisation for such a graceful bird. The fisherman has less success with his shrimp lines than with spotting flamingos; the water is shallow in places, and he hops out, wades through thick mud and pushes the boat. I lie back and enjoy the ride, my skin frying under a blowtorch sky.

Crossing into Venezuela from the desert-ringed, rubble-strewn border town of Maicao, it feels good to leave behind the melee, from the fist fights and billiards bars to the bleating herds of scruffy goats. I tentatively press my pedal to the metal – the road is notorious as a hangout for corrupt speed cops. On the Venezuelan side of the border, there are ten – yes, ten – police checkpoints, where it is customary to 'tip' for an easy passage. As Venezuela has a black market for US dollars, at a much better exchange than the official rate – a legacy of Chavez's pricing for the world oil market – this all costs little more than a handful of loose change. Meanwhile, the checkpoint keeps up the pretence of saving the Venezuelans from the scourge of contraband rice cookers. (Although the most profitable black-market goods right now are mega-packs of toilet roll. Since the nationalisation of the toilet-paper industry, Venezuelans have suffered from a country-wide shortage of toilet tissue. Queues of people start forming outside stores before breakfast for the quota of a dozen rolls, with scuffles erupting on the pavements when stocks sell out.)

In Central and South America, in my experience, the police are even more likely to rob you than street muggers. For this reason, I keep a stash of low-denomination cash in my wallet, but no big notes. Those are folded into a hollowed-out paperback novel in the bottom of my backpack. An 'emergency fund' of a few hundred dollar bills has been taped into each bra cup.

Nearby Maracaibo Lake, virtually undiscovered by tourists on account of its dodgy location, is wedged between lands owned by the Venezuelan mafia and oil companies. But as one of the largest freshwater reserves in South America, it offers hours of birding in a glow of exotic bird species, from golden tanager and blue-capped tanager to scarlet-fronted and rose-headed parakeets. On learning that there has been a spate of knifepoint muggings near here lately, I decide not to stop after all, and turn back. I pass a string of burning oil drums – a roadside reminder that I'm now in a nation where oil is cheaper than bottled water. Another reminder is my watch. Venezuela is half an hour ahead of Colombia – an important thirty minutes as far as Hugo Chavez is concerned because it places Venezuela in front of every other South American nation.

Everyone around this part of Venezuela makes a living from the contraband market that operates a slick service 24/7. As I wait, patiently, soaking in a dripping sweat, for my passport to be checked on my return into Colombia, a succession of people carrying various vessels move by and skip the line without question. Venezuela's most lucrative commodity – petrol – travels to Colombia in any container in which it can be carried. Men, women and children ferry it across using empty coke bottles and jerry cans. Profits are easily made by selling it to Colombians at half the local price. A 'petrol street market' runs right along the Colombian side of the border, with petrol sold from old tables and car bonnets. I've never been to any market more terrifying, not because of criminality and violence, but because of the smoking habits of the men touting the fuel. Each has an ash-heavy glowing cigarette clamped between his lips as he hangs over petrol in open vessels. The whole place is an incendiary tinderbox, moments away from fireballing.

So, where to head next? That's the burning question, and one, believe it or not, which I often decide by unfurling a map. Panama, a geographical 'piggy in the middle', offers excellent land, sea and air routes to the whole of South and Central America. Sometimes I travel somewhere I can reach with a tank of gas (Costa Rica), or a cheap flight (Colombia). Or I might feel like heading somewhere on foot (Costa Rica) or by boat (Colombia), or venturing further afield.

I am in full distraction mode as I try hard not to think about harpy eagles. It looks as though there'll be no harpy trip for now, because no guides are available where I am, so I plough my energies into a recycling programme in Bocas del Toro and help to fundraise for the hospital. I catch up with old friends, such as Agnes Santomenno, the Scottish-born owner of a company specialising in reproductions of pre-Colombian art. My lawyer friend Ernesto entertains me, as always, with salacious tales about his dynastic clan: his wife is the niece of Roberto Arias, the infamous Panamanian husband of the English ballerina Margot Fonteyn. When the Panamanian Ambassador to London is next in town, we share a fresh fruit breakfast at the Hotel Bristol. Ana Delgado has been unfailingly supportive of every project I've undertaken be it books about Panama, magazine articles, public talks or TV programmes.

I try to track down Heloise, a journalist from London, whom I met in Isla Colón, where she was whipping up passion-fruit margaritas in a cocktail bar. When I discover she has left for Costa Rica, I join a volunteer programme with the international charity SOS Children's Villages, working with abandoned children in Panama City. The capital does its best to hide the uncomfortable truth about its street kids – a few years ago I was astounded to find myself threatened with arrest for trying to share a sandwich with a desperately hungry little girl. Being homeless here is to be an illicit species, often considered beyond help. Children as young as three sit aimlessly by the roadsides watching belching diesel trucks thunder past to places far beyond the life they know. All they know is hunger, sadness and pain. In a wind like hot breath,

I play skipping games with fifty adorable children who, with the love and care of the charity, are discovering laughter and peace.

Then a harpy is spotted in Venezuela's Orinoco rainforest and, although the sighting is unconfirmed, I have my heart set on going. My desire to see a harpy in the wild is an itch I still can't scratch. I have a mountain of work to finish before I leave: an article for the *Independent*, a column for CNN and an entire chapter for a book. When I tally up all my boarding-pass stubs, I have flown thirty-six domestic and international flights in just eighty days. Though taking notes on my travels has become second nature, the deciphering of my inky scribbles and re-crafting of spidery scrawls takes time. For three long weeks I work to a punishing schedule, starting at around four each morning and writing until gone midnight.

I arrive at the Colombian border hollow-eyed, with dark shadows above each sunken cheek, to find that a political spat between President Chavez and Colombia's President Uribe has intensified. Diplomats have been withdrawn, allegations made, threats issued and an age-old slanging match resumed. Legions of armed troops and two battle tanks guard the border, which is closed – indefinitely. I drive home, wearily, and sleep.

Blood, Sweat and Tears

Panama
2010

Turning forty has made time all the more noticeable. Not long ago, the calendar meant little to me. It was a way of dividing up weather, or following patterns of migration. Now it charts time passing. Another dimension, in which the relationship between age and happiness is questioned. I look the same, feel better than ever and can't imagine this will ever change. I will resist everything to stop myself disappearing with age. But, the reality is, women my age often do. For the first time ever, I feel as if I'm on the back-nine of my life, to borrow a golfing term. It's a nostalgic place to be.

As a lifelong morning person, the first meal of the day has always been my favourite. For as long as I can remember, I've always preferred to sit and savour breakfast properly in glorious peace and quiet. In South and Central America the morning meal is a large one of exotic fruits, freshly squeezed tropical juices, eggs (usually fried or served scrambled with peppers and ham), often with a small piece of steak. In Panama tortillas – around ten times thicker and half as wide as the corn rounds found in Mexico – come piled high with eggs and melting cheese on top. Also served with eggs are *hojaldras*, delicious flattened Panamanian doughnuts, deep-fried and sprinkled with sugar. Every morning I lick my lips at the prospect of a long, leisurely breakfast in what is a predictable routine. After flicking through the headlines in *La Prensa* and trawling my inbox for potentially heartening news of harpy eagles, the onset of morning heralds the start of another amazing day. Nothing is more enjoyable than contemplating the possibilities and opportunities it offers.

The ping of my phone tells me I have a text waiting.

'Chek email. GOOD LUK!!'. The text is from Solange, a zoologist friend from Quito, Ecuador. But why is she wishing me luck? Reluctantly, I pull myself away from my breakfast table and and saunter a couple of blocks back to the charming small hotel in Casco Viejo, Panama City's colonial old quarter, which has been my home for the past few weeks. After many exhausting months spent bashing out copy on my laptop computer, I've been enjoying doing very little – a restorative counterbalance to the constant drain of daily newspaper and magazine deadlines. But doing very little isn't something I can sustain for long before the fidgeting kicks in.

Back at the hotel I re-read Solange's text and log into my email. For almost three months I have been sending out emails daily, following up on harpy eagle leads that have amounted to zilch. First, constant heavy rains brought landslides to parts of Nicaragua, then unrest in Guatemala made nervous guides reluctant to travel. I've lost count of the number of times a phone call has told of a sighting of a harpy in Costa Rica. Dropping everything to hotfoot it across the border is exciting, until you arrive to learn that you have 'missed out' yet again. Guyana, another country that taunts me with its harpy activity – the bird they call the 'flying wolf' is believed to have active nests in far-ranging parts of the Rupununi region – is simply too expensive to visit. Disheartened, I posted some last-ditch messages on Facebook, placing every last hope in social media. My pleas zoomed around the globe to several thousand people in less time than it takes to roast a chicken.

Solange's message makes sense once I read her email. She has put me in touch with Manuel, a friend of a friend. And he has agreed to guide me in the Darién. Although he is only young, he has spent more than a month living in the jungle and has good links with the Emberá people. Even more impressive, he has a lead on a harpy eagle nesting site. As a botany graduate who is now shelf-stacking in a supermarket, his long-term plan is to work in ecotourism; he just needs an all-important break. Reassuringly, he has some ground rules, which he lays out in his own email. He stresses how essential it is that we take time to understand the Darién; that we both outline our goals so that misunderstandings are swept away; that we pledge to cause no harm or disruption to the jungle, or anything in it, so that nothing can tug at our consciences. He insists that our focus be environmental, and in no way skewed by fixation or obsession. This trip should not be a trophy hunt.

Without knowing it, this stranger has corked all my worries. I feel sane and optimistic. It feels good no longer to bubble like a brew pot in a stew of uncertainty. As is so often the case, it takes a distant mind to unmuddle a problem that has grown too big and too close to manage. Nature is big-hearted with the gifts it bestows. All I need to do in return is keep a cool head. To know my place. No reels of camera footage; no ladder to secure the ultimate close-up; minimal noise, maximum respect and a commitment to leaving the nest in peace. Hope swirls round me like joyous flute music and I am flooded by a sense of well-being. Unwittingly I catch sight of my reflection. My smile is wider than a well-stretched hammock.

Later that day, with plans underway, I re-read Solange's email. Her final paragraph is an ominous reminder of the scale of the mission. 'Sara, I wish you luck, great luck – and you'll need it. Remember, the powerful harpy eagle is not easy to see. It rarely, if ever, soars.' It brings me back down to earth with a bump. She's right: this is no easy challenge. Without pausing to allow the mental cartwheels to start, I make a list: packing, permissions/ letters to various authorities, planning, maps, new jabs, jeep – as ever, there is a lot to do.

Though local people don't refer to the Darién as 'the gap', the name given to it by outsiders rings true. Its inaccessibility is best appreciated from the sky. The thick sweep of dark green forms an unbroken barrier as far as the eye can see. Without roads, paths, cars, buses, coaches or tour buses, this is a region that can be explored only on foot, horse or primitive boat. Vast tracts of this primeval jungle are so tangled, twisted and knotted that a route must be cut in order to pass through. Giant trees, soaring palms and oversized bushes grow rapidly in this unmapped land, spurting shoots, closing paths and leaving no trace of exploration within a few days. Its crude accommodations are tents, hammocks and simple wood-and-thatch shacks. There are no shops, no air ambulances, no signs, no maps and no fleet of kindly jungle rangers. You enter with a few basic supplies and keep your wits about you. The human species is low-ranking here: a humbling lesson in humility that I enjoy. Meekness is mellowing, I find.

Leaving Panama City by jeep before sunrise turns out to be a wise move – by daybreak it will be hot and humid beyond belief. Initially I barrel along at about fifty kicks in the dim glow of the capital's outer suburbs. At the roadside, dark heaps form higgledy-piggledy mounds in the gloom – they are not discarded piles of rubbish, but the bodies of sleeping, rag-clad vagrants, huddled together for safety and snatching the last few minutes of sleep before the police uproot them from the kerb. I feel uneasiness bubble up inside me as I selfishly drive by in a leather-upholstered, air-conditioned four-wheel-drive.

Once the buildings begin to thin out and are replaced by glades of trees, the adventure begins. The city air gives way to farmland smells: a mix of manure, grass and wet soil. Within less than an hour, the grease and grime of traffic fumes turn into bitty platelets of dust and grit that cloud the windscreen. I swing the wheel to ride the final curve of a wide, banana-shaped freeway, rumbling onto a rutted road. The wet, hot burliness of the approaching Darién hangs like damp washing. I glance upward: the brilliance of the early-morning sky is still another hour or so away.

As I cross into the new province, a green-and-white municipal archway straddles the road to proclaim 'Bienvenidos a Darién' in welcome. It signifies a move into the mystery zone of an extraordinary region riddled with legends. The gleaming sophistication of Panama City feels a long way away. At the village of Las Aguas Frias, I pull over for an ID check and watch as a small boy shins up a coconut tree with a machete almost as tall as he is. This long village is split into two, as if one half of the community has fallen out with the other. A cracked riverbed forms the divide between each part, with just enough of a turning circle in which to swing a jeep. After slashing at a bough the boy frees a coconut, climbing back down the tree at breakneck speed.

He hacks the top off, sticks in a straw and hands me the fruit. His dirty face beams like a lantern as I press some coins into his tiny hand. I watch as he disappears into the dawn on a squeaky, clapped-out bicycle.

I pass untidy piles of second-hand tyres, plantains and chopped wood for sale by the roadside. From the truck-stop town of Meteti all the way to Yaviza, the potholes double in size, ensuring that the unlit fifty-kilometre stretch is an unforgiving bum-bruiser. My jeep lurches from one gaping hollow to the next, over lump and bump like a crazy slalom course. In these rain-rich stretches, newly laid asphalt doesn't last long. Every few metres the road tapers to a narrow black ribbon. The ruts multiply. My patience dwindles.

After I've rollicked around on a rough gravel-mud mix for a few minutes, the road levels once more, only to disintegrate again. Even in the amber glimmer of sunrise, I pay little attention to the scenery, for here the jungle is no more. It is lost to buzz-saw invaders and the farmer's flame, machete and plough. Where the forest once crept, dark and thick, there is now flat pasture covered in large, glassy puddles. With the root system gone, the fertile topsoil has washed away, erasing the natural catchment. Waterlogging and run-off from the rain is immediate, hence the lake-like puddles and crumbling roads. Focussing on the deeply furrowed road ahead spares me the visual tragedy of the blighted fields. I trundle on in trepidation, paranoid about picking up a puncture miles from anywhere. Apart from a rusty old truck, gasping its few last miles in plumes of smoke over a cattle crossing, the road is empty. I pass a solitary vehicle every twenty minutes or so, hurtling towards me – generally on the wrong side of the road.

I pull up by the roadside, sending a thick cloud of rust-coloured dust up to the heavens. Although the marauding vandals of progress have ridden roughshod here, too, felling the jungle to make way for farmland pasture, there is just enough tree cover to attract the birds. I unfurl a blanket on springy grass sheltered by a small wooded clump set behind a living fence. Lying back, I gaze up at the blue sky. Like a lizard, I position myself to optimise my exposure to the sun's UV rays. A golden dose of vitamin D soon soaks in deep. Without a sunshine rush, I feel lethargic, sickly and slow, so I've become an expert sunbather over the years. A ten-minute basking session yields the intense sunlight I need. The invigoration kicks in and I'm re-energized like a rechargeable battery after a power surge. In colder climates this type of idling is considered lazy. In the warmth of the tropics it is both expected and encouraged. I'm thankful for that.

'Sara?' A voice snaps me out of my dreamy state and forces my eyes to open. A round, smiley face offers me an outstretched hand. 'I'm Manuel,' he says, giving my hand a gentle shake. He's spotted me sun-napping by the roadside and asked his bus driver to pull over and drop him. His palm is wet and warm but a joke about being nervous to meet me helps to break the ice. 'Hey, Manny, it's great to meet you at last,' I say, with absolute truth. We've been trading emails for weeks now. Manny is quite tall for a Panamanian, at around five foot ten, and powerfully built – he clearly visits a gym. We ready ourselves to drive on to Yaviza, where we will meet our Kuna guide.

'You will need to smile very sweetly at the checkpoint guards, Sarita,' he urges. 'We may need to persuade them to let us through.' The Darién is not an easy place to visit. Manny has heard that something has spooked the police at Yaviza, although exactly what it is remains a subject for conjecture. For more than a week now, they have even been turning back gringo travellers. There is a very real chance they will do the same to us. It's the kind of bombshell I've been dreading. As Manny slops a bucket of water at the windscreen, I gnaw at my nails in quiet despair and watch him scrape at a sticky massacre of splattered flies.

At every passport stop I have managed to convince the jungle police that I'm an adventure-crazy British girl on a pre-menopausal wildlife trip. My bag of bird books, binoculars and first-aid kit supports these innocent intentions. Yet there is still a rigmarole of paperwork to complete. At Meteti I was gestured at to pull over and stop, but a flea-bitten dog cocked his leg at the guard and peed all over his shiny jackboot. Its timing was impeccable, and I was shooed away with foul-mouthed irritation in the same breath as the nuisance dog. Further along the road a truck overloaded with green bananas had collided with a cow. As I squeamishly inched the jeep around a bloodbath of entrails and squashed fruits, I was surprised to see a woman attempting to squeeze milk from the carcass's teats. In the Darién, nothing goes to waste.

The public body charged with guarding the Darién Gap is SENAFRONT, Servicio Nacional de Fronteras (National Border Service), a poorly paid arm of an already underpaid police force. Wearing military fatigues slung with automatic weapons, the guards man a string of checkpoints on the approach to the Darién jungle. Each has a lined book in which he registers every traveller, documenting name, nationality, destination and purpose of visit. Usually, although not always, the guards insist on searching all bags and your vehicle. Sometimes this is just a cursory glance, but it can be a good deal more. I ready myself for the car seats to be pulled out and the trunk to be emptied, hoping against intense interrogation and a full rubber-glove body search.

Yaviza's population of around six thousand people seems completely unaware that the town boasts landmark status. If it was in Florida, the southern terminus of the Pan-American Highway would be celebrated with an 'End of the Road' theme park. In the Darién, there is a man who flogs cheap shots of rum from a painted wheelbarrow filled with watermelon and eggs. After thousands of miles, the road just fizzles out. It is rather unspectacular. No fancy sign. No photo booth. No car park for coaches or cafe for sightseers. No explanation as to why. No directions as to where you can rejoin it again. Nothing. Just the end of the road.

A woman nursing a baby is surrounded by sparsely clad children playing a game of tag. A grandmother is scolding a teen-age girl for using too much soap on the clothes she has washed in the river. After parking the jeep in a shed draped with leaves and sticky vines, Manny slips the older woman a handful of notes to watch it while we're away. When he asks if our pirogue (boat) is ready, she nods with a single dip of the head.

At the checkpoint, with fingers crossed, smiles fixed and stories straight, we hand our passports and papers to *el comandante*. He is standing, rod straight, in full camouflage, on an elevated platform behind a podium. Like a priest delivering a sermon, he embarks on a lengthy lecture about the jungle's many dangers. Then, just as we suppose he is finished, his attention turns to the town itself and the dubious morals and intentions of all men found here. Evil

lurks everywhere, he stresses. Here. Here. Here. And here. With
face flushed crimson and arms waving, he is clearly warming to
his theme. Foretelling of divine punishment and the torment of
damnation, he describes the Darién as 'Lucifer's lair'. I nod,
knowingly, as he refers to a painted icon on his woodworm-
ridden bureau of the Virgen del Carmen, who is, I think, the
Catholic patron saint of fishing boats. He runs out of puff, and
the doom-laden prophecies come to an end. Steely, he looks me
in the eye, unblinking. Though it feels as if he is laser boring my
pupils, I dare not look away. After an eternity, he nods, satisfied
that we understand the perils. Banging his fist down hard, he
motions that he is finished. For not rolling our eyes or attempting
to contradict, correct or interrupt the righteous, Manny and I are
allowed to pass.

Despite smirking flippantly, Manny and I know too well that
the commandant has a point. This lawless land entices the good,
the bad and the dreadful to become immersed in its unruly wilds,
and some never resurface. At half a million hectares, the Darién is
five times the size of Los Angeles, but is patrolled by less than a
dozen rangers. They don't have walkie-talkies, vehicles or GPS
and are paid a pittance, which makes them susceptible to bribe-
taking and corruption. Each is expected to police, conserve,
supervise and patrol their respective territories and all they may
contain, which could include thousands of species of plant, rare
and endangered wildlife, remote ancient tribes and all manner of
illicit activities, from drug-growing, smuggling and people-
trafficking to logging.

Every jungle in the world has a story about a tourist who
walked ten feet away from a clearing and was never seen again.
Many of these stories are true. Despite the red tape, checkpoints
and stark warnings, even the most experienced travellers can get
lost in these ungoverned wilds. In May 2013, twenty-six-year-old
Swede Jan Philip Braunisch, a determined and adventurous
traveller, vanished without trace on a solo trek across the Darién –
his last contact with family was an email to his wife. Despite a
year-long search by the Swedish authorities with the help of both
Panamanian and Colombian police, he hasn't been heard of since.
Manny and I both know to guard against being reckless, especially
after recent reports about narco-traffickers, bandits and smugglers.

In truth, I fear the drug traffickers more than anything else, because the stories I'm told are laced with brutality. The cartels in Mexico set the sorry standard for this: decapitated bodies, hog-tied and disembowelled, intestines protruding, ears and fingers mutilated. The level of violence is gruesome.

Well-worn trails run through the Darién jungle as part of the route used to move bundles of cocaine from Colombia into Panama. Each large, plastic-wrapped pack contains about fifty pounds of cocaine – about the most that one man can carry. Traffickers carry weapons, and are jumpy with nerves and fiercely protective of their booty. The result is often a deadly encounter with a trigger-happy assailant who, fearful of being robbed himself, will shoot first and ask questions later. These unkind, boggy swamps aren't the place to beg for mercy or cry for help. Should your calls land within earshot of an official, he is likely to be corrupt. Or deranged. Or both.

Yaviza is an ugly place full of unattractive souls. Sallow and sour in daylight, when night falls they all appear to be drunk, pimping, smuggling or hustling on streets scattered with broken bottles. Glassy-eyed prostitutes stand barefoot in gloomy doorways. Dogs paw at piles of rubble. Toothless teens have mobile phones, small wraps of cocaine and porn DVDs for sale. Old men shuffle aimlessly outside the Chinese-run store. Only the docks seem to serve a valid purpose. After buying some bottled water and a tarp to protect us from the sun, I soak up the scene while Manny loads the boat. As usual, my cash and valuables are hidden deep down in my bag. Yet in Yaviza, I feel vulnerable. It feels as if every person around me has X-ray eyes. Can they tell I am weighed down with money?

There is no alternative to carrying cash in the Darién. Nobody takes traveller's cheques or credit cards. And while most things in the Darién are cheap, travel isn't one of them. The only way to get around reasonably quickly is in a dugout canoe powered by an outboard engine. But a day's journey can easily cost one hundred dollars in fuel alone. Chartering a boat has a price tag of another hundred a day, an unavoidable cost unless you're happy to wait several days until someone happens to pass your way. Then there are the fees for guides (another hundred dollars per day). And it's wise to budget for unforeseen 'expenses', in the event that you may need to grease a few palms. So, in a place full of poachers, drug runners and criminals, your wallet needs to be bulging. What's more, everyone knows this. Even in jungle scruffs and tatty boots, I am an advertisement for ready money, a *gringa* millionaire.

At the dock a small army of men run around like busy ants. Boys stack propane bottles. Crates layered with banana leaves are hauled from one canoe to another along wobbling planks. Baskets heavily loaded with plantains are counted at a steady pace. Sacks are pulled into waiting boats. This neck of the river is a watery freeway of commerce, plied with goods from coconuts and cans of diesel to mattresses and rope. Old women with furrowed faces balance trays of deep-fried pastries on their knees. Children sell bowls of candy. On a wooden table, a man has primitive tools for sale. Everything is upcycled, nothing is wasted, from screwdrivers crafted from old crankshafts to hammers made from metal piping.

In Yaviza the river Chucunaque is narrow enough to be spanned by a footbridge, but where we are heading it grows to a breadth unimaginable in a country as small as Panama. Because of its close proximity to the coast, the region's powerful tides alter twice daily. Water levels can rise and fall by as much as twenty feet, making areas inaccessible at low tide. Bordered by extensive lowland forest, shrubs and grasses, mudflats and small beaches, the riverside is home to an astounding variety of birds. Within twenty minutes of arriving at the jetty, Manny has excitedly pointed out several eastern Panama specialities, together with a spectacled parrotlet and large-billed seed-finch. For its feisty sparkle alone, I always enjoy encounters with spectacled parrotlets. They are birds with attitude. In captivity they can be coached to talk, whistle and learn how to play dead. In the jungle they are utterly fearless. Characterised by bright green plumage and (in males) distinctive blue rings around the eyes, they love a fight and are fierce defenders of the nest, squaring up to any threat. But I always imagine these little tough nuts will take their specs off before a ruck.

Our Kuna guide, Eli, meets us by the dock. A live chicken peers out from a zip in his backpack. We are on our way. For the first twenty minutes or so, Eli manoeuvres our canoe out of the dock using just a paddle, sparking the engine into life once we enter the jungle's mossy undergrowth. The Chucunaque is Panama's largest river, running 231 kilometres across the province of Darién. As I stare down into its murky brown depths, the water licks the boat like molten toffee. It's hard to believe that this dark sludge is the same river that starts off life as a sparkling mountain stream in the peaks of the Serrania del Darién. More than three million years ago, a natural waterway linked the Pacific and Atlantic oceans. Eventually, shifting tectonic plates created a mountain range that blocked the channel in the Darién. The jungle became a bottleneck for the continent's wildlife, with deer, tapir, bear and cat heading south, and sloth, monkey, marsupial, armadillo and anteater going north. Today, the river snakes in an eternal curve along a sweltering route riddled with parasites, malaria and botflies.

We scull along, past enchanting glades filled with tiny yellow butterflies and sally around a broad elbow flanked with gullies of naked rock. At a purl in the river cradled by bushy palms covered in ants, Manny spots a richly coloured bare-throated tiger heron, whose large frame and sand-and-chestnut stripes are wonderfully complimented by the spongy red-brown marsh. Chasing dragonflies among the reeds is a yellow-backed oriole, its wasp-like livery instantly recognisable. The motor shudders against the current, prompting Eli to increase the gas feed while the boat drifts backwards and sideways. Thudding the motor powers us through the marshy ripple. A trickle wets the bottom of my boots.

As we plough through syrupy depths, vultures hover overhead. A lazy necklace of bubbles suggests a lethargic crocodile beneath the surface, but there is no sign of fish. Bamboo floats downriver beside us in a stew of limbs and leaves. It is almost an hour until we can gun the engine again, make real progress and leave the tiny dugouts of the fishermen behind. We glide past swampy forests that are home to large numbers of beady-eyed black-billed and yellow-breasted flycatchers, as well as one of the tiniest and most unassuming flycatchers in northern South America and Panama: the olive-and-grey sooty-headed tyrannulet, with its jet-black skullcap. We hear the sharp 'peeo-pee-peeo-pee-pe-pe' of the rufous-tailed jacamar, catching a glimpse, eventually, of its metallic

green and tangerine plumage through great tufts of leaves. Dead
branches collect in crooks to form huge flotillas of bobbing
driftwood. Like mysterious clawed hands, balls of exposed tree
roots jut out from the riverside and grasp towards the sky. An
entire tree trunk barrels past us at one point, its branches
beautifully interwoven with a wispy white climbing orchid in full
flower.

In a stark and grotesque contrast, a dirty polythene bag bobs
to the surface and snags itself on the bark. 'Beauty and the beast,'
Manny says ruefully, his eyes on the telltale remnants of duct
tape on the plastic. These dense, lawless waterways are used for
trafficking narcotics from Peru, Bolivia and Colombia to North
America. Local indigenous people are often persuaded to act as
guides and mules. Since Manuel Noriega was overthrown in
1989, Panama hasn't had a standing army, so it struggles to
maintain control of its porous border with Colombia. Now
that increased sea and air surveillance has prevented easy passage
northward, drug runners favour isolated coastal overland routes.

However, while it is the narcotics trade and guerrillas that earn
this region its headlines, I am mindful of Manny's observation
that the Darién's human dangers should be put into context. The
wild animals, killer bees, scorpions, poisonous snakes, leeches,
rabies, fungus, mosquitoes and ticks that lurk here should be at
the forefront of the traveller's mind. Everyone who comes here is
blazing a trail and stepping, in some way, into an unknown. Even
on the better-known paths, the leaf litter is so deep that a boot
will sink down a good few inches with no clue of what may be
lying beneath. In poor light the mile-long trailing vines can
ensnare, throttle or choke. Breathing the air of the Darién is like
inhaling steam. And shop-bought insect repellent is useless here,
unless it has the toxicity of napalm.

I'm not squeamish about bugs. I've handled slugs, spiders,
snails, worms and beetles since I was a child. But in the Darién
it is often a biting dot-sized fly that causes the most damage.
During the boat ride from Yaviza to La Palma, I feel a sharp nip
at my wrist. Within an hour a bite as small as a pencil point has
swollen up into a gooseberry-sized globe. It is red, sore and,
judging by the way it is bulging and wriggling, it contains some
sort of burrowing worm. Gross. Only swallowing one of the

Darién's vomit-inducing flies would make me feel queasier. By the time we arrive in La Palma, the throbbing bulb on my wrist is the size of a plum. In the hotel that night, Manny rolls up my sleeve and inspects it with quizzical concern. From a first-aid kit he pulls out some neat alcohol, which he uses to clean the skin purposefully. A minuscule dark speck at the top of the bump is the cause of my discomfort, he reassures me. Tearing a short stretch of sticky tape from a roll with his teeth, he flattens it down onto my skin. The lump squirms. We both shudder. As incursions by skin-penetrating foreign bodies go, this is pretty grim. The next morning, before breakfast, Manny whips the tape off in a single tug. An ugly, dead grey worm is stuck to the tape's sticky underside, trapped during its attempt to gasp for air. This wasn't what I meant when I said I wanted the Darién jungle to get under my skin.

La Palma, Darién's capital, lies on the Pacific coast surrounded by caiman-topped sandbanks, mammoth glades of trees and mudflats baked by a punishing sun. Built on stilts, the houses of the town stagger up a slope, from which petrol to refuel the boats is winched, slowly, down. Today, a group of gold prospectors from California has arrived with plans to dredge a small river, once they've built an airstrip on which to land. They've travelled to La Palma by boat from Yaviza – an eight-hour trip in a boat full of live chickens, goats and plantains, which tested their sanity but cost them three dollars apiece.

Our boat departure from La Palma is without any of the life-threatening drama of my last trip with Hernan. The waters are gently lapping, languid and limp. Under bright blue skies, we delight in the company of four small bottlenose dolphins, which leap in perfect synchronicity beside us all the way along the mangrove-dotted coast. Surfacing often, their curved mouths – as if in a permanent smile – make my heart sing. These charismatic stars of the ocean slice through the water at speeds of more than thirty kilometres per hour, super-sleek torpedoes executing perfectly choreographed twists and turns. After one particularly spectacular series of jumps that has us applauding for an encore, the aquatic ballerinas disappear into the deep blue.

We are heading to a spot earmarked by Eli as a place to camp overnight, a full day's hike from where a new harpy eagle nest has been sighted. The nest is bunkered by a camouflage of thick swaddling leaves and rope-like trailing vines, Eli says. A chick of around eighteen months old is still entirely dependent on its parents for food, so there is a regular hunting ritual – although these can be a week or more apart. Manny is cautious in his assessment, offering me no encouragement to dare hope to see the birds at all. 'It will be good to see the nest intact – that means the chick is probably thriving and all is fine. Strong winds have toppled several trees in the area, so the most we can hope for is that the nest has survived.'

We pass a toothy American crocodile the length of a fully extended ladder. Large and leathery, with a distinctive bulge in front of each eye, he is 'gaping', with all sixty-something of his china-white gnashers on show. The American crocodile is an endangered species in nearly all parts of its North, Central, and South American range, including Panama, where males have been recorded at lengths of more than six metres. Records are poor, but there are believed to be few more than 2,000 left in South and Central America, a pathetic figure given that they have inhabited the Earth since prehistoric times. Like the harpy eagle, the American crocodile is one of the Darién's living fossils. Once, while washing my socks in a river, I watched open-mouthed as an American crocodile glided past me with a single hatchling sitting upright on its head – a comical sight. Being around him, with his silvery stare, makes my palms sweat.

Later, after we've been entertained by the bloated, stinking carcass of a dead manatee infested by winged maggots, Manny – his voice a low whisper – points out a foraging Neotropical river otter, to my absolute delight. At first it looks as if we will see only its back and elongated tail, while it forages in the crook of the river. But then, in a movement as fluid as silk, the otter does a 180-degree turn to stare straight at us, head tilted to one side, nostrils inquisitive and ears twitching. The tail of the Neotropical otter (also known as the long-tailed otter) makes up more than a third of its total body length. Short limbs and webbed feet make it an efficient swimmer, slick and fast. I hold its gaze for a few precious moments and study its greyish-brown fur.

'It's strange to see one here, so low down,' Manny observes. 'They prefer clearer water than this slow-moving brown stuff.' He speculates that human disturbance may have pushed it here to seek out fish, molluscs and insects. 'They're really adaptable; they'll eat armadillo, even capybara or birds if they have to. That's what happens when there is no parental care. You hunt alone and learn to look after yourself, however you can.'

As our canoe curves masterfully into a shallow sponge of marshland, we pull ourselves up out of the boat using the bromeliad-covered roots of a giant kapok tree. A shadow overhead alerts us to a kettle of broad-winged hawks and a pair of great green macaws. With boots submerged in sinking sludge, we peer into our spotting scopes, inwardly rejoicing at the magnificence of being in one of the top ten birding sites on the planet.

Eli, a small man with a rail-thin body and pudding-bowl haircut, has a deep knowledge of curative plants. When Manny slices his hand with a machete, he disappears into the forest, returning with freshly squeezed sap that stems the blood flow. When my stomach gurgles menacingly one day, he boils a tea using mossy bark to soothe the bacteria that line my gut. As we walk and talk, he collects berries, shoots, lichen and plants that he claims will treat cancer. He also carries most of the gear, runs ahead to check fragile paths and prepares our dinner. One day, he hunts down a paca – a beagle-sized rodent – and slings it across his shoulders, from where its glassy eyes stare vacantly at me for hours. Before light falls he skins it and rubs it with sweet, young grasses. Once it has been roasted with yams on an open fire, we dine like kings.

Manny reminds me to check for ticks during every toilet break in the bushes. It's a thrice-daily inspection routine that I utterly despise. Yet, when a parade of inch-long ants catches my eye in the same instant that I splat another mosquito, I am reminded again that everything in the jungle demands attention, however small and insignificant it may seem. A tick can burrow down deep into the skin and cause life-lasting lethargy. So, behind a fan of palms, and with well-practised ease, I peel back sections of clothes to scrutinise every freckle and dirt speck. Around me, green-and-black poison dart frogs hop about in the leaf litter, while tamarins rustle overhead. I flick a discarded tick into the path of a procession of leafcutter ants armed with tiny white flowers. In the distance I hear a pair of toucans fly by.

Our camp for the night is without manicured landscaping, so we collectively swipe at the long grasses with our scythes. Eli chops wood and creates a makeshift toilet using the sawdust – he will add ash later. As I wriggle my body free from my backpack, an orange flower on a trailing bough catches my eye. Without thinking, I reach out to touch it, spotting the small, branch-brown snake coiled around its tip in the nick of time. Eli kills the chicken and splays it flat with his fist so that it will cook quickly on the fire. We eat it with salted crackers and just-cooked rice. Weariness sets in as soon as I spot the moon. Rubbing my eyes, I stifle a wide-mouthed yawn and bid everyone good night.

My hammock, anchored on sturdy dog-leg branches, has just the right curve. The canopy will shelter us from any overnight showers and there's a mosquito net around my bed. Darkness is complete in the rainforest at night. It's so much more active, and noisy, when it's dark than during the day. Yet despite hollering monkeys, screeching owls and a deafening fuzz of insects, I wake up fully rested. I've got harpy eagles on my mind as I swill my mouth with black coffee and smear all areas of exposed skin with repellent. As I wait for Manny, I switch on my iPod and smile as the distinctive bouncing reggae-beat of Bob Marley fills my head. 'Rise up this mornin', Smiled with the risin' sun . . .' Bang on cue. It's 'Three Little Birds', the perfect melody to start an eight-hour hike. Except, unlike Bob's birds, the ones on our doorstep aren't so little.

We have all washed without soap this morning and are wearing clothes laundered in the river and cleaned without detergent. Being free from strong artificial smells may make us less easy to detect. Well, that's the theory. Our bright faces radiate hope. Our churning stomachs betray anxieties.

The day will be almost entirely an uphill climb that Eli warns us may be tough. Thankfully, my legs are eager to get going this morning. I feel agile and strong. At Manny's request, I have spent the last few weeks boosting my cardiovascular fitness. I've also tweaked my diet and learned more about conserving and managing energy levels. As we blindly push through stretches of trackless forest, the sound of insects – like a pneumatic air pump – drowns out any heavy breathing. Certainly, my stamina is improved and I feel robust. Breaking a leg or snapping an ankle isn't an option here. Limping back to safety in excruciating pain would surely bring on infection, delirium or madness – and that's if I didn't succumb to an agonising death after a one-legged struggle across the uneven mud, bogs, marshes and decaying detritus. The Darién jungle has never been kind to the sick or the feeble. In 1854 an American expedition began hacking through the forest's snarl of knotted creepers and deadly snakes. The land had been fictitiously mapped so the route charted for them was wholly unrealistic. Disorientated, the men lost their way, wracked with a terrible fever. Suffering from a chaos of hallucinations, mutinous temptations and cannibalistic impulses, they wound up so hungry they ate their dead. Only a handful of the men survived the 97-day ordeal – a warning to us all against entering hostile wildernesses poorly prepared.

Today, I don't waste time sweating the small stuff: there's too much of a challenge to deal with ahead. We are less than an hour into our trek when Eli catches the scent of white-lipped peccaries ahead. We switch direction to take an alternative loop across a deep, rocky ridge. After zigzagging round half a dozen river crossings, near-missing swamps, vipers and brown-green towers of thorny foliage, my fatigued limbs are yearning for a flat, soft breast of land. We rest up by a leaf cotton tree; the buttress of its roots is taller than me. Our pace has slowed now that our clothes are weighted with river water. To the beat of each step, I swat the hot, damp air around me with a leafy branch that serves as a mosquito splat. From behind me, Manny swipes another branch across my back, confirming that thousands of the bastards are piggybacking me for a ride. Later, when I peel off my clothes, I discover a fire-red mosaic of pillowy welts.

Meanwhile, I have another nuisance to contend with – my debilitating dislike of heights. Until now I have managed to control it, somehow. But today I am faced with a plunging ravine that I need to cross. Eli didn't think to warn me. That this could pose a challenge simply hadn't entered his head. Like most Kuna, he walks at double time, trotting along in rubber boots without socks. Uphill or downhill, he carries a heavy sack and a five-gallon jerry, his thin limbs slack and easy. It looks effortless. In a handful of nimble skips he is across the other side of the chasm, the tree trunk wobbling in his wake. Some kind soul has rested it over the gorge so the crossing can be made, tightrope-style, above the river.

After pulling myself up across moss-patched rocks using leg-grabbing vines and rootballs, I peer down past conical reeds, grasses, spikes and brushes. Sprouting ferns that are impossibly green peek out from silvery gullies lined with mulch. An uprooted hollow carries the face of a goblin, complete with pointed hat, large nose and beard. In this enigmatic wilderness, rich in legends of foreboding, every trunk hides a story in its burls, grooves, scars and peeling bark. I linger at the edge of the abyss, the dizzying depths below now a sickening blur. Step by step, backwards, I recoil slowly. I can feel the blood draining from me. My head feels heavy and limp.

'I don't think I can do it, Manny. Sorry.'

My brain goes into rewind in an attempt to locate a resource – a tip, some advice, an inner force, a trick or a magical solution. Whatever it takes to get me across. I remember the self-hypnosis that helped me to relax while broadcasting on the radio or appearing live on TV. In truth, I'm not sure whether I achieved a hypnotic state or not. But I am convinced it helped me conquer mind over matter. Silly anxieties about freezing mid-sentence or swearing accidentally on daytime telly were calmed. My heart stopped thumping. My breathing steadied. All I needed to do was exhale slowly after a five-second pause for breath. 'Dig deep and breathe big,' I whisper to myself.

I stand up, stiff and awkward, to focus on the crossing itself, not death at the edge. I have weird pins and needles in my hands and feet. There is not a drop of saliva in my mouth. Manny's voice reaches me from the other side – he's made it over, so I can too. He seems far away, like a distant dot. 'On the count of three, walk to me, Sarita,' he coaxes.

With my nails digging into my palms, I step out over the canyon, my eyes fixed forward on the fraying collar of Manny's jacket. Crossing the three-metre void isn't graceful. My legs are wobbling like barely set jelly. On the last step I lose my footing, and a poorly judged jump onto a slippery rock sends the log into an alarming rattle-spin. It's ungainly, but I am across. Inwardly I hum the soundtrack to the film *Where Eagles Dare.*By the time we reach the upper ridge, where a large section of lowland forest buffers against a ragged slope, seven river crossings have soaked us to the skin. Not that we notice. Not one bit. My stomach is churning like a washing machine on spin cycle. If Eli has pinpointed the nesting site with accuracy, we are less than two hours away. We stumble upon an empty lean-to made of palm fronds, abandoned by a poacher. Seeing evidence of human life is unnerving. We throw off our packs, gather our breath and flop to the ground, lying silent for a few minutes. Manny is surprised to spot a dot-winged antwren, unmistakable in its striking black plumage with snow-white patches and handsome tapered tail. He doesn't expect it to occur so deep into the interior of the forest. He grins in encouragement, handing me a banana. 'What a great day, eh? Fantastic.' He is buzzing. 'Nothing makes me feel so alive as this place. You too, Sarita, no? Absolutely incredible! Tomorrow will be even better, *si*? An early start, a cup of coffee, then *vamos* — let's go!'

My thigh muscles are feeling the strain as we build a fire together. Then, as Manny cooks, Eli makes the camp, sharpening wooden stakes to pummel into the ground and weaving them with strips of peeled palm. We hang a tarp from the boughs above to make a waterproof roof and drape mosquito netting almost down to the jungle floor. With our hammocks slung in between, the result is a covered pod of suspended cocoons. By the time we've eaten tinned tuna, rice and salt crackers, the jungle seems extra wired. All around us, a whirring, spitting buzz sounds like high-tension electric fencing. After a torchlit trip to the 'bath-room' — a clump of shrubbery within hollering distance — I crawl into my hammock. I'm exhausted, so once my eyelids have shut out the darkness I am soon asleep.

Without warning, I awake with a jolt. I can hear the sound of snapping twigs close by. I stay static, trying to make sense of the noise. A puma, maybe? No. Something bigger. Motionless, I hold my breath, while my brain throttles into overdrive. Then I detect the faint smell of cigarette smoke. It is noxious and pungent in the hot jungle air. Humans. Just a few metres away. Two, possibly three. And they are wearing heavy boots.

The urge to fight or flight is coursing through my veins, powered by free-flowing rushes of adrenalin. Yet all I can do from a prone position is wrinkle up my nose and stay perfectly mute and still. At night, the jungle engulfs you, which I've always found a comfort. It lives, breathes and has a voice and a pulse entirely of its own. Before now, I heard the jungle's sounds as a song and viewed its beauty as a gorgeous spread of patterns in dazzling daubs of colour. Tonight, it is a solid black wall looming in front of me. I feel tightly bound by it. Captured. I hear no song, just an evil hiss. My nagging bladder is little comfort.

An eternity later, an hour or more I'm guessing, I can no long hear or smell a thing. Have they gone? My chest cavity widens, my racing heart slows to a jog. After a while, I dare to breathe normally again. But I don't move. The men may be there, still and silent. Watching and waiting for a sign of life. My eyes are shut, but I dare not fall asleep. I lie, fretful and tormented until the night turns to light.

Over strong coffee the next day, I nervously check around our encampment, but Manny says our visitors are long gone. Eli is sure they were FARC scouts on a reconnaissance mission. They were sent by a captain to suss out who we are. Manny nods in agreement. The boot prints around the camp are conclusive, Eli says. Fewer than 1,300 humans live in the jungle, and most have bare feet or wellingtons. But to traipse through the undergrowth, the FARC wear rubber-soled boots. They now know we don't pose any sort of armed threat. But by hanging around for a while, they have delivered a message: we've seen you, we know you're there; we'll be watching you. In silence, we pack up our gear, eager to be on our way.

In the further reaches of the Darién, the threat of spillover trouble from the Colombian border is very real. Violence can flare up at any moment, making safety in this belt of forest unpredictable. Fighting between Colombian paramilitaries, the army and rebel insurgents can place it off limits at any time. The closer to the border you get, the greater the likelihood of bumping into an M16-toting policemen – or worse. Landmines are also a real risk here, and this thought terrifies me. In South and Central America, landmines have a devastating effect on human life, much of it well documented. Less known about is the prevalence of mine-triggered injuries that maim or condemn wild animals to slow and agonising deaths. Panama's landmines have been seeded by Colombian guerrillas along the snaking cocaine corridors on the shared border, where, it is believed, they have planted coca fields.

In the midst of this mercenary mayhem, travellers have been snatched for ransom simply by being in the wrong place at the wrong time. Guides I have travelled with have shared their own stories of encounters with the FARC. Some were fleeting, others more intense. One was so surreal that the guide in question wondered if it may have been a dream. Flooding pushed him off course along an arching trail of thick foliage. Though spikes snagged at his clothes and pierced his skin, he battled on because he was sure he would reach the coast. When he heard female voices echo under the tree cover, the high-pitched trill of girlish chatter puzzled him until, suddenly, he was staring down the barrel of an AK-47. The women he had stumbled into were an all-female battalion of the FARC – except they looked as if they were on a Pirelli calendar shoot, having swapped their camouflage fatigues for skimpy bikinis. Coughing in apology, he strode confidently past them and towards the sea, nodding his head in a casual greeting. The girls followed him, producing a pack of cigarettes and handing them round. For about an hour they grilled him on his political views and personal life. Did he have a girl? Was he afraid of the FARC? Did he think they might shoot him? When did he last have sex? How did he feel about being ruled by a puppet government with its strings pulled by Washington? Before long, they tired of him and signalled that he was free to leave.

In keeping with its vision of equality, the FARC bills itself as a community where men and women are equal. In practical terms this means that its female soldiers feel able to be more violent and ruthless than its men. The guerrilla group is forty per cent female. It often times its press releases to coincide with International Women's Day, to tailor stories in support of a feminist society. Females play a strong role in Latin America, despite the traditions of machismo within its culture. The region has several female presidents, a number of female ambassadors and numerous women in other high-profile political roles. In the past twenty years,

South and Central America have welcomed more than seventy million women into the workforce, which has reduced extreme poverty in the region by thirty per cent during the last decade. In 2011 as many girls as boys in Latin America finished primary school for the first time. But gender-related violence remains a leading cause of injury to women in Central and South America. Girls caught in poverty and domestic violence often join organisations such as the FARC, because a culture of war is all they know. Conversely, many towns are now all-female because of the loss of male lives in the conflict.

On the Colombia–Panama border, stories abound about horrific attacks on villagers in the 1980s and '90s. In later, safer years, when I crossed the frontier region on foot, I travelled the jungles and rivers from Colombia's semi-lawless frontier towns northward along the palm-trimmed sands of the Caribbean coast. I walked through small settlements of simple adobe houses covered in chilling blood-red graffiti threats. Four out of five homes lay abandoned, charred with the brutal scars of flames and petrol. All the people who remained were female, because every man and boy had been rounded up, taken into the Darién gap and shot. In the decades that followed, mass graves were recovered. One, a lady told me with tears rolling down her cheeks, was full of children. It was covered in the pure-white blooms of Panama's national flower, the holy ghost orchid, its Greek name *Peristeria* derived from the Greek word *per* ('from dove') because its petals – like dove wings – symbolise purity and peace.

War and nature coexist often. So many of the world's most volatile armed conflicts occur in areas that are rich in biodiversity. The instability in Panama's vine-tangled stronghold of rebels, the Darién, has sheltered its wildlife from illegal poaching and logging for more than five decades by rendering the area out of bounds. For example, the Darién's abandoned Cana gold mine, now overgrown with a knot of jungle orchids and tentacle-like creepers, was once considered too dangerous to visit. Midway up a mountain, encircled by coca fields and narcotics camps, the site has been protected and conserved by the dangers of its locale. As a result, it is an untroubled oasis of staggering Neotropical bounty that dazzles and puzzles scientists in equal measure.

Only the hardiest ecotourists and research scientists have braved the trip through near-impenetrable forest to visit this World Heritage Site. Facilities are basic and the atmosphere can be dark and miserably wet. The tiniest generator offers minimal oomph; there is barely enough power to generate an hour of electricity at sunrise and sunset, resulting in a mad dash to recharge cameras and torch batteries at first light. Sheets, pillows and blankets soak up moisture like bathroom tissue and are impossible to dry. Yet the rewards of voyaging to this rust-encrusted mining relic just five miles from the war-torn Colombian border are immense. Santa Cruz de Cana, to quote its full name, clings to the eastern slope of Cerro Pirre (Pirre Hill) in a wilderness that seems to stretch on and on. The landscape, and its eerie remoteness, is remarkably unaltered from the way it was when the Spanish found gold here in 1665. The mine became one of the richest in the Americas, swelling the population of the settlement to more than 20,000 people. It was mined heavily until plundering pirates and deadly disease caused the Spanish to abandon the town in 1727. After the mine lay discarded for more than a century, it was reopened by the Darién Gold Mining Company, established by the British, from the 1890s until 1907, producing four tonnes of gold.

It is birders and wildlife-watchers who strike gold here now. I was lucky enough to join them once, nipping in by charter plane, skirting over mountains and lush lowland rainforest before descending between cloud-cloaked, razor-sharp peaks. Where a lifetime's unstunted jungle growth chokes a set of rusting locomotives, vast knots of foliage and towering trees are home to such species as tooth-billed hummingbird, stripe-cheeked woodpecker and black-crowned antpitta. Rough trails skate round where the ore carriages once rumbled, fresh tracks in the mud indicating a rich variety of mammal species, including tapirs, peccaries, pacas, deer, anteaters and monkeys. These, of course, mean that there are also considerable numbers of jaguar, puma, ocelot, fox, eagle and hawk. Bugs crawl between every rusty crevice, attracting large numbers of birds. Flapping wings and excitable flutters fill the air as beaks probe every crack and fissure.

Ongoing conservation monitoring and scientific research is a big part of Cana's modern-day role. Every year researchers from the Smithsonian arrive to discover species new to science, and never leave empty-handed. Giant anteaters, a rare sight, have been recorded here feeding on plentiful nests of bullet ants. Wildcats are also found here, in healthy and thriving numbers, and this population of apex predators, and the positive mark they make on the ecosystem's overall health, creates a big buzz throughout the ecology community worldwide.

Nothing could have prepared me for my visit to Cana, a magical place that, both geographically and spiritually, took me closer to Pachamama. From the top of a wooden veranda I could see the entire eastern section of the National Park, stretching away in all directions like a giant bed of dark green broccoli. Behind me, a large fruiting tree was a 'must-watch' feature. In just one day I spotted half a dozen blue cotingas there, within sight of two black oropendolas – found only in the Panama-Colombia border region. The blue cotingas were displaying in the slanting afternoon sunlight, ruffling their gorgeous blue feathers and flapping their wings to create reflective circular discs to dazzle females.

Around the clearing trees played host to perching black-tipped cotingas, spot-crowned barbets and cinereous becards, while quietly tucked away in the darker stretches of forest were white-whiskered puffbirds and slaty spinetails. Flowering shrubs attracted green thorntails and the endemic dusky-backed jacamar. And just when I didn't think it could get any better, a tooth-billed hummingbird visited some straggly flowering vines just a few yards to my left.

I rested my pack down and perched on it under a centuries-old tree cloaked in creepers and downy white bromeliads. A toucan hopped down from nowhere to join me, jumping onto the large exposed rootball of an upturned tree. As always, I was entranced by its comedic waddle and curious features – it was so vivid and glossy that it looked as if it had had a coat of lacquer. By now, more than a dozen hummingbirds were swooping and darting in the foliage around me, sending a broken flower head falling to my feet. I picked it up and inhaled the perfume, sucking in so deeply and exhaling so slowly that I could almost taste the sweetness. Within seconds, a scaly-breasted hummingbird with shimmery snakeskin-like plumage had spiralled towards my hand to follow my lead, dipping its slender bill into the velvety pink petals for a honeyed feast. Its feathers were inches from my cheeks as I marvelled at its rod-straight bill. Not to be outdone, the toucan hopped closer until it was staring up at us both with its bright blue eyes. At that precise moment, a frilly orange butterfly landed on my shoulder, just as a pair of great green macaws landed in the canopy to my right, eclipsing everything around them with their dazzling emerald hues. A warm feeling of well-being flooded all my senses and I wished – more than ever – that someone could capture this moment on film.

Of the 530 species of bird in the Darién region, around twenty are hummingbirds, from the common blue-chested and snowy-bellied hummingbirds to the rare rufous-crested coquettes and ruby-topaz hummingbirds. They thrive in the jungle, brushing against wet palms and foliage to create a misting of water to fly through, darting from flower to flower to dip their long bills into nectar. At Cana large numbers of hummingbirds begrudgingly share a feeder, swarming round together in a dazzling iridescent blur. Though they appear social, hummingbirds have been known to body-slam one another in mid-air and even lock bills together while spinning. They guard territories fiercely, chasing bumblebees and hawk moths away from their feeding spots. They have a preference for red, tubular blooms, which they hang on or hover over while feeding.

Everything about these incredibly smart little birds fascinates me, from their ingeniously fit-for-purpose drinking-straw tongues and sugar-bowl nests to their solitary outlook: they neither live nor migrate in flocks, existing alone around one another – profoundly single. They engage in the briefest coupling possible: the mating is concise, without any pairing bond. After copulation, the birds part. There is no joint decision about nest location, no shared effort in building the nest, no co-parenting. Chicks leave the nest after little more than a week. In every respect, the hummingbird is as different from the harpy eagle as it is possible to be.

The smallest UK coin, the five-pence piece, is so small that it is barely there, yet at 3.25 grams it weighs a whole gram more than a ruby-throated hummingbird. Of the 320 or more hummingbird species on Earth, the bee hummingbird is the smallest, at less than six centimetres long. The largest, aptly named the giant hummingbird, is the size of a large starling at around twenty centimetres. Other than insects, hummingbirds have the highest metabolic rate of any creature. They visit many hundreds of flowers each day in order to consume more than their own weight in nectar, and are always only hours away from starving to death, storing just enough energy to survive overnight.

A hummingbird's pectoral muscles account for about a third of its body weight. Principally, these muscles are responsible for powering flight: its average forward flight speed is nearly fifty kilometres per hour. In a dive, these diminutive dynamos can reach up to 100 kilometres per hour, their wings beating like the clappers at up to 200 flaps per second. It is hard to believe that these feathery little puffs can survive migratory flights of between 500 and 5,000 miles, during which they battle against strong winds and fly low over turbulent seas. Those that follow the route over the Gulf of Mexico, travelling between North and South America, have no place to stop and break the journey, meaning that these two-gram birds do the whole trip in a single shift.

The Darién is the largest national park in Central America, extending along virtually the entire border with Colombia. A UNESCO World Heritage Site and biosphere reserve, it is the crown jewel of all of Central and South America's rainforests. No other place offers an opportunity to see North American species at their southernmost range or vice versa: a legacy of an exchange of plants and animals between the Americas over millions of years as sea levels rose and fell. This isolated mountainous expanse is home to an extraordinary number of species – a fifth of all Darién plants occur nowhere else. Even now, after decades of intense study, the IUCN (International Union for the Conservation of Nature) admits that thousands of species remain undiscovered.

I feel the flood of gratitude that unexpected privilege brings, even with stinking gunk up to my knees. A small stream gives us a chance to clean up a little, but it is deeper than we expect. We link hands to slosh our way through, unsteadily, in waist-high water, making sure we are less than a man apart. It is a bit like the blind leading the blind. Our steps lack any surety or steadfastness in this muddling web of rivers.

Every hour, without fail, the Darién delivers a jaw-dropping surprise. When a rufous-vented ground cuckoo pokes its head through the bushes, Manny is close to tears. With its black beady eyes, russet-copper plumage and large frame, it is one of the most difficult-to-spot birds on Earth, a 'Holy Grail' of the Neotropical birding world, I have since met many birders who have been visiting Panama for decades and are yet to encounter this rare and beautiful bird.

It is times like these – after a rush of pure elation – that you throw up your hands in the air in utter exasperation at what the future may bring. Plans still exist to tear up the Darién National Park to make way for an ultra-sleek freeway, and it is not hard to imagine what will happen to birds like the rufous-vented ground cuckoo if this type of road proposal gains traction.

At least a dozen road plans suggest ripping down a protected forest to build a mammoth strip of asphalt linking Panama City with Colombia. In readiness, a greater number of juggernauts have already starting shipping lumber: I passed a couple stacked with logs the colour of honey rumbling along the road between Metetí and Panama City. As I stared at the piles of freshly sawn timber, I worried for the future of the Darién rainforest, which has resisted five centuries of encroachment but is in danger of being whittled away for profit before our eyes. My skin prickles at the sound of someone shaving away at the forest. Based on losses to the Brazilian Amazon – currently at the rate of almost 78 football pitches per hour – fears for the Darién are very real. I struggle to comprehend the mammoth scale on which the world's rainforest is being lost.

'There is constant talk of replacing cleared ground with teak trees around here.' Manny's sigh is tinged with anger. 'Teak is fast-growing, reaching up to twenty feet in a year, so people think they'll make big bucks from it. They think it is "green" because it's a tree. The thing is, they're an alien species – from South-east Asia. So they're practically useless to local wildlife.'

★ ★ ★

Whistling is an important skill for an eagle spotter. Manny, in a bid to lighten the mood, asks Eli to teach him how to mimic the harpy's call. As the species isn't particularly vocal, the harpy's screech is unlikely to notify us of its presence – we'll need to look for other clues, too. If they call at all, it is usually when they are close to, or in, the nest. It is a penetrating, high-pitched, wispy, wailing scream that is repeated in a series of about half a dozen calls. Once we're closer to the nest, Eli will mimic the whistle again.

We are within about a hundred metres of the nest site, Eli says. So we squeeze down into a soft, spidery bush that offers us good cover and unrestricted views. Paranoid that I'll rustle the leaves and frighten away all wildlife, I squat on my haunches and dare not move. The excitement conveyed by the guttural sounds of howler monkeys echoes my own growing anticipation. I am as hot as Hades, with an incredibly thirst. Families of flies are stuck to my nostrils, eyelids, cheeks and forehead. With my scope by my side, lens cap unflipped, I am primed for action. All eyes are fixed on a heavy bough of a giant hardwood tree. We patiently wait.

It takes about an hour, but all of a sudden there is a mighty flap of wings. In an instant we are snapped from drowsy inactivity to full alert by a mammoth bird. With its piercing dark eyes boring a hole into my soul, the harpy is standing close enough for me to see it clearly. I struggle to take it all in: the majesty, the stature, the strength and the power that this creature conveys. Stocky legs are perfectly placed for a supercharged high-speed take-off. The branch is grasped by talons as sharp as knives. Light specks of blood spatter his grey-white plumage. He continues to stare straight at us, his double-pointed crest raised: a menacing hunting machine, perched ready to kill. After about fifteen long minutes, the bird tilts its ruffled head and allows his eyes to survey the wider forest. Then, having grown more comfortable with our presence, he part hops and part flies to a higher bough, where we can just see the edge of a giant, saucer-shaped nest. Manny and I creep forward; I push my face through the brush, parting the leaves to make space for my scope. We have a perfect view of the harpy eagle and its nest in the leafless crook of a huge ceiba tree, the eagle's dramatic profile dark against the sky. I turn to Manny. We are both beaming from ear to ear.

For about two hours we study the harpy and observe him crushing bones with his beak. He scouts for food, appearing rapidly from low over the canopy to swoop on a tamarin monkey. With deft agility, he snatches up the creature in a single forceful swipe, carrying it, flaccid like a rag doll, to the nest. Harpies prefer to hunt for medium-sized mammals – mainly monkeys and sloths – but will take other prey as well, including reptiles and certain birds, such as curassows, parrots and macaws. Cardinal-red droplets splash down from on high, daubing the greenery with globules of blood. The harpy wrestles with the carcass, shaking it at the neck like a dog would a toy. In this feral landscape, it feels transcendental to witness this primitive avian powerhouse follow its most basic instinct.

For a moment, it ghosts into the tree with its back to us, and I fear it may have gone. My palms are clammy, adrenalin has flushed my cheeks and I can feel the blood surging through every vessel. Woozily, I will the bird back with a barely audible mutter: 'Turn your head; turn your head.' Within seconds it obliges, triumphantly executing a dramatic two-point turn to face us head on. I am utterly awestruck. From his position, slightly in front of me, Manny reaches back through the bushes to blindly give my shoulder an excited squeeze. His jet-black hair is sodden with sweat.

The harpy tilts his head, slightly parts his fearsome hooked beak and fixes me with a steel-eyed stare. It has legs thicker than gateposts and claws like a T-Rex. A battle-ready headdress of feathers and breastplate of dark grey warpaint markings add to its formidable appearance. Although it is about half my height, I am dwarfed by the harpy's presence. Under its gaze, I feel weak and exposed. My heart flies around my insides and my mouth feels as dry as cork. While I ogle with open-mouthed wonder, not daring to move for fear it might leave, Manny erects a tripod. The harpy stretches his sturdy legs and seems totally unperturbed. The carcass of the brown-furred primate hangs limp and bloodied in his beak. Meeting Panama's national bird fulfils all my wild expectations. Just when we are making plans to leave, Eli whistles loudly. In flies the mate, a shadowy grey blur. Our hearts soar. The female is heftier and even more formidable.

They share the kill, tearing off the fur and ripping the flesh into manageable chunks. Bones, skin and claws fall to the forest floor. At about the size of a turkey, the chick is already showing tinges of juvenile colour. We gawk at the ripping, clacking, stabbing, pecking and shredding of the monkey. It is a savage feast. I have never wanted to kill an animal. I don't have a hunter's instinct. But to watch the consumption of the spoils in this way is extraordinary. With silent stealth, Eli – barely creating a shadow – collects up a scattered graveyard of bones, skulls, claws and mandibles, then returns to hunt the forest floor for the harpy's distinctive regurgitated pellets, containing hair, bones, teeth and all. The plan is to pass it all on to the staff at Summit Zoo. It will provide a wealth of information on feeding behaviour, health and diet.

Reluctantly, we tear ourselves away. Eli is insistent, because the clouds are beginning to darken. As we trudge away from the nest, I turn back to scan the branches, screwing up my eyes to bring the distant birds into focus while pushing back the tears.

At first the raindrops are light and refreshing and we grin at each other in moisture-drenched jubilation. But when the downpour quickens and the heat rises, our pace starts to slow. The clouds grumble and the skies shake. There's enough room for us to walk two abreast but Manny and I are too wired to talk. So after a high-five and a joyous, jumping hug, we fix our eyes on Eli's shoulders. He is watching for fer-de-lance while hacking at the trail. My legs are heavy, but I feel as if I am dancing a light-footed quickstep. My spirits are soaring high up in the clouds.

The long trek back to our overnight camping spot is downhill, but in the rain is it treacherous. A sucking river of sticky mud is pulling me downwards. Biting insects have caused my wrists to swell and my hands are being torn by sharp thorns. My eyes are blinded by the rain and a sweat that never stops running. My backpack seems doubly heavy as I shuck it high onto my shoulders to keep it dry on raging river crossings. On a rest break I lightly brush against the bush under which I am sheltering, sending a patchwork of angry blisters racing across my forehead. While I'm trying to cool them down with some splashes of bottled water, a horsefly stings me on the neck. The pain is excruciating.

Yet I am so buoyant with euphoria that the discomfort doesn't register fully. Despite the sores and grazes, I'm pumped with joy. I don't see the mud or the rainy gloom, only the vivid splendour of our surroundings. I'm blissfully unaffected by all that is here to torment me and cannot feel the pain. The green of the leaves and the perfect globule of each raindrop thrills me. My heart leaps in time with each dull patter. A giant morpho butterfly flitters by, looking every inch like the piece of fallen heaven that the ancient Mayans believed it to be.

I have hit the wildlife jackpot. I have eyeballed one of the rarest winged creatures in one of the wildest rainforest regions on the planet. I turn to Manny and declare myself the happiest woman alive. He stoops as we stride, planting a kiss on the top of my head. There is a kinship formed in shared travel that is impossible to replicate. Our mission took us to a deadly jungle to seek out a bird that is fighting for survival in the modern world. Our journey took us deep into a place where money, status and material worth count for nothing. In our eagerness not to miss a moment, we walked long days and slept short nights. It tested, challenged and terrified me in equal measures. In every sense, I am as far away from home as it is possible to be. But, for all its gruelling hardship, it has been an adventure that I wouldn't have missed for the world.

If an angel had come down from heaven, I could not have been more enraptured than I was to see a wild harpy eagle framed by a kapok tree in front of my eyes. My quest to see the most powerful wild eagle on the planet has been fulfilled. The euphoria of the thrill floods my memory as I replay the encounter in my mind; I cannot imagine that I will ever tire of reliving it over and over again. Before this trip to the Darién, I had allowed myself to wonder whether, in setting high standards for myself and constantly challenging the norm, I had raised the bar too far. Thankfully, it is not in my nature to dwell on failure for long. But in these moments of doubt, I felt as if I was trudging along a frustrating road to disheartenment.

That evening we toast our success with a ceremonial chink of two cans of Aguila beer. It is particularly fitting, because the brand name means 'Eagle' in Spanish. After snapping a photo for posterity, I hand my tin to Eli, who grins in gratitude and savours each last drop.

Since I started travelling in the 1990s, my voyages have taken me along rivers, through jungles, across mountains and over desert sands. Every part of me has been challenged, and improved, by travel. Through my journeys, I have discovered a great deal about myself. My fitness and stamina have been tested; my stomach for adventure questioned. Travel has emptied my bank account; estranged me from friends, family and lovers; terrified and thrilled me to the core. I have grown to realise how, like a two-bit gambler, I live my life around an ingrained belief in good fortune and hope. I am an optimist, open-gaped with wonder, who sees the world, and its wildlife, as utterly amazing.

Though I pored over the bird pictures in encyclopedias and relished the outdoors as a child, I never dreamed I would see so many exotic species first-hand. That I was able to fulfill my dream of encountering Panama's national bird in Panama itself, a country that means so much to me, has been particularly satisfying. Accepting it was beyond the control of circumstances helped in managing my expectations. As Hernan Arauz says: 'Mother Nature rolls the dice and holds all the aces.'

I didn't lose my Cheshire-cat smile for almost a month; inwardly it still stretches broadly across my face. The taste of success was all the sweeter for having no bitter aftertaste. Our observance left no trace and the harpy nest continued to be well protected by the indigenous people who fulfill the role of the harpy's modern-day guardians. Looking back, I am glad that I didn't meet a harpy too soon – it wouldn't have been anywhere near as rewarding. My journey enriched my affection for and deepened my understanding of this incredible bird. After following in its footsteps, surveying its territory, I know the mighty challenges it faces in terms of habitat loss and predators. I've grown a lot, in every respect. I am not just a better birder.

Where I once failed to hear and see the many species of bird around me, my head now whirls at the smallest sound of an unidentified warble. I love it that birdwatching can be done on impulse, wherever you are on the planet. I've seen beautiful burrowing owls on wasteland in São Paulo; striking vermilion flycatchers on a built-up municipal estate in Mexico City; a blue-crowned motmot in the middle of San José's urban sprawl; nesting peregrines outside the Tate Modern gallery on London's South Bank. Though I prefer to travel solo, I've enjoyed pairing with fountains of birdy knowledge. I've learned from the masters, shared the buzz and learned to see places in all their wild glory.

Fulfilment eludes so many of us, until we take the time to understand ourselves better. Most of us fumble around, groping in the dark until we strike against a purpose. But, with so many projects to complete, great discoveries to be made, extraordinary wildlife to see, amazing lands to explore and incredible peoples to meet, travelling the world remains an inviting prospect – even after all this time. Fulfilment comes from sating the desires deep within ourselves. For me, this has always been to listen to my heart – and put my travel boots on. To have goals, final destinations, is important. But the challenge – the getting there – must be part of the happiness.

As I fly over the British Isles, I look down over patchwork pastures and the stone-spired churches that punctuate every English village. It is less than twenty-four hours since I said good-bye to Manny in the sweet light of a Darién dawn. Only a sighing breeze disturbed the blizzard of morning flies fizzing around us. I was overheated, overtired but overjoyed as we embraced one another, already reminiscing about our mind-blowing escapades. Around us, a collection of trogons had gathered alongside some brown-throated barbets to feed on fruiting mangos. When a gaggle of giggling local children emerged from the bushes – and a horse joined in – I snapped a picture of us all for posterity under a floss of twirling vines.

On the M25 motorway from London Heathrow, I join a sea of gridlocked traffic. As the car inches along in a slow staccato of stops and starts, I dream of rufous-tailed hummingbirds battling for supremacy with scaly-breasted hummingbirds, and imagine I am watching with a sapphire-throated and a snowy-bellied hummingbird in either hand. I think back to standing on lands first visited by Vasco Núñez de Balboa, the first European to gaze upon the Pacific, and I pray that the mighty forests he saw then will last another five hundred years. I conjure up images of ridge-skinned crocodiles and the frenzied waters of feeding piranhas. And I allow my mind to wander through dark, knotted jungle trails filled with flame-coloured serpents, blue butterflies, giant golden spiders and orange frogs. I recall the joy, the fear and the sheer elation. Smiling at the memories, I picture the mighty harpy eagle with its wings outstretched, hooked beak open and feathered dark grey crest. With the MP3 player mounted on the dashboard, I flick the output. Lynyrd Skynyrd starts to play. To the sound of 'Free Bird', I dream of doing it all again.

I voyaged a million kilometres for excitement and fulfilment. But my adventures have brought me so much more than passport stamps and air miles. By venturing into inhospitable deserts and caves, crossing rising rivers and dense jungles, I not only got to see a harpy eagle in the wild. I learned a lot about myself, and about life itself. Life, as the seasons. Life, as procreation. Life, as nature's cycle. Life creating life.

Epilogue

I run, barefoot, through an enchanting rainforest that I've never been in before, a magical, colourful place of giant ferns, crimson flowers and huge emerald trees. I am looking for a place to hide. A place in which I can be safe, comfortable and immersed in the soothing sounds and sights of the natural world. The sun is barely up; it's just a pale yellow glow, like a dimmed light bulb yet to find full power. Eventually I find a small clearing, a vibrant glade sheltered by soaring palms and a swish of vines. Gently, I lower myself to the ground, smoothing a patchwork quilt on which to lie. Birdsong filters through the rustling leaves and I catch a glimpse of a quetzal's red, gold and emerald plumes shimmering behind a jutting bough. The pain is intense now, yet I am completely silent. I breathe gently, holding my swollen stomach: it is tight and hard like a balloon about to pop. I close my eyes, raising my face up to the heavens to feel the morning breeze against my lips. In a low, hushed whisper, I ask the spirits of the forest to take care of me, before plucking a bloom to hold in a clenched palm. Then, gently and silently, surrounded by birds, creatures, plants and flowers, I give birth to a beautiful baby girl. She looks just like my younger self.

Childbirth, for me, took place in a British state-run hospital. But my experiences among the indigenous tribes of Central and South America had clearly left their mark. I required little coaching. I was calm throughout. And the meditative practices I'd learned in the jungle ensured I needed no drugs to ease the pain. Without concern or calculation, I let nature guide the process. I felt no tension or anxiety, just an astounding sense of well-being. Though wrapped in a hospital gown with half a dozen wires linking me to various beeping machines, I imagined myself into the wild jungle setting. Average labour times in many tribal communities are shorter than in Western societies. And just like the babies of my forest-dwelling friends thousands and thousands of miles away, my daughter came into the world in less than four hours.

   Though I never felt that life was slipping through my fingers, I did suddenly feel an overwhelming grief for the child I had never had. It hit me without warning, like a sucker punch, and I assumed, initially, that it would be a passing phase. But it wasn't, and I feared that regret might become my closest friend. To discover that I was expecting a child, my first baby, at 43 years of age, was a miracle moment. I felt like the luckiest woman in the world. That a little pea-sized being had formed inside me seemed too incredible to comprehend. I wondered: would he or she be a traveller like me?

   Travel changes a person in more ways than one. It can be instant, profound or slow-burning. And travel itself is an evolutionary process. When I first started journeying across the world in my late teens, I travelled very differently from the way I do now. Over the decades I have realised that I need a slower, more in-depth trip to fulfill me. I may see a lot less, but I take away considerably more. I no longer feel enriched or gain great value from an action-packed visit that flashes by in the blink of an eye. It can take a willingness to step away from travelling in order to properly assess your direction. In my forties, for the first time in my life, I knew myself so deeply, so intimately and so honestly that I didn't have to go afar to search for answers. They were already within me, waiting to be discovered.

   So do I have any regrets now? Not one. Sure, I mourn the passing of time occasionally, when my once-great memory fails me – when I forget a basic phrase in Spanish or can't recall the name of a favourite place. But as for the way that I've travelled, I only have incredible gratitude. Even in recent history, say, five decades ago, it wouldn't have been so easy as a woman to travel alone. For me, travelling solo isn't a deficient experience. It is rich, rewarding and remarkable. As a lone female, I am convinced that I have had greater access than I might have had in a group. The wildlife I have seen, the stories I have heard, the meals I have shared, the kinship I have enjoyed, the friends I have made, the chances I have taken and the inspiration I have felt: each trip has been an amazing, beautiful, one-of-a-kind experience that I continue to cherish to this day. To dig deep is so much better for the soul than merely scratching the surface. Take it from me: there is no shame in admitting that you're holidaying by yourself.

My first major trip alone was without the consent of my parents. I didn't even consult a friend or colleague. I was so concerned that I may be talked out of it that I kept the whole thing to myself, passing up every opportunity to ask anyone if it was a good idea. I didn't suggest anyone tag along. It was a ticket for one – booked in a swell of excitement. When I study photos from that trip, my face mirrors a peaceful contentedness. My smile is broad and genuine and reaches right to the back of my eyes. I was there, in the thick of life. It wasn't passing me by.

It felt amazing to be far, far away from the conservative town of my childhood, where it was rare even to hear of anyone leaving the country. Maybe that was what fuelled my rampaging curiosity. My childhood fascination with maps, encyclopedias and foreign countries made me daydream constantly about exotic places. My imagination took me to wonderful worlds that I yearned to see. Soon, I wanted answers to questions that no one could give me. About this world that existed far away from me.

Will my daughter, Milly, wonder about the world? Will she learn about the people of the planet, like me, from travelling and meeting them herself? With her in tow, I hope to do some of the gazillion amazing things I still haven't done with some of the phenomenal people I've yet to meet. It is through her big brown eyes that I now watch amber-red sunrises over the Caribbean Sea. With her chattering non-stop by my side, I have undertaken epic European road trips by public transport. She shows all the signs of being hungry to make her own discoveries. Aged four, she is already asking about such things as the population of China, the languages of the jungle and if we can go on holiday to the moon. She has yet to realise that our enormous world can be small enough, on occasion, to ensure you meet a neighbour in a remote desert. It will also be a while until she understands that it is so big, diverse and full of incredible people and creatures that it would take a million lifetimes to encounter it all.

Acknowledgements

No two days of travel are ever the same and it's this unpredictability of travel that undoubtedly forms part of its excitement. Buses run late. Rivers flood. Bridges crumble. Tyres explode. And planes are cancelled. So, I am indebted to a whole host of local knowledge for helping me plan and unravel some of the confounding logistics involved in getting from A to B. And an even greater array of folk with better memories than I also deserve a massive thank you. You helped me make sense of a jumble of vivid recollections with forensic patience. And have allowed me time to trawl slowly through rain-soaked notes smoked dry and crinkly over camp fires. Though I like to think my reflections haven't been coloured and faded by time, I can offer no guarantee. Memoirs like mine are never an exact science so apologies in advance for any names mis-remembered, muddled dates, and inky omissions or errors. The wonderful hours I spent idly gazing up into the clouds, following harebrained schemes and wandering through dense rainforest foliage have done little to sharpen my mind. I have, however, managed to calculate the distance I've travelled since my adventures started. Not only have I criss-crossed the planet in several directions but I have also clocked up around one-million kilometres along the way.

I owe considerable thanks to Hernan Arauz, Mario Bernal and Alejandro Navas for encouraging my harpy eagle daydreams – their passion and support to my plans and schemes are more than they know. I have never forgotten their kind words of advice and look back with fond affection on where it took me. Tellingly, Hernan and I shared a candid conversation about our desires to have a daughter each one evening whilst in adjacent hammocks in the Darién – it was the first time I'd acknowledged my maternal urges, to myself let alone to anyone else. We both went on to fulfil our yearning: me in 2010, when Milly came into the world; and Hernan in 2012, when he became a father again to beautiful Victoria born in Melbourne, Australia.

Few travellers have the means to solely concentrate on nothing other than travel. Most have other demands – a job, bills to pay, a family to spend time with and work to complete. I have too, of course, but I've been able to do this whilst 'on the road' in some of the most amazing countries on the planet. For this, I am grateful to the publishers and magazine editors who continued to ask me to pen stories about my travel quests and exploration of many of the most wildlife-rich regions of South and Central America. I know I have been incredibly fortunate. Hilary Bradt – founder of the excellent Bradt Travel Guides – deserves a special mention.

Writing this book is the product of a series of extended journeys and a catalogue of epic challenges that have tested me to my physical limits and truly opened my heart and my eyes. Thank you to the many tour guides, operators (especially Acon Expeditions and EcoCircuitos in Panama, Sunvil, Steppes Travel and Traveller in the UK and the folk at Proexport in Bogota and London), regional tourist offices, embassy and consulate staff, friends, acquaintances and colleagues that chipped in to help trips run as smoothly as possible. When juggling a busy schedule it's never easy to orchestrate journeys to reconcile it with seasons, deadlines and calendars, but you helped me iron out some of the glitches.

An extra-special *gracias* goes to the very lovely Julie Bailey at Bloomsbury for trusting me to write this book. I am eternally grateful, also, that she appointed editor Rachael Oakden to help the book take shape. Rachael must surely be one of the UK's finest copy editors. She is a truly phenomenal and energetic force of nature in every sense and ploughed great effort into this tome.

Lastly, I'd like to thank my husband Matthew, for helping me burn the midnight oil and get this book written, and the Royal Society for the Protection of Birds (RSPB), my inspiring place of work since 2012. To be surrounded by so many dedicated wildlife conservation professionals is an absolute dream come true – you all understand first-hand the yelping joy, weeping despair and rejoicing triumphs of my quest to see iconic wildlife in amazing places.

Index